Indigenous Educatí

CW00820971

This is an essential, practical resource for pre- and in-service educators on creating contexts for success for Aboriginal and Torres Strait Islander students. Based on the latest research and practice, this book provides an in-depth understanding of the colonised context within which education in Australia is located, with an emphasis on effective strategies for the classroom. Throughout the text, the authors share their personal and professional experiences providing rich examples for readers to learn from.

Taking a strengths-based approach, this book will support new and experienced teachers to drive positive educational outcomes for Aboriginal and Torres Strait Islander students.

Marnee Shay is a Senior Lecturer in the School of Education and a Senior Research Fellow in the Centre for Policy Futures at the University of Queensland.

Rhonda Oliver is Head of School in the School of Education at Curtin University.

Indigenous Education in Australia
Learning and Teaching for Deadly Futures

Edited by Marnee Shay and
Rhonda Oliver

Routledge
Taylor & Francis Group

LONDON AND NEW YORK

First published 2021
by Routledge
2 Park Square, Milton Park, Abingdon, Oxon OX14 4RN

and by Routledge
52 Vanderbilt Avenue, New York, NY 10017

Routledge is an imprint of the Taylor & Francis Group, an informa business

© 2021 selection and editorial matter, Marnee Shay and Rhonda Oliver; individual chapters, the contributors

British Library Cataloguing-in-Publication Data
A catalogue record for this book is available from the British Library

Library of Congress Cataloging-in-Publication Data
A catalog record has been requested for this book

ISBN: 978-0-367-20774-8 (hbk)
ISBN: 978-0-367-20775-5 (pbk)
ISBN: 978-0-429-26345-3 (ebk)

Typeset in Times New Roman

by SPi Global, India

Printed in the UK by Severn, Gloucester on responsibly sourced paper

Access the companion website: www.routledge.com/cw/Shay

Dedication

From Marnee: My dedication is to all of our young people, as it is they who have provided me with the inspiration and motivation to edit this book. I have been privileged to work with many young people as a youth worker, teacher, and now researcher, and it is the young people who I have worked with over the years that motivate me to advocate for a more equitable system that recognises and highlights their strengths, identities, and aspirations. There are far too many names to mention but I will say that young people are our future – they are our next generation of knowledge holders, leaders and storytellers. I believe in the excellence and talents our young people possess.

I would also like to dedicate this book to our Elders who have paved the way for myself and for our future generations to grow, learn and contribute. I would like to pay my respect to and honour our ancestors who have been here for millennia and achieved great things at a time when books like this did not exist. Special mention goes to Aunty Denise Proud: thank you Aunty for being such a strong, proud, and staunch role model and for seeing our vision for the book so clearly and representing this story in the painting on the front cover of the book. To Boori Monty Pryor – a magnificent storyteller/keeper/doctor that I have been privileged to work with. Thank you for your yarns and gentle reminders of the strength we get from our culture, country and stories.

From Rhonda: I dedicate this book to a number of special friends who have taught me so much – especially the power of resilience, something they have all demonstrated to me with grace, dignity, but especially with good humour. Thank you for being you – strong Aboriginal women.

First to sisters Selina and Glenda Kickett – we met at school and although we rarely see each other these days, memories of you both are strong and when we do meet, the years melt away. Next to my very dear friend Debra Bennell – we met working at a regional university over a decade ago and connected over our shared Diet Cokes. We have shared many laughs together since that time, in many places. Deb, you know you'll never be 'just a black duck' to me! To dear Gaye Graham, who I met through my research at Wongutha CAPs – I love your passion and will always be grateful for our times spent yarning. Finally, to Bianca and Katelyn who I also met through my research – fancy convincing the boarding house master to drive all the students six hours to watch my son play basketball! I continue to follow you both avidly on Facebook and you know we will always be your 'Perth family'.

Contents

Figures

Tables

Artist bio

Aunty Denise is an Honorary Research Senior Fellow of The University of Queensland and is an internationally renowned presenter, educator, author, and artist. Aunty Denise is a proud Aboriginal woman who was born and raised in Cherbourg. As a consultant, Aunty Denise delivers cultural and educational workshops across a range of sectors and industries nationally and internationally to better support organisations in engaging and collaborating with Aboriginal and Torres Strait Islander peoples and communities.

Cover art

The painting uses Aboriginal symbols to tell the story of this text book, *Indigenous Education in Australia: Learning and Teaching for Deadly Futures*. The painting deliberately uses black and white to represent black and white peoples coming together to share, learn, partner, and collaborate for brighter futures for Aboriginal and Torres Strait Islander and non-Indigenous young peoples. The circles represent meeting places, the coming together of peoples from all walks of life. The small symbols of people are children on the inner circle and adults around them, supporting them, and nurturing them with the rich knowledges and wisdom. The black lines from the outer edges represent Indigenous knowledges, our ways of knowing. The white lines represent white knowledge, which for too long have only recognised one way of knowing, and often excluded the 65,000 years of knowledges that have existed, and still exist, here in this country. The painting reflects what is possible if we all work together.

Contributors

Karen Adams
D'harawal Traditional Descendants and Knowledge Holders Circle

Jacqueline Amagula
Northern Territory Department of Education

Gavin Andrews
D'harawal Traditional Descendants and Knowledge Holders Circle

Danielle Armour
La Trobe University

Claire Bartlett
Batchelor Institute of Indigenous Tertiary Education

Frances Bodkin
D'harawal Traditional Descendants and Knowledge Holders Circle

Gawaian Bodkin-Andrews
Centre for the Advancement of Indigenous Knowledges
D'harawal Traditional Descendants and Knowledge Holders Circle

Noressa Bulsey
Batchelor Institute of Indigenous Tertiary Education

Kathryn Coff
La Trobe University

Tomzarni Dann
Koya Aboriginal Corporation

Ross Evans
D'harawal Traditional Descendants and Knowledge Holders Circle

Bronwyn Ewing
Queensland University of Technology

Mike Exell
Clontarf Foundation

Simon Forrest
Curtin University

John Foster
D'harawal Traditional Descendants and Knowledge Holders Circle

Shannon Foster
Centre for the Advancement of Indigenous Knowledges
D'harawal Traditional Descendants and Knowledge Holders Circle

Graeme Gower
Curtin University

Ellen Grote
Curtin University

Cheryl Kickett-Tucker
Curtin University

Beth Madsen
University of Queensland

Helen CD McCarthy
Curtin University

Jodie Miller
University of Queensland

Lillian Miller
Catholic Education Services

Ann Morgan
Griffith University

Robyn Ober
Batchelor Institute of Indigenous Tertiary Education

Rhonda Oliver
Curtin University

Norah Pearson
Teacher
Torres Strait Islands

Ren Perkins
University of Queensland

Jay Phillips
Charles Sturt University

Aunty Denise Proud
University of Queensland

Grace Sarra
Queensland University of Technology

Marnee Shay
University of Queensland

Carly Steele
James Cook University

Annette Woods
Queensland University of Technology

Introduction

Marnee Shay and Rhonda Oliver

We introduce this book firstly by acknowledging the traditional owners of this country, Aboriginal and Torres Strait Islander peoples. We recognise the 65,000+ years of custodianship, knowledges, wisdoms and connections of First Nations Australians and understand that it is a great privilege and responsibility to edit a book on Indigenous education. We recognise the diversities, strengths, resilience and sovereignty of all Indigenous Australians. We use the terms Indigenous, Aboriginal, Torres Strait Islander, and First Nations throughout this book. In doing so, we recognise that these are imposed terms and that before colonisation the many hundreds of nations throughout the country had their own languages, lores, cultures and customs and that many First Nations Australians prefer to use their languages when identifying themselves, their people and knowledges. The term deadly is used in the title of this book as it is an Aboriginal English word that means very good or excellent.

In line with Indigenous protocols, we introduce who we are and how we have come to edit such a book.

Marnee Shay

My family connections are to Wagiman country (Daly River, Northern Territory) on my Mum's side and I have strong Scottish and some English ancestry on my Dad's side. I was born in Brisbane and raised in South East Queensland, where we have many family and community connections. I was not raised on Country but am fortunate to know who we are, where we come from and how we are connected. My journey in education is a long one that spans a 20-year career. I have a diverse professional background, working in community roles as a youth worker (within schools) before going back to university to retrain as a middle school teacher quite early in my career.

My teaching experience was in secondary settings, mostly in a schooling context called 'flexi schools' – for young people who had been disenfranchised from mainstream schooling. I noticed immediately that there were high numbers of Indigenous young people enrolled in these schools and I saw it as an opportunity to use my cultural knowledge, my youth work experience and teacher training to try and give these young people who were failed by the system a positive experience with learning. I grew so much from my time in flexi schools and owe much of what I learned about myself as an educator and learner to the young people I worked with during those years. I have always been interested in Indigenous education. Having trained early in my undergraduate degree with a Bachelor of Indigenous Studies, I wondered how a field such as education has been so resistant to understanding how rich Indigenous knowledges are and how important it is for all young people to learn about them, in this place. Education as a discipline should include all ways of knowing and it is limiting the potential and imaginations of our future custodians and leaders if we don't do a better job in all aspects of Indigenous education.

Rhonda Oliver

I am an Australian of many generations. When you come to my chapter with Simon Forrest, you will see that the Oliver family has been in Australia since at least the beginning of colonisation. I grew up in Perth and went to primary and then high school with peers representing considerable cultural diversity, including a number of Aboriginal students. Perhaps this is why I was drawn to become an 'English as a Second Language' teacher (as it was called then – now EALD) where I worked teaching in schools for more than a decade. As an academic working in universities teaching teachers, I have continued to visit classrooms undertaking research and working alongside educators ever since. My research has involved studies of child second language acquisition, but from there I have found myself also working in the Indigenous education area. In various projects I have examined how children who have English as an additional language go through the process of learning that language (or dialect in the case of Aboriginal English speakers), how they feel about it and how this impacts on their learning in the classroom and in their lives beyond the classroom. I have been particularly interested in how they interact when learning and working with others.

Over more than 40 years of being in classrooms I have seen the some of the best teaching practices, but also sadly some that have not been so good. I have seen Aboriginal children's language and culture embraced and used as a springboard for effective teaching, but I have also seen their knowledges and backgrounds ignored or at least not utilised well within the classroom. I have observed how when there is a strong connection between schools and teachers and the communities or families of students who attend those schools, good things are achieved. I have witnessed Indigenous and non-Indigenous educators working closely together and learning from each other in ways that have supported young people to do well.

As an Aboriginal/non-Aboriginal collaboration, we hope to demonstrate what is possible in working together in partnership. Our common ground is always our distinct and unwavering commitment to improving the schooling experiences of every Aboriginal and Torres Strait Islander student in every classroom in this country. Although through different lenses, we both have our experiences of witnessing what is possible if systemic change occurs; and we believe that Indigenous knowledges and education will benefit all students, not just Indigenous students.

We edit this text book at a time when we have had strong policy reform in Indigenous education, but the data tell us consistently that these policy reforms have not resulted in significant improvements in educational outcomes for Indigenous young people. Changes to the national Australian Professional Standards for Teachers through the inclusion of standards, "1.4 Strategies for teaching Aboriginal and Torres Strait Islander students", and "2.4 Understand and respect Aboriginal and Torres Strait Islander people to promote reconciliation between Indigenous and non-Indigenous people", have seen a significant paradigm shift from placing the blame for educational failure on Indigenous young people, their families and communities to emphasising the professional accountabilities and roles of teachers in improving educational outcomes for Indigenous young people. The inclusion of Indigenous knowledges as a cross curriculum priority in the national curriculum has also signalled a shift for educators about the significance and importance of including Indigenous knowledges and perspectives into the curriculum.

In this book we support the notion that Australian histories are our shared histories. Phillips (2012a) challenges the persistence of binaries when we think about Australian history and asserts that "by reframing the dispossession of Indigenous people as something that affected only 'them' (Black History), the national systems built because of this oppression can ignore this crucial fact in contemporary deliberations about who 'we' are" (p. 12). Part of the futures of Indigenous education must include truth telling and healing, and this is particularly important as we grapple with the identity crisis of who 'we' really are as Australians. The impact and ongoing legacy of racism with its roots grounded firmly in Australia's colonial foundations tell us where we have come from, but there are many possibilities of what these futures could be, if institutions such as education contribute to addressing pervasive injustices caused by our shared histories.

We acknowledge the tireless work of so many people to get Indigenous education to where it is today. We cannot, and must not, forget the legacy of Australia's histories that in the not-too-distant past excluded Indigenous Australians from accessing education. From Indigenous Elders, parents, young people and families, grassroots community members to educators, leaders and policy makers, their tireless advocacy in making space for a book like this to be used in pre-service and in-service teacher education is also not forgotten. There is a growing number of excellent texts in the field of education that are Indigenous-led or ensure that there are significant Indigenous voices within the texts. Texts such as *Introductory Indigenous Studies in Education* (Phillips & Lampert, 2005; Phillips, 2012b) and *Aboriginal and Torres Strait Islander Education: An Introduction for the Teaching Profession* (Price, 2012) set the foundations for the futures of Indigenous education that are Indigenous led, collaboratively driven with non-Indigenous teachers and leaders and that centre the lived experiences, voices, knowledges and aspirations of Indigenous peoples.

Many Indigenous people have expressed the desire for Indigenous education to move beyond gaps and deficits to strengths and excellence. A strengths approach underpins the philosophical and ideological structure of this book. Strength-based approaches bring about change through understanding people's "dignities, capacities, rights, uniqueness and commonalities" (McCashen, 2005), whilst recognising resources in people's environments (such as their community) is a strength from which that person is able to draw. Strengths approaches in education have been around for some time, but due to the political, racial and social constructs in Australia, often played out in the media, Indigenous people have been subject to deficit approaches in education for far too long. Our intent in this book is for pre-service and in-service teachers to understand that:

- All Indigenous people – students, their families, Elders and communities have strengths, abilities and capacities;
- Indigenous people are experts in their lives;

- The problem is the problem; the person is not the problem;
- People and situations can change;
- Indigenous students and their families are doing the best they can;
- There is a power in stories that bring about possibilities for change and reimagining what is possible.

(McCashen, 2005, p. 9)

Indigenous and non-Indigenous authors have together contributed to this edited book. We have attempted to cover a diverse range of topics that cover many elements of practice in Indigenous education from a large range of authors. It is of course impossible to cover every aspect of Indigenous education, and indeed Indigenous knowledges, and we recognise that there is so much more to learn in the context of Indigenous knowledges and education. We further acknowledge claims that a particular way of effectively teaching Aboriginal and Torres Strait Islander students contributes to homogenising a diverse group of learners. The idea that there is one magic pedagogical solution to addressing why Indigenous students are more poorly served by schools than non-Indigenous students can result in racialised ideas that form a perception by teachers that Indigenous students are fundamentally 'different' to non-Indigenous students. We want to strongly convey that excellent teaching practices can serve all students in positive ways.

We recognise and value a range of knowledge holders in this text, including Elders, community perspectives, practitioner voices, as well as scholars in the field of Indigenous education. This book is applied in nature with a balance of theory and research to support the practice approaches put forward in each chapter. We have purposefully ensured the language used in the text is accessible to a wide audience whilst maintaining rigour in the ideas and approaches put forward in the text. The book aims to provide pre-service and in-service teachers with the knowledge and skills they need to support the *deadly futures* of all Aboriginal and Torres Strait Islander students in all classrooms across the country, and indeed, all Australian students. As we've indicated, we have purposefully encouraged a strength-based approach throughout this text. We have also tried to demonstrate how through collaboration we can work to improve the outcomes and life opportunities for Indigenous people.

The first eight chapters of the book are aimed at providing a description of different perspectives about foundational skills and knowledges that are considered essential in teacher education. The first chapter, 'Foundations of teacher knowledge and classroom practice in Indigenous education' by Jay Phillips provides discussion on essential practices on working with Indigenous students and the development of Indigenous-focused curriculum. Chapter 2 by Gawaian Bodkin-Andrews, Shannon Foster, Frances Bodkin, John Foster, Gavin Andrews, Karen Adams and Ross Evans, 'Resisting the racist silence: Understanding the evidence for when racism and education collide', outlines an evidence-based story of how racism impacts on student learning and wellbeing and how teachers can address the issue of racism in their classrooms. The third chapter, 'Practising critical self-reflection as a foundational skill' by Aunty Denise Proud and Ann Morgan provides teachers with practical resources so they may consider their own cultural standpoint, worldviews and histories in relation to Indigenous people, cultures and communities.

Identity and wellbeing are discussed in Chapters 4 and 5. In Chapter 4, 'Cultural learnings: Foundations for Aboriginal student wellbeing', by Cheryl Kickett Tucker, explores how Aboriginal knowledges form the basis of decolonising pedagogy and curriculum and how this is connected to the identity and wellbeing of Aboriginal students. Chapter 5, 'Strong identities, strong futures: Indigenous identities and wellbeing in schools' by Marnee Shay, Grace Sarra and Annette Woods, broadens the discussion on the criticality for teachers to understand the connections between identities and wellbeing for Indigenous students. It explores how Indigenous identities are constructed outside of Indigenous experiences and how teachers can proactively support identity-affirming work within their classrooms. Chapter 6, 'Weaving Torres Strait Islander language and culture into teaching and learning' by Robyn Ober, Noressa Bulsey, Norah Pearson and Claire Bartlett, provides an explicit outline of the history, context, and strength of Torres Strait Islander education and perspectives. Chapters 7 and 8 provide further foundational skills to working in partnership with Indigenous peoples. Chapter 7, 'Developing strong relationships with Aboriginal students, their families and communities' by Mike Exell and Graeme Gower provides case study examples of how to develop strong partnerships with local Indigenous communities. Chapter 8, 'Supporting the diverse language background of Aboriginal and Torres Strait Islander students', by Rhonda Oliver and Simon Forrest provides teachers with the essential skills for understanding diverse languages and what this means for building relationships, teaching Indigenous students, and designing the curriculum.

The final six chapters of the book provide suggestions for specific skill sets of teachers in their classrooms in relation to pedagogy and curriculum development. In Chapter 9, 'Teaching and learning – there is no one right way, but there are right things to do', Lillian Miller and Carly Steele outline a range of approaches to supporting students, including a relational approach to developing personalised learning plans. In Chapter 10, 'Critical selection of curriculum materials for embedding Indigenous knowledges and perspectives: tools for teachers', by Beth Madsen, Ren Perkins, and Marnee Shay, the authors provide a practical tool for teachers to critically evaluate curriculum materials and resources in embedding Indigenous knowledges and perspectives into the curriculum. In focusing more on the maths curriculum, Grace Sarra and Bronwyn Ewing outline in Chapter 11 'Culturally responsive pedagogies and perspectives in mathematics'.

Chapter 12, 'Relational pedagogies and co-creating curriculum with students' by Danielle Armour and Jodie Miller, provides some examples of what can be achieved when centring relational approaches to teaching and learning to co-create learning experiences with students. Chapter 13, 'Aboriginal and Torres Strait Islander students at school – strengths analysis' by Ellen Grote and Tomzarni Dann, outlines a holistic framework for teachers in mapping students' strengths. Chapter 14, 'Learning on and from Country: teaching by incorporating Indigenous relational worldviews' by Kath Coff, highlights what learning and teaching on Country has to offer all students. The final chapter by Jacqueline Amagula and Helen McCarthy, 'Red ochre women: sisters in the struggle for educational reform', outlines the experiences of two educators working to improve educational provision in a remote community and provides some poignant ideas for teachers to consider in contributing positively to Indigenous education.

We hope that this book provides pre-service and in-service teachers with information that spans the past, present and future in order to incorporate the many dimensions of Indigenous education into their practices as teachers in Australian classrooms.

References

McCashen, W. (2005). *The strengths approach: A strengths-based resource for sharing power and creating change*. Bendigo: St Luke's Innovative Resources.

Phillips, J. (2012a). Indigenous knowledge perspectives: Making space in the Australian centre. In J. Phillips & J. Lampert (Eds.) *Introductory Indigenous Studies in Education* (2nd edition). Frenchs Forest NSW: Pearson.

Phillips, J. (2012b). *Introductory indigenous studies in education*. London: Pearson Education Limited.

Phillips, J., & Lampert, J. (2005). *Introductory Indigenous studies in education: The importance of knowing*. Frenchs Forest, NSW: Pearson.

Price, K. (2012). *Aboriginal and Torres Strait Islander education*. Cambridge: Cambridge University Press.

Chapter 1

Foundations of teacher knowledge in Indigenous education

Jay Phillips

Who I am

Jay Phillips
Jay Phillips is a Wakka Wakka educator and researcher who has worked across all sectors of education, predominately in the university sector.

Introduction

This chapter will focus discussion on some fundamental principles for teacher practice whether working with Indigenous learners or in relation to the design and development of Indigenous studies curriculum. These principles are framed by the findings of a large-scale empirical study of teacher knowledge and class-room practice in Aboriginal and Torres Strait Islander education conducted from 2009–2012 (Luke et al., 2011, 2013). This longitudinal study was informed by over 1200 participants in or associated with over 200 primary and secondary schools from around Australia, and included Indigenous and non-Indigenous teachers and principals, Indigenous community groups, Elders, students, and parents. This research deliberately centred Aboriginal and Torres Strait Islander voices, concerns, and perspectives as the lens through which to understand and highlight institutional barriers to achieving sustainable change to schooling for Aboriginal and Torres Strait Islander people. Foundational to improving the provision of education for Indigenous students is ensuring that an evidence base is used in understanding what has improved outcomes and where the gaps are. This study provides educators, leaders and policy makers with informed guidance on where to focus efforts to address education inequalities that Indigenous people continue to face.

Key research findings of relevance to this discussion about schools and schooling in Indigenous education show the following:

- High value placed on education by Aboriginal and Torres Strait Islander peoples;
- Low recognition and acknowledgement by schools and teachers of the social and cultural values of Aboriginal and Torres Strait Islander children and youth;
- Low engagement of schools and teachers with local Indigenous peoples and communities;

- High level of broad support for the integration of Indigenous knowledges and perspectives into the curriculum, however teachers report a lack of knowledge and cultural experience to teach in this field;
- Higher rates of inclusion of Indigenous topics and knowledges in curriculum from teachers who report regular social and community engagement with Indigenous peoples;
- High level of deficit perspectives of Aboriginal and Torres Strait Islander children, families, and communities informing classroom practice, including classroom management; and,
- Less time spent on behaviour management and in the teaching of basic skills in the classrooms of more experienced teachers (>10 years).

(Luke et al., 2013)

The common response from Indigenous people and educators who read these research reports is, 'this is not new; we have always known this'. As a Wakka Wakka educator and researcher I echo this response. There *is* a proliferation of research on Indigenous education, echoing the above and more. A recent systematic review of 18 studies into pedagogies that support Aboriginal student engagement and outcomes in education found that the significant challenges still to be addressed were: the structural barriers inherent to schools and schooling; the lack of attention to exploring and addressing the impact of deficit discourses; and the culturally loaded assumptions in measurements and definitions of 'success' (Burgess et al., 2019). In view of this, the discussion that follows will highlight the significance of teacher knowledge and present a pedagogical framework to establish an alternative approach to curriculum development in schools.

Traditions of schools and schooling in Australia

Australian schools and classrooms are not culturally or historically neutral sites. They acculturate individuals by reinforcing dominant social and cultural practices, authorising particular forms of knowledge and knowledge production, and guiding students to develop a sense of their place in, and belonging to, the world around them. Schools are complex bureaucratic institutions which, alongside other powerful institutions, such as the media, churches, and government, are grounded by ideologies and practices that have been deemed critical to and for the national interest. Schools also reinforce a history and a national identity that only selectively considers Indigenous peoples' contributions or experiences to both.

The act or art of teaching is also not free of the impact of politics or ideology although the institutionalised norms of schools are often invisible to those whose social and cultural values mostly align with the dominating cultural framework. Subsequently, mainstream education systems have distinct ways of transmitting, defining, authorising, and applying knowledge, and for the most part, this framework reflects and reproduces dominating non-Indigenous cultural values, practices, and worldviews which continue to be framed by settler-colonialism.

Settler-colonialism refers to an enduring process whereby particular knowledges and understandings about the founding of Australia are circulated through social, cultural, historical, and institutional fields. The international doctrine through which the colonisation of Australia was deemed justified was that of *terra nullius* – empty land – and this continues to be an invisible, but powerful regulator of contemporary thought. While January 26, 1788 was the start of an invasion on Indigenous countries that was executed with violence, contagion and targeted legislation, the persistence of *terra nullius* thinking continues into the 21st century. *Terra nullius* philosophies in curriculum and pedagogy reinforce notions of the enduring resilience and pioneering spirit of settler-colonists and their descendants, and pair it with contemporary national identity and prosperity. Once they enter the schooling system, Aboriginal and Torres Strait Islander children are also exposed to these one-dimensional representations of Australianness which render Indigenous peoples invisible or inconsequential, or exoticised; rarely equal and almost never sovereign.

Indigenous education policy in Australia can be seen as a reflection of the political agenda toward Indigenous peoples that has spanned Australia's history. From the first decades under the guise of civilising, Christianising, and educating for domestic servitude and service to the colonies, to assimilating to integrating, and more recently toward reconciling, schools have been central to the attempt by the colonies to resolve "the Aboriginal problem" (Fletcher, 1989). The multiple and intersecting legacies of this history have manifested in alienation and exclusion for Indigenous peoples, and they continue to mar Indigenous participation in education today.

With notable exceptions, a large focus of Indigenous education research is oriented to the identification of issues stemming from the culture, family, and socioeconomic backgrounds of Indigenous students. In their research with families in the Northern Territory, Lea et al. provided a notable exception (2011), with research that busted the tenacious myth that Indigenous peoples lacked interest in education. The families included in the study made a clear distinction between their responsibilities within the home-space and what they saw as schools' responsibilities to educate their children. A subsequent conclusion the researchers drew was that "to the bureaucracy which produces policies and strategies for education reform, unequal outcomes in Indigenous education are not about social hierarchy but about lingering cultural deficit" (Lea et al., 2011, p. 335). The cultural deficit discourse refers to discourses

> that represent people or groups in terms of deficiency – absence, lack or failure. It particularly denotes discourse that narrowly situates responsibility for problems with the affected individuals or communities, overlooking the larger socio-economic structures in which they are embedded.
>
> (Fogarty et al., 2018, p. vii)

The prevalence of cultural deficit discourse in the education policy field can also strongly manifest in teacher-talk and action. In a national 2010 survey with 233 respondents (Luke et al., 2011), teachers were asked to summarise what advice they would provide to new teachers that would assist them in working with Indigenous students. Approximately 45% of responses to this question highlighted issues informed by deficit notions of Indigenous families, communities, and students. Examples included that there was a lack of value placed on education by Indigenous parents, inter-community issues that students bring into schools, low self-esteem, and poor food choices (Phillips & Luke, 2017). These statements interact with the minimal focus placed on the importance of teacher professional development (5%), pedagogy and curriculum (6%), and systemic factors (15%) to correspond with a view that in relation to Indigenous student achievement, family and cultural issues were most responsible. There are social, cultural, and political assumptions at play here that emerge from a history of positioning Indigenous peoples as the problem. This foundation neglects to scrutinise the complex trajectory through which the normalisation of particular values and assumptions have been embedded in various systems.

Fundamentally, the inflexibility of mainstream education systems to recognise or acknowledge its colonial foundations and how particular worldviews are privileged, or at the very least presented as an unspoken norm, contributes to the lack of sustainable strategies to 'close the gap' in Indigenous education. The resulting lack of systemic change contributes to decades of failed efforts to improve overall outcomes in Aboriginal and Torres Strait Islander education, while paradoxically confirming the 'problem' lay mostly with Indigenous peoples. Where there is success, this is often reliant on the goodwill and commitment of individual teachers to accommodate alternative student experiences, worldviews, and knowledges.

Not only does the marginalisation of Indigenous cultural perspectives in classrooms impact on Indigenous student beliefs that their cultural knowledges and experiences are not as important as others, this exclusion also perpetuates cultural dominance. This has obvious implications for participation in mainstream education by Aboriginal and Torres Strait Islander students because it requires their additional and consistent effort to mediate their learning in the school – this includes the mediation of classroom content that deems Indigenous peoples as non-existent or irrelevant. How then do we as educators reorient our perceptions of our roles and consider alternative explanations for the systemic educational gaps that circumscribe Indigenous participation in mainstream schooling? The first step is to consider the existing frameworks that govern ideas about what constitutes a culturally responsive educational environment for Indigenous learners. The second is to consistently question assumptions that the socio-economic conditions of Indigenous lives, emanating from a long history of marginalisation in Australia, are representations of our cultures.

Western systems of education are usually linear, compartmentalised, time-based, adult-centred, institutionalised, and, in many cases, resources that are used in classrooms are not representative of Indigenous peoples, let alone the *diverse* cultures of Indigenous peoples. In the home, most Indigenous students are taught at a young age to be independent, to be self-reliant, to solve their own conflicts and rely less on adults. This creates different expectations for Indigenous learners as they are not presented with the opportunity to transition/scaffold their cultural ways into the alternative space of learning that schools provide. This also implies the need for those children to adopt another cultural lens within the classroom, to make connections between what they know and what they are learning, and to mediate their learning to preserve inherited cultural knowledges. An additional hurdle for Indigenous children is managing the consequences of these cultural differences that occur when a teacher with limited cultural competence is in charge of managing learning and student behaviour.

Today there is evidence of schools developing and maintaining strong community partnerships with local Indigenous communities, which assist teachers and students throughout the schooling years. Disbray's (2016) report found cross-cultural knowledge was created when programs were planned and had the support of both the school and the local Aboriginal and Torres Strait Islander community working to establish a strong, effective, and Indigenous knowledge-informed curriculum. Through mutually beneficial partnership, schools are able to tap into the wealth of Indigenous knowledges that communities hold, benefiting the whole school. Home-school transition also becomes easier with this community backing. It also helps overcome the reticence of parents to engage with schools, which has been identified as based on historically informed negative views and contemporary interactions with schools (Barr & Saltmarsh, 2014; Chenhall et al., 2011; Cleveland, 2008). The reticence of Indigenous parents and communities is also informed by their awareness of, and experience with, the deficit discourses that are seen to be embedded in schooling. All of this has reinforced parent views that most teachers have little understanding of how pervasively negative attitudes impact directly on their classroom practices.

A story from practice: Integrated practice in school leadership

At Dirranbandi P-10 State School in the years 2010 to 2013, the school Principal established an Indigenous consultative committee made up of members from the local Aboriginal community. The committee consulted on school policy, school behaviour data, teacher professional development needs, events, school budget, and the school curriculum. Two 'Elders in residence' were elected from the group who became regulars at the school. Uncle Sonny Draper and Aunty Lenense Cooper conducted 'Welcome to Country' at school parades, organised cultural days, took cultural lessons in classes, walked and talked with at-risk Aboriginal students and shared many skills with all students. They, and the members of the Indigenous consultative committee, became advocates of the school within the community, as they were integral to the success of programs and processes of the school. This community partnership wasn't tokenistic as had been tried before, but rather involved the community within deep and meaningful decision-making at the school level. Classrooms welcomed Aboriginal parent attendance and the role Elders played within the school, seeing a rich benefit to their involvement.

Implications for practice: 1

The capacity for the school to change is multi-faceted. Teachers and school leaders need access to quality training that provides opportunities to understand Country from Indigenous perspectives in order to be able to connect deeply with Aboriginal and Torres Strait Islander peoples. In their 2014 study with practitioners on embedding Indigenous perspectives, Lampert et al. identified critical factors that highlighted how one community developed local opportunities for the professional learning of teachers. These included the establishment of a cultural program that increased appreciation for and knowledge of the local community's connection to Country, the significance of transmission of culture to local people, and the positive effect of teachers supporting cultural connections between Elders, students, and schools (Lampert et al., 2014). School leaders require an openness to consult and work alongside Indigenous community, including Elders, in making decisions within the school for the benefit of all students.

Teacher knowledge and reflexivity

The deconstruction of how particular ways of knowing become socially, culturally, and institutionally embedded to create normative knowledge structures that reproduce colonial ideas about Indigenous peoples and Australian culture and values is a critical first step. An interdependent activity that sits alongside this is teacher reflection on practice and, more critically, teacher reflection on the socio-cultural and institutionalised dimensions of their existing knowledge and the examination of pre-existing assumptions emanating from this space. There is value in this self-reflexive enquiry into hidden or institutionalised assumptions about Indigenous peoples and cultures and in the analysis of how popular discourses can work against the sustainability of good practice in Indigenous education. While this preparation and guidance would be more effectively achieved through pre-service teacher education or in-service programs, there are steps that practising teachers can take to test the impact of their assumptions – whether these are in relation to teaching or supporting Indigenous students, planning for family involvement, and/or making decisions about the curriculum (also see Chapter 3, Proud and Morgan on critical self-reflection).

Deficit discourse and non-Indigenous teacher practice

A study completed by Edith Cowan University in 2001 reported that one of the key barriers to Aboriginal student success was teacher attitude towards Aboriginal students (Gray & Beresford, 2001). A lack of depth in much teacher awareness of the social and cultural contexts of Aboriginal student lives attracted critical comment in the study, with the unresponsiveness of teachers and administrators to the racialised attacks that students experienced being particularly emphasised. The misconstrual of Aboriginal dialects as a poor form of English was also emphasised in the study undertaken by Oliver et al. (2011) as having a critical impact on the quality of the learning environment for Aboriginal learners. Suspensions of Aboriginal students were more frequent than the punishment of perpetrators of the attacks, which further reinforced a sense of mistrust of the system by Indigenous students and their parents. The findings from the 2011 Luke et al. study found that approximately 45% of teachers surveyed had "no contact with Indigenous peoples outside the school environment, with less than 25% having visited an Indigenous organisation" (Luke et al., 2012, p. 23). It is not surprising then that teachers will rely on public discourses and anecdotal data to establish the knowledge base from which to teach the Aboriginal and Torres Strait Islander students in their classrooms. This means that teachers also need to have the skills to critically select resources that accurately reflect the lived experiences, cultures, and values of Indigenous peoples (see Chapter 9).

Connecting and building relationships with Indigenous parents and communities (see Chapter 7) helps to broaden a teacher's perspective on Indigenous knowledges. This coupled with reading Indigenous literature and research will assist in providing broader perspectives within the classroom. When teachers are knowledgeable about the family lives and cultural backgrounds of students, they are more likely to effectively engage a child's existing knowledge in classroom activities (Villegas & Lucas, 2002).

There has been increased emphasis on the Aboriginal and Torres Strait Islander history cross-curriculum priority through the inclusion of new elaborations in 2019, and the substantial resources that have been compiled on the Australian Institute for Teaching and School Leadership (AITSL) website. Educators have increasing access to a wealth of exemplars for practice so in this section the discussion will attend to the consequences of teacher knowledge and practice to effective curriculum design. The two main ways that teacher knowledge impacts on practice is in the choices and decisions they make in the prioritising of content of Indigenous studies programs, and the capacity to teach through the invariable conflicts and tensions which arise when teaching that content. In some cases, there is a heavy reliance on inserting content with limited scaffolding across the curriculum. In this example, secondary students reflect on their experience in a classroom where the film Samson and Delilah was included as a learning activity.

> Samson and Delilah. That's a really good movie. I love it... While we were watching it [non-Indigenous students] were so racist... There's this one part where Delilah gives Samson food, and he would follow her. And then [non-Indigenous] student compared him to a dog. The teacher laughed at that, and I was like, 'wow'... It was pretty sad.
>
> (Phillips and Luke, 2017, p. 971)

Samson and Delilah is the recount of a national story, one in which the dispossession and disenfranchisement of Indigenous peoples is circumscribing contemporary circumstances. This gap in cultural knowledge contributes to a cycle of partly told stories in the classroom and affects the learning of Indigenous and non-Indigenous children. Over time, choices which are made in the development of the Indigenous studies curriculum have confirmed a particular forgetfulness about Australia's shared and interdependent history. A step toward resolution in this respect is the inclusion of Indigenous peoples' narratives inside the existing space of teaching across learning areas to re-engage new ways of understanding the connectedness of Indigenous peoples' knowledge and experiences. Consistently, research shows that teaching does not reflect culture (defined as worldviews and artefact), does not commemorate Indigenous achievements or histories, lacks acknowledgement of local language, and shows negative stereotypes of Indigenous peoples when or if included in the curriculum (Gray & Beresford, 2001; Phillips & Luke, 2017).

Traditional and contemporary approaches to teaching Indigenous studies often lacks a reflexive and relational approach. Indigenous studies programs most frequently position Indigenous peoples as the objects of study. When curriculum content is delivered in a decontextualised learning environment and focused on sharing 'knowledge' *about* Indigenous peoples and cultures it assumes a motionless, homogeneous, non-evolving culture and conceals the intersecting relationships between Indigenous and non-Indigenous peoples over Australia's colonial history. It assumes that all that's required for learning is for 'new' ways of seeing Indigenous peoples to be revealed through explicit topics focused on Indigenous issues or experience. As one example, the Historical Knowledge and Understanding content area in the Year 10 HASS curriculum contains in-depth studies on World War II, Rights and Freedom, Popular Culture, and Migration Experiences (Australian Curriculum, Assessment, and Reporting Authority (ACARA), n.d., pp. 2–7). Aboriginal and Torres Strait Islander peoples' histories are contained in the topic of Rights and Freedom with no Indigenous perspectives (or ACARA elaborations) applied to the other topics, reinforcing an enduring normative understanding that our histories as Indigenous and non-Indigenous Australians are disconnected, rather than shared and interdependent. The contributions of Indigenous peoples to Australian nation building are extensive and were performed through wartime, under dehumanising policies designed to facilitate and support dispossession and continue today through economic endeavours, popular culture, creative industries, law, and education, to name a few.

This is not just true for historical events; the lack of Indigenous Australian perspectives in other parts of the curriculum, for example science, reinforces colonial discourses. Yet colonisation was the process that not only introduced, but sustained these discourses, and there was privilege bestowed upon non-Indigenous cultures and their future ancestors as a consequence. Indeed, Western disciplines and discourses have long plundered Indigenous peoples, lands, cultures, and traditions through the pursuit of colonisation. Thus, any calls to create space for Indigenous cultural knowledge inside of institutions requires an incredibly complex entanglement of history and legacy to be unravelled. Non-Indigenous learners are rarely offered the opportunity to consider their own experiences inside a critical relational context in terms of Indigenous studies, although if non-Indigenous learners are offered the opportunity it is usually a consequence of individual teacher commitment and goodwill rather than systemic design. Therefore, a crucial part of decolonising the curriculum is the equitable inclusion of Aboriginal and Torres Strait Islander people within the development and delivery of curriculum and curriculum policy. Indigenous input and leadership assist in repositioning equity and disadvantage to genuinely embed Indigenous systems of coming to know the world, and Indigenous understandings and perspectives of the world, at the core of the curriculum (see Chapter 10).

Fundamentally, learning spaces in Indigenous studies must seek to re-contextualise what Langton refers to as the "stories told by former colonists" (Langton, 1993, p. 2) and to consider a design that does not rely on particular forms of content that more often than not rely on colonising discourses. These studies must be integrated with other areas of the curriculum, as without scaffolding this tack-on approach is merely an add-on to existing knowledge (and assumptions) held by students without guiding self-reflection and critical thinking. For many, the most important first stage in any Indigenous studies program is the 'unlearning' of particular ways of reading and interpreting existing knowledge and assumptions.

Challenging students to explore and interrogate their *own* way of seeing with a view to understanding how and why these have evolved over their histories will assist to facilitate deeper ways of viewing the world and the relationships between Indigenous and non-Indigenous Australians. This will enable non-Indigenous students to take personal responsibility in realising the limitations of particular positions and cultural understandings, and to provide opportunities for them to develop new tools for interpreting, and in many cases, subvert existing knowledge and understandings (Phillips, 2011). For Aboriginal and Torres Strait Islander students, this will create new spaces for interacting and involvement as the systemic factors that currently impact upon their engagement in the classroom and school environment are mitigated.

An Indigenist Standpoint Pedagogical framework

Given the normative and normalising discourses and practices of settler-colonialism, merely including content about Indigenous Australian peoples' experiences, cultures, and knowledges is not sufficient to ensure deep learning. Any new content that is added to the curriculum will be contaminated by the existing powerful socio-cultural, institutional, and historical frameworks of schools and classrooms. Indeed, this decontextualised integration of Indigenous studies content serves to confirm popularised notions about the separatist positioning of Indigenous peoples.

The extent to which any Indigenous studies curriculum can achieve goals of transforming understandings and creating new ways of knowing is dependent on the willingness of students to engage in the process. This need to provide opportunities to create, explain, and manage the conflict emerging from re-authorising Indigenous knowledge perspectives provides the basis for Indigenist Standpoint Pedagogy (ISP). The learning space must create critical subject positions for all students – including non-Indigenous students. Whether you are poised to develop new content, or are grappling with integrating existing content into your curriculum, an ISP framework will assist you with scaffolding and integrating Aboriginal and Torres Strait Islander studies content within other key learning areas, and in establishing a critically reflective framework for students to connect their own cultures and experiences to their learning in each curriculum area, when relevant. This framework also can be applied to teacher reflexivity – assisting with curriculum planning in ways that avoid including disconnected and compartmentalised information-packages about the experiences, cultures, or knowledges of Indigenous peoples.

Through her Aboriginal lens, Phillips (2019, p. 9) explains the core concepts that are foundational to ISP:

- Historical disenfranchisement and the subsequent objectification of Indigenous peoples position us to be "known" rather than "knowers";
- Contemporary assumptions that apprehend historically constructed deficit and essentialist discourses reinforce colonial ideals about the relationship between Indigenous and non-Indigenous Australians; and,

- Institutionalised colonial knowledges reproduce justifications for Indigenous peoples' disenfranchisement and continue to socialise and empower contemporary discourses.

While the colonial dispossession of Indigenous peoples is mostly accepted as valid, the objectification of Indigenous peoples through deficit and essentialising discourses is still prominent. In this final section, an overview of the theoretical aspects of the framework will be provided. When used to guide teacher reflection and classroom practice, the framework will enable: a re-thinking of the foundations of teaching across all learning areas; the identification of inherent dominant values or beliefs that are taken for granted as an unassailable truth; and, the development of a critical teaching and learning framework for key learning areas also in what is considered more traditionally as Indigenous studies. Space does not permit all aspects of the framework to be discussed so the focus remains on teacher knowledge and curriculum design.

Critical standpoint enquiry and Indigenist perspectives

In ISP, standpoint does not mean perspective. Rather, it signals a process of enquiry where individuals first identify existing knowledge then through critical and planned questioning that can be related to any content, they deconstruct the social, cultural, historical, and institutional forces that aid in its (re)production. Critical standpoint enquiry is, therefore, a significant tool for teacher reflection and in the development of learning approaches for students in the Indigenous education space. The enquiry repositions teachers and students, non-Indigenous in teachers and students in particular, in relation to the systems of knowledge that inform their worldviews. The purpose of these enquiries is to facilitate critical reflection and thinking around how knowledge about Aboriginal and Torres Strait Islander experiences of Australian history and subsequent contemporary experiences are framed by normative and normalising discourses. Additionally, this also enables the emergence of understandings about cultural dominance. As such, standpoint enquiry is effective for all students, including Aboriginal and Torres Strait Islander students. Specific questions that can be asked in a classroom to facilitate this are: What do you know? Where do you know it from? Why do you hold that knowledge? Why do you see it as complete? What advantages are there to understanding a particular concept in that way?

In respect of institutionalised knowledges, this refers to overt knowledge as well as to the invisible culturally dominant norms and to the positioning of content *about* Indigenous peoples. Indigenist is a theoretical approach first developed by Lester Rigney in the 1990s and has been applied by other Indigenous researchers and theorists to their educational and research work (Martin, 2003). Rigney's Indigenist theory encapsulates research that is undertaken by Indigenous people for Indigenous peoples, with a primary goal of self-determination for Indigenous peoples (1999). The key elements of Indigenist frameworks are summarised by Martin (2003) as the acknowledgement and privileging of Indigenous worldviews, experiences of Australian history, and contemporary priorities as a path toward identifying and redressing issues of critical significance to Indigenous peoples.

Indigenist approaches are responsive to change – that is, they will evolve and adapt as they attend to structural change, functioning to re-centre the views, perspectives, and knowledges of Indigenous peoples. This re-centralisation causes a logical shift in the social, cultural, and institutional frameworks that govern settler–colonial contexts. As such, Indigenist approaches have a dynamism that shifts, and in turn responds to shifts, that the re-integration of Aboriginal and Torres Strait Islander knowledges and cultural knowledge will facilitate. In the application of Indigenist theory to curriculum design and teacher practice in ISP, there is a broadening of this scope to position Indigenous and non-Indigenous teachers/students to emphasise the significance of Aboriginal and Torres Strait Islander worldviews, and particularly, the role of all to the deconstruction of normative knowledges to create space for this privileging.

A story from practice: Indigenist Standpoint Pedagogy

By many standards, the school I teach in could be considered 'disadvantaged'. Thirteen per cent of our students are Indigenous, 35% of our students first speak a language other than English, only around 20% of the parents at our school completed high school themselves, and nearly half of our families sit in the bottom quarter of the Index of Community Socio-Educational Advantage. As a woman of Irish and Scottish heritage with post-graduate qualifications and an above-average household income, I occupy a different social and cultural space than many of my students and their families. Therefore, an Indigenist Standpoint framework is integral to my teaching practice. For me, this means continually interrogating my 'taken-for-granted' knowledge of Australian society so that I can identify and disrupt hegemonic practices and ideas in my classroom.

So, what does that look like? For example, before teaching a Year 8 unit focused on Indigenous representations in media texts, I spoke privately with three Indigenous students in my class. I told them that the unit was coming up, I shared my cultural background with them, and I told them that I would like them to help lead this new phase of learning. I asked if they would like to contribute resources or ideas, and I took cues from them in the classroom. They relished the chance to share their cultural heritage and past family traumas with their peers, and as a result, all students benefited from a more relevant and nuanced unit of study than I could have led alone.

Interestingly, I find Indigenist Standpoint Pedagogy is most helpful as a reflexive framework for the times I 'get it wrong'. For example, one of my students started routinely falling asleep in class. At first, I thought it was funny but after about the third time I was privately wondering why his parents let him stay up so late. One day after class, I asked him if he was feeling okay. He haltingly asked, "Miss, have you heard of Ramadan?" At a different time in my life, I might have felt confused or embarrassed. Instead, we had a positive conversation about how I could support his studies. Privately, I reflected on how I was unable to anticipate his needs from both my personal and professional standpoints. It is this kind of reflection that I believe makes me more responsive to students in the classroom and more critically aware of my role within this profession.

(Secondary Teacher, Queensland 2020)

Implications for practice: 2

The role a teacher performs as head of the classroom is multifaceted. With some regularity, competing priorities vie for teacher attention. In this context, it is often easier to look for examples of content when developing learning activities across key learning areas, or when considering good pedagogical practice for engaging and supporting Indigenous learners. Aboriginal and Torres Strait Islander educators and communities have consistently advised across many contexts that there is no 'one-size-fits-all' approach – which continues to be borne out in Indigenous education research.

In considering the colonial foundations and structures of schooling in Australia, alternative approaches that situate Indigenous peoples as knowledge-holders and reconceptualise this knowledge as evolving pre-and post-Invasion are necessary. Dominant knowledges that frame education must also be understood as institutionalised colonial traditions which have cemented a particular relational dynamic. In her 2012 PhD research on English literary studies, Sandra Phillips analysed how exploring First Nations' writing "runs the risks of contemporary colonisation if encountered as a literary object for close reading without context or reflection on the role of the reader" (cited in S.R. Phillips and Archer-Lean, 2019). The implications of non-reflexive teacher practice, wherein dominating structures are not questioned, and deficit framings of Indigenous peoples, cultures, and knowledges are taken for granted run this same risk, whether in reference to curriculum design or managing learning and classrooms.

Conclusion

This chapter has focused on principles to guide re-setting existing foundations for practice, and/or evolving a more nuanced approach to the perception of teachers' roles in Indigenous education. It situates teacher knowledge and reflexivity as critical for developing alternative approaches in Indigenous studies curriculum design and the integration of Indigenous knowledge perspectives into other learning areas. Deficit discourses that frame and reproduce assumptions about Indigenous peoples and cultures are institutionalised and are rarely questioned, particularly if they are framed with good intentions. There are also structural impediments in the organisation of schooling that when left unacknowledged or unaddressed work against effective evolution of effective educational experiences for Aboriginal and Torres Strait Islander learners.

Reflective questions

1. Select three examples of media or social media that relate to Indigenous education. What are the discourses that are used to frame Indigenous learners and communities, the Australian education system, and connections and responsibilities to 'closing the gap'?
2. In the sample articles, are institutional factors clearly identified as requiring change? How and why?
3. When you develop learning activities in key learning areas how do you approach the integration of Indigenous Australian perspectives and link them to the discipline content (e.g., STEM, HASS, Creative Arts, English, PDHPE)?

Acknowledgement

Thank you to Dr Mayrah Dreise for her thoughtful discussion and commentary around critical issues central to the writing of this chapter.

References

Australian Curriculum, Assessment and Reporting Authority. (n.d.). The Australian curriculum: Humanities and social sciences. https://www.australiancurriculum.edu.au/f-10-curriculum/humanities-and-social-sciences/

Barr, J., & Saltmarsh, S. (2014). "It all comes down to the leadership": The role of the school principal in fostering parent-school engagement. *Educational Management Administration & Leadership*, 42(4), 491–505.

Burgess, C., Tennent, C., Vass, G., Guenther, J., Lowe, K., & Moodie, N. (2019). A systematic review of pedagogies that support, engage and improve the educational outcomes of Aboriginal students. *Australian Educational Researcher*, 46, 297–318. 10.1007/s13384-019-00315-5

Chenhall, R., Holmes, C., Lea, T., Senior, K., & Wegner, A. (2011). *Parent–school engagement: Exploring the concept of 'invisible' Indigenous parents in three North Australian school communities*. University of Wollongong, Research Online: https://goo.gl/xb1Cyx

Cleveland, G., (2008). *The voices of our people: Aboriginal communities across Western Australia speak out on school and community partnerships*. Osborne Park, WA: Western Australian Aboriginal Education and Training Council.

Disbray, S. (2016). Spaces for learning: Policy and practice for Indigenous languages in a remote context. *Language and Education*, 30(4), 317–336.

Fletcher, J. (1989). *Clean, clad and courteous: A history of Aboriginal education in NSW*. Sydney: J.J. Fletcher.

Fogarty, W., Bulloch, H., McDonnell, S., & Davis, M. (2018). *Deficit discourse and Indigenous health: How narrative framings of Aboriginal and Torres Strait Islander people are reproduced in policy*. Melbourne: The Lowitja Institute.

Gray, J., & Beresford, Q. (2001). *Alienation from school among Aboriginal students*. Mount Lawley, Australia: Edith Cowan University, Institute for the Service Professions.

Lampert, J., Burnett, B., Martin, R., & McCrea, L. (2014). Lessons from a face-to-face meeting on embedding Aboriginal and Torres Strait islander perspective: 'A contract of intimacy'. *Australasian Journal of Early Childhood*, 39(1), 82–88.

Langton, M. (1993). *"Well, I heard it on the radio and I saw it on the television…": An essay for the Australian Film Commission on the politics and aesthetics of filmmaking by and about Aboriginal people and things*. North Sydney: Australian Film Commission.

Lea, T., Thompson, H., McRae-Williams, E., & Wegner, A. (2011). Policy fuzz and fuzzy logic: Researching contemporary Indigenous education and parent–school engagement in north Australia. *Journal of Education Policy*, 26(3), 321–339. Doi: 10.1080/02680939.2010.509813

Luke, A., Cazden, C., Coopes, R., Klenowski, V., Ladwig, J., Lester, J., et al. (2011). *A formative evaluation of the stronger smarter learning communities project: 2011 report*. Brisbane: Queensland University of Technology.

Luke, A., Cazden, C., Coopes, R., Klenowski, V., Ladwig, J., Lester, J., Phillips, J., et al. (2013). *A summative evaluation of the stronger smarter learning communities project: 2013 report – volume 1 and volume 2*. Brisbane: Queensland University of Technology.

Luke, A., Shield, P., Theroux, P., Tones, M., & Villegas, M. (2012). *Knowing and teaching the indigenous other: Teachers' engagement with Aboriginal and Torres Strait Islander cultures.* [Working Paper] (Unpublished)

Martin, K. (2003). Ways of knowing, ways of being and ways of doing: A theoretical framework and methods for Indigenous re-search and Indigenist research. *Journal of Australian Studies*, 76, 203–214.

Oliver, R., Rochecouste, J., Vanderford, S., & Grote, E. (2011). Teacher awareness and understandings about Aboriginal English in Western Australia. *Australian Review of Applied Linguistics*, 34(1), 60–74.

Phillips, J. (2011). *Resisting contradictions.* PhD Thesis. Brisbane: Queensland University of Technology.

Phillips, J. (2019). Indigenous Australian studies, Indigenist Standpoint Pedagogy, and student resistance. *Oxford research encyclopedia of education.* https://oxfordre.com/education/view/10.1093/acrefore/9780190264093.001.0001/acrefore-9780190264093-e-257

Phillips, J. & Luke, A. (2017). Two worlds apart: Indigenous community perspectives and non-Indigenous teacher perspectives on Australian schools. In W. T. Pink, & G. W. Noblit (Eds.) *Second international handbook of urban education, Volume 2* (Springer International Handbooks of Education). Cham, Switzerland: Springer, pp. 959–996.

Phillips, S. R. (2012). *Re/presenting readings of the Indigenous literary terrain.* PhD thesis. Brisbane: Queensland University of Technology.

Phillips, S. R., & Archer-Lean, C. (2019). Decolonising the reading of Aboriginal and Torres Strait Islander writing: Reflection as transformative practice. *Higher Education Research & Development*, 38(1), 24–37. Doi: 10.1080/07294360.2018.1539956

Rigney, L-I. (1999). Internationalization of an Indigenous anticolonial cultural critique of research methodologies: A guide to Indigenist research methodology and its principles. *Emergent Ideas in Native American Studies*, 14(2), 109–121. doi: 10.2307/1409555

Villegas, A. M., & Lucas, T. (2002). Preparing culturally responsive teachers: Rethinking the curriculum. *Journal of Teacher Education*, 53(1), 20–32. DOI: 10.1177/0022487102053001003

Chapter 2

Resisting the racist silence

When racism and education collide

Gawaian Bodkin-Andrews, Shannon Foster, Frances Bodkin, John Foster, Gavin Andrews, Karen Adams and Ross Evans

Who we are

Gawaian Bodkin-Andrews

Gawaian is currently employed at the University of Technology Sydney (UTS), and despite being trained as a Western academic across the disciplines of psychology, education, and sociology, he was born and raised as a descendant of the Bidigal (through his maternal grandmother's bloodline) and Nataimattagal (through his paternal grandfather's bloodline) peoples within the D'harawal nation.

Shannon Foster

Shannon is a Sydney D'harawal Saltwater Knowledge Keeper, educator and artist who is currently doing her PhD at the University of Technology Sydney. She has been teaching her family's stories for over 20 years to a range of audiences in learning institutions such as Sydney Olympic Park, Taronga Zoo, Australia Museum, and multiple universities (including UTS, University of Sydney, and the Australian Catholic University).

In respecting and centring the Aboriginal voices within this chapter, the representatives from the D'harawal Traditional Descendants and Knowledge Holders Circle (hereafter referred to as The Circle) are included as co-authors. The D'harawal nation is one of five Aboriginal language groups recognised within the broader Sydney Basin, and The Circle are a group of Elders, Knowledge Holders, community representatives, and researchers (ages 42 to 85 years – including the lead author) whose varying bloodlines are connected to Bidigalo (Bitter-waters, e.g., Salt-pan Creek) Nattaigalo (Fresh-waters, e.g., Nattai Valley), and Garigalo (Salt-water, e.g., La Perouse) Country linked by the Georges River and the Nattai River. The Circle representatives have participated in a research project (ARC Indigenous Discovery – IN130100051) involving in-depth yarns about the nature of racism and bullying today, and so their voices will act as the foundation for this chapter.

Introduction

This chapter aims to provide a clear outline about the nature of racism today and its presence within Australia's education systems, and will use the guiding voices of Aboriginal (D'harawal) Elders and Knowledge Holders who speak of their own lived experiences of racism. It also seeks to provide teachers with strategies and methods to help them address racism and to support their Aboriginal and Torres Strait Islander students.

Racism within Australia is often seen as a 'hot topic' – one that draws attention from a wide diversity of media commentators, politicians, and researchers. Unfortunately, a vocal portion of these people too often centre on attempts to minimise, trivialise, and even deny the existence of racism today (e.g., Price & Price, 2013). Sadly, these attitudes are also reflected in some Australian classrooms. For example, Aveling (2006) found that students often expressed defensiveness when race, racism, and privilege were recognised and critically explored in their own learning environments.

This chapter takes the position that such minimisation and denial of racism effectively silences the voices, lived experiences, and ultimately trauma of many Aboriginal and Torres Strait Islander peoples (Bessarab, 2017; Bond, Mukandi, & Coghill, 2018; Carlson, 2019; Carlson, Jones, Harris, Quezada, & Frazer, 2017; Moreton-Robinson, 2015; Paradies, 2017; Porter, 2019). And it is important to hear these voices and recognise that Aboriginal and Torres Strait Islander students (across all levels of education) continue to feel the impact of racism (Bodkin-Andrews, Clarke, & Foster, 2019; Brown, 2019; Moodie, Maxwell, & Rudolph, 2019). Therefore, in this chapter we seek to reverse this silence by examining the evidence about racism that has continually targeted Aboriginal and Torres Strait Islander peoples and communities, and we do this not only by examining the literature, but also by reporting the lived experiences of Aboriginal (D'harawal) Elders and Knowledge Holders. From this, we hope to identify tools to address the issue of racism and respond to Aveling's (2002, p. 126) lament about racial ignorance in the classroom:

> Just how to move beyond such defensiveness with those few students who continued to see racism as something that did not apply to them because they did not engage in what they perceived to be acts of racism, is a question that continues to haunt me.

A story from practice: Indigenous yarning

Our chapter is informed by a research project that was concerned with bullying, racism and identity. We did this respectfully drawing on the voices of many Aboriginal people through Indigenous yarning, and for this chapter we chose to honour the voices of the D'harawal Elders and Knowledge Holders Circle who supported this research project. Yarning is an Indigenous research method introduced by a Bardi and Yjindjarbandi scholar Dawn Bessarab (Bessarab & Ng'andu,

2010). It is a method that helps ensure cultural safety in research by making sure interviews and focus groups are conducted in a manner that is transparent, relaxed, collaborative, and culturally responsive. We began our research with social yarning (Bessarab & Ng'andu, 2010), which helped us develop trust in the research for the Circle members. This included a gift of seeds native to D'harawal lands (e.g., flannel flower, wattle, waratah), and the sharing of a Gurawanga (Ancestral story) connected to these seeds (e.g., Talara'Tingi – How the flannel flower came to be). Next the yarns moved on to the research questions of what is racism, how it may have been experienced, and implications for future generations. It is the themes that emerged from these yarns that we share in this chapter (the Circle members chose to use cultural pseudonyms for individual quotes).

What is racism?

> Racism results from the transformation of race prejudice and/or ethnocentrism through the exercise of power against a racial group defined as inferior, by individual and institutions with the intentional or unintentional support of the entire culture.
>
> (Jones, 1972, p. 117)

Many Indigenous scholars from around the world have noted there are diverse and pervasive forces that continually seek to minimise, and even erase meaningful attempts to discuss and understand racism affecting Indigenous peoples today (Carlson, 2019; Moreton-Robinson, 2015). One mechanism for the denial of racism is the denial of race itself, where some researchers have noted that as a biological construct, race does not exist (Littlefield et al., 1982). Rather they argue that race is an 'illusion' created by social norms – the very norms that saw the 'emergence' of scientific and evolutionary racism (e.g., phrenology, racial/biological superiority). Whilst the idea that 'race does not exist' may seem appealing, critical scholars have suggested that the denial of race is a key feature of colour-blind racism (e.g., I treat/hate everyone equally' – Bonilla-Silva, 2013; Moreton-Robinson, 2015; Walter & Butler, 2013).

What cannot be denied is that the social construction of 'race' is a powerful tool for colonisation itself (Feagin, 2006) and because of our 'race', Aboriginal and Torres Strait Islander peoples have been (and continue to be) subjugated through systemic inequalities. For example, we experience discrimination in relation to access to goods and services, even to our Traditional Lands, and there is a systemic lack of support for our culture and languages. We have also been denied essential human and Indigenous rights. This was signified in 2007 when out of 144 nations, Australia was one of only four nations opposed to the United Nations Declaration of Indigenous Rights. In this way, denying race can be dangerously synonymous with denying racism: beliefs about 'racelessness' do not erase the existence of racism, but rather obscure the ability to see racism itself (Jones, 1972). In our own research, we have consistently found for all the Circle members that racism was a repeated lived experience throughout their entire lives.

And yet racism is often not seen, or in many cases, explicitly denied by non-Indigenous peoples.

> I have been talking to people over the years, you know, about racism… and I don't think they believe me. They didn't even think that they were that, you know, cruel, or stupid.
>
> (Wugan the Raven)

Australia is not unique in this respect. In 1972 African American scholar James M. Jones argued, "Racism in America is as old as the Country itself, and older" (p. vii). He also argued that the origins of racism targeting African Americans today are directly linked to racialised biases embedded within early British colonial beliefs and attitudes. As a result, American society (and other British colonial societies), has racism embedded in its values and cultural principles (e.g., political, religious, and economic systems). Racism then goes beyond simple beliefs and attitudes, but racism manifests in the power to exercise and perpetuate oppression through the racialised structures of society.

In our study, for example, after speaking of their repeated experiences with various government institutions, all members of the Circle, including Wiritjiribin, have come to the conclusion that racism is a perpetual component of Australian society today.

> My attitudes to racism is that it is fundamentally embedded - now, whether natural or acquired; I tend to think it's an acquired skill… it's embedded in the Western system, at least in the human psyche. So the acceptance of the existence of racism is to me the real issue, not the continued denial that it exists. Because I think it fundamentally exists.
>
> (Wiritjiribin the lyrebird)

Furthermore, racism is not just a thing of Australia's colonial past. A little more than half a century ago – within the lifetime of some people still working in schools – one of the early research studies on prejudice and racism found that a significant portion of a sample of NSW residents held attitudes that belittled Aboriginal and Torres Strait Islander peoples (Western, 1969). This included 20% who reported being *unwilling to be friendly* to Aboriginal Australians, 28% who thought that White culture was *more advanced* that Aboriginal Australian 'culture', and 40% who thought that Aboriginal Australians were *best suited to manual labour.* Other research has suggested that these negative attitudes are persistent across time. For example, Beswick and Hills (1972) found that of 1066 people in NSW and Victoria, 51% reported that they would *not like a family member to marry* an Aboriginal person; and 26% thought that if Aboriginal people moved into their community, *its hygiene would decrease.* In 1994, Walker found that around 20% of Perth people would *feel uncomfortable if an Aboriginal person sat next to them,* 46% believed that Aboriginal peoples *were dirty,* 52% would *not like a family member to marry* an Aboriginal person, and 28% would *not like an Aboriginal person as their boss.*

Some research has focused on the question concerning attitudes about a family member marrying an Indigenous Australian. As can be seen from Table 2.1 for over four decades there has been a persistent and substantial percentage of

A snapshot of racist attitudes ('concern' if a family member were to marry an Aboriginal person)

Author (Date published)	# of respondents	State	% opposed to marriage
Beswick and Hills (1972)	1066	New South Wales and Victoria	51%
Walker (1994)	257	Western Australia	52%
Dunn (2003)	5056	New South Wales and Queensland	28%
Dunn and White (2008)	455	Australian Capital Territory	22%
Dunn, White, and Gandhi (2010)	1486	South Australia	32%

non-Indigenous Australians who would be opposed to the very inclusion of an Aboriginal person within their family.

We argue that such segregation-oriented beliefs (not wanting to mix Indigenous and non-Indigenous peoples) clearly demonstrate racist values. In a more recent 2014 phone survey of 1000 non-Indigenous people across Australia (Beyond Blue, 2014), whilst only 6% of respondents would *verbally abuse* an Indigenous Australian, 21% of respondents reported that they would *move away if an Indigenous person sat nearby*; 37% think Indigenous Australians *are lazy*; and 20% *feel okay with racist labels* for Indigenous Australians. Clearly there has been, and still is, a substantial portion of the Australian population who are willing to support racist attitudes and/or enact racism that targets Aboriginal and Torres Strait Islander peoples. In fact, over a long period of time research consistently shows at least 1 in 5 Australians holds some form of racist attitudes against Aboriginal and Torres Strait Islander peoples.

Racism: More than sticks, stones, and words…

> It's an embedded part of who we are as a nation and you'll see it every day from the most minute interaction or lack of interaction, you know, to politicians going off their nut under political privilege. That's what racism is to me. It's something that needs to be fought. I don't think we'll ever win it but it just needs to be fought.
>
> (Kannabi the 'storyteller')

Whilst racism has existed, both at the individual and cultural level over many years in Australia, it was not until Mellor's (2003) seminal work that the voices of Aboriginal and Torres Strait Islander peoples began to be included in research on this topic. Mellor found that not only was racism an everyday occurrence for Aboriginal Australians, but it was also blatant in nature and not limited to simplistic words and threats. Instead, racism is multi-faceted and multi-levelled in nature (Jones, 1972; Paradies, 2017). Since then these results have been replicated and extended by many researchers (Bodkin-Andrews & Craven, 2013; Bond et al., 2018; Brown, 2019; Moodie et al., 2019). This finding was also apparent with the Circle representatives. We found when speaking of their everyday lived experiences, the representatives experienced racism in four major ways: verbal racism, behavioural racism, institutional discrimination, and macro-level racism.

Verbal racism

This is a form of interpersonal racism that includes name-calling, jokes and taunts, intimidating comments and threats, and comments that either implicate themselves or Aboriginal peoples, in general. For example, Garrawi speaks of his first clear memory of racism at three years of age.

> ...they'd have a community feed... the whole community would sit around a big circle – all white people, we were the only black people that I know of that were there – and one night they had vegemite sandwiches... But I remember when I got my sandwiches, the bloke who gave it to me said, "Here, eat all these," he said, "It'll put colour in your cheeks... as if you need it," and everybody laughed, and I felt discrimination there for the first time, and at three years old, you wouldn't think that it would affect me, but it's something that I'd never forgot. (To this day, Garrawi has not eaten vegemite again.)
>
> (Garrawi the sulphur-crested cockatoo)

Behavioural racism

This is a form of interpersonal racism that includes behaviours where the participants are ignored, avoided, stared at (e.g., suspiciously), patronised, segregated, harassed, assaulted, and have their identity denied. An example, from the Circle representative Wiritjiribin, told of a school excursion program where some families refused to host Aboriginal children:

> When I was a kid and I didn't understand, you know, why this other family who were pretty prominent around town wouldn't have a, you know, an obviously black kid staying in their house. I couldn't understand... .
>
> (Wiritjiribin the lyrebird)

And again such experiences are not confined to history, as contemporary research shows housing discrimination directed at Aboriginal and Torres Strait Islander peoples (Andersen, Williamson, Fernando, Eades, & Redman, 2018).

Institutional discrimination

Strongly related to interpersonal racism, this form of racism includes unfair treatment and denied access to basic services across a diversity of institutions (e.g., shops, government agencies). This includes not being allowed to sit on buses, allocation of sub-standard housing, refusal of entry to hotels or being served in shops, and selective application of rules (e.g., police arrests, fines, and failure to deal with racism in schools and sporting events). It also includes discrimination in the judicial system, reflected in the high levels of incarceration amongst

Indigenous youth today (Behrendt, Porter, & Vivian, 2016). In the following example Wugan speaks of his experiences working within the police system:

> The latest one would be in the police area. White youth come into the station and they get all the support that they need, and they do a conferencing sentence [an allegedly restorative process used in the justice system that has received some criticisms from Indigenous scholars, e.g., Kelly & Oxley, 1999]. Black kids get caught, come in, don't get all the support they require and get forced to do a conferencing sentence without understanding what it's all about... .
>
> (Wugan the raven)

Macro-level racism

This is where racism occurs within broader society and is underpinned by the perpetuation of overarching racist values. Examples listed by the Circle representatives included a lack of concern about Aboriginal communities, a denial of Aboriginal views about history, the dominance of White values and structures, the denial of the right to commit to Aboriginal beliefs and practices, and the misinformation conveyed by the media and politics about Aboriginal and Torres Strait Islander peoples. Beela, for example, described how racism clearly links across varying knowledge production agencies (e.g., education, media) within Australia.

> ...I think of how there was this lack of education, Aboriginal education or Indigenous education at all, in school. So there's no talk about it. No discussion of it. So then I had to have conversations with kids where they said, "You can't be Aboriginal. They only come from Alice Springs..." which then leads back to what's the view of Aboriginal people, and that's [from the] media and government... .
>
> (Beela the yellow-tailed black cockatoo)

Beela's sentiments are a re-occurring theme within contemporary research, such as poor representations of Aboriginal and Torres Strait Islander peoples within education (Brown, 2019; Hogarth, 2017), and widespread negative and stereotypical representations in the media and by politicians (Bond et al., 2018; Moreton-Robinson, 2015).

A powerful example of the various manifestations of macro-level racism is offered by Munanjahli and South Sea Islander woman and scholar Chelsea Bond and her colleagues in their critique of Australia's national anthem. They object to the expectation that Aboriginal Australians 'rejoice' in a nation being 'young and free', and suggest that singing the national anthem not only reinforces the myth of the birth of this nation, but it "is tantamount to demanding Blackfullas be complicit in, and celebrate, the effacement of those who are here prior to 1788" (Bond et al., 2018, p. 416). They also describe how Aboriginal and Torres Strait Islander peoples are continually being erased through assimilative 'close-the-gap' narratives (e.g., comparison to Western non-Indigenous norms), attempts to weaken the Racial Discrimination Act that is designed to protect minorities (instead protecting the 'right to be a bigot'), and the implementation of public nuisance charges to more easily arrest and detain Aboriginal peoples. These legal and cultural forces effectively are vehicles for the perpetuation of systemic racism within Australia. Even the simplest attempts to resist racism can result in fierce pejorative media and political abuse (e.g., the experience of Australian rules footballer Adam Goodes when he 'called out' the racism he was subjected to).

As already noted, all levels of racism are of considerable concern to the Circle members, as racism is not just for now, but is an ongoing force that will oppress our future generations. After highlighting the demeaning attitudes that she has faced over the years within her work place, the struggles to keep her own place of residence, and government policies that make it increasingly difficult to survive, Bookerrikin spoke of her fear for her grandchildren, and the sense of isolation she feels in relation to this:

> You know and this kind of thing lays heavy on my heart. When I said before, I'm heartbroken, I think a lot of it – maybe I'm not literally heartbroken, but my heart is heavy because that's a constant thing for me, being aware of how do I help them become decent people when all the odds are stacked against them…? But again, I'm just nan, and I'm the female, and there's no other Elder in my community that I feel that I should just go to – or could go to, and say can you help me with this one.
>
> (Bookerrikin the green wattle)

In a similar manner to Bookerrikin's lament, Bond et al. (2018) rightfully liken Australia to a cage for Aboriginal and Torres Strait Islander peoples. With that being said though, Bond highlights a critical element that is often forgotten in Aboriginal and Torres Strait Islander people's struggles with racism, and that is our ability to resist:

> To sing of freedom from within the cage that is the Australian nation-state is an act of grieving for Blackfullas, and the insistence that we rejoice is most obscene and absurd. However, the resistance of Blackfullas to singing joyfully of the fiction of freedom is not a failing or a weakness, rather it testifies to the strength of the warrior to fight back.
>
> (p. 423)

Racism is not some benign construct that people can simply shrug off and 'get-over'. In its many forms, racism creates a significant and detrimental risk over the physical, social, emotional, economic, aspirational, and cultural wellbeing of Aboriginal and Torres Strait Islander peoples. Racism is, for instance, strongly linked to depression and suicidal thoughts (De Maio et al., 2005; Larson, Gillies, Howard, & Coffin, 2007; Paradies et al., 2015). Therefore, it is imperative that racism not be ignored and that teachers and schools play their role in addressing the issue.

But Australia is more educated now – right?

Gomeroi/Gamilaray scholar Nikkie Moodie (Moodie et al., 2019) recently led a systematic review of research that has investigated racism experienced by Aboriginal and Torres Strait Islander students (ranging from pre-school to K12). She identified a variety of ways in which racism was understood (e.g., verbal assault, exclusion, stereotypical attitudes, oppression, denial of Indigeneity), but two clear trends emerged. Firstly, racism was prominent across the lived experiences of those students who took part in the research, and secondly, the negative impacts of racism were exceptionally strong. The negative consequences of racism included a weakening of academic performance, poorer engagement with school, weaker positive self-perceptions, lower sense of social and emotional well-being, and a weaker sense of positive identity and confidence.

Members of the D'harawal Circle also spoke of how racism has travelled through generations of families through their lived experiences of racism, particularly within the education system.

> … I've seen at home through my father and my sister… I heard the stories of my grandfather and all the different things coming down through the family, and then you go to school and then someone says, "Oh, all Aboriginal people are, you know, dirty or alcoholics," or whatever… So, I think racism has, and that intergenerational thing, has a lot more layers and a lot more long-standing damage through the generations than just the run-of-the-mill bullying… .
>
> (Beela the yellow-tailed black cockatoo)

More recent studies have continued to highlight the ongoing and damaging presence of racism within schools. Gumbaynggirr scholar Lilly Brown (2019), for instance, points to the ongoing presence of colonial violence and its intrinsic links to racism across classroom pedagogies. Specifically, Brown identified evidence of intergenerational trauma (e.g., family members were part of the Stolen Generations, history of family denial/shame of Indigeneity), the white-washing of Australian history, the denial of Indigenous perspectives, the appropriation and Eurocentric misrepresentation of Indigenous Knowledges, and the glossing over of historical relations between Aboriginal peoples and colonial invaders. Brown indicates these are a continuing source of trauma for students, as too often their shared Aboriginal histories, standpoints, frustrations, and pain are ignored, denied, or blatantly resisted within the classrooms.

Mixed-method research by Bodkin-Andrews et al. (2019) also centred on the perspectives of Aboriginal students. The students voiced direct experiences with racial slurs, stereotypes about them and their families, the erasure of Aboriginal perspectives in school knowledge production (e.g., history), physical abuse (e.g., being spat on), and even racism emanating directly from teachers (e.g., ignoring Aboriginal students, name-calling, denying the harm racism can cause). In addition, the students felt that racism in schools reflected their experiences in the wider community. A survey that the students responded to also found that it was the negative impact of the teachers' racist attitudes and actions that had the greatest effect on the students' emotional wellbeing and school engagement. Not surprisingly, students who are subjected to diverse forms of racism had an increased risk of higher levels of stress, anxiety, and depression, feeling hopeless at school, believing that school is pointless, and wanting to skip school. These detrimental effects were independent of the age of the students, their gender, and the school's socio-economic status. "And so racism lives on, and ... it is our children and youth who will suffer" (Bodkin-Andrews et al., 2019, p. 21).

On the basis of such research findings, it must be recognised that a long line of Aboriginal and Torres Strait Islander scholars advocate the need for racism to be strongly fought within our education systems (Bin-Sallik, 2003; Rigney, 1999).

Fighting racism

> If anything, in terms of teachers and/or counsellors, but especially teachers, the ... advice I'd be asking them or giving them is to look at themselves, their own feelings and their own behaviour and to see that inadvertently... racism is so embedded in society, much of society would deny that they're racist.
>
> (Wiritjiribin the lyrebird)

Racism must always be addressed, but the question for teachers is how this can be done. Anti-racism 'interventions' often centre on the prejudicial attitudes and behaviours of individuals (e.g., perpetrators) and have had mixed levels of success. In addition, individual-based anti-racism interventions rarely address the existence of racism as a powerful and systemic entity across the whole nation (Moreton-Robinson, 2015). Some research has also attempted to identify methods to lessen the negative impact of racism by identifying methods of resisting the oppressive forces of racism whilst remaining personally and culturally strong (Baez, Isaac, & Baez, 2016; Bodkin-Andrews & Craven 2013; Bodkin-Andrews, Newey, O'Rourke, & Craven, 2013; Campbell & Smalling, 2013).

A suite of anti-racist strategies is recommended by Australian social psychologist Anne Pedersen and her colleagues (Pedersen, Walker, & Wise, 2005; Pedersen, Walker, Paradies, & Guerin, 2011) as key components to address racism. These include:

- *Combatting false beliefs:* provide accurate information about minority groups to combat false stereotypes;
- *Involving the audience:* create a respectful environment for frank and open discussions from 'both sides';
- *Being empathic:* carefully invoke consideration of the lived experiences of marginalised groups;
- *Emphasising communalities and diversities:* explore shared beliefs and values and respect differences;

Gawaian Bodkin-Andrews et al.

- *Focusing on changing behaviours:* move beyond attempts to change beliefs by also promoting more egalitarian behaviours;
- *Meeting local needs*: be aware of the contextual specificities of the anti-racism strategies (e.g., classroom, workplace);
- *Evaluating:* whilst this component is targeted at the research context, because one-off strategies rarely have long-term effects on reducing racism, there is a need to continually monitor anti-racism strategies over time;
- *Being aware of the broader context:* be aware that racism is not just about individual beliefs, but that there is also a need to address how beliefs can be reinforced across institutions and broader cultural settings;
- *Exploring dissonance*: look at the incompatibility between prejudicial beliefs and attitudes and more egalitarian values and behaviours;
- *Managing emotions*: explore feelings other than guilt, such as outrage and compassion;
- *Correcting beliefs*: address the idea that racism is endorsed by the majority of the population;
- *Promoting intergroup contact*: promote controlled positive intergroup interactions;
- *Addressing personal experience*: acknowledge and respect possible negative personal experiences (that may reinforce stereotypes) whilst also discussing the dangers of false generalisations and self-fulfilling prophecies;
- *Addressing group identities*: increased nationalism is often associated with increased racist values, so more meaningfully explore what it may mean to be Australian;
- *Recognising White privilege*: examine the often invisible advantages afforded to whiteness (including intersectionality with class, gender, sexuality, age, mobility, etc);
- *Providing alternative ways to talk*: explore strategies for not only more respectful conversations, but also to intervene when witnessing racism;
- *Addressing the source*: examine and unpack individual values that lead to racism, in addition to critiquing outside sources that may reinforce these values (e.g., the media);
- *Including multiple voices*: work with a diversity of people and disciplinary sources (e.g., psychology, sociology education) to provide a wider breadth of anti-racism strategies.

Pedersen et al. (2011) recommend that these multiple strategies should be used in combination, as no individual anti-racism strategy has been found to be truly effective on its own. It is also vital that the complexities of local contexts be considered and carefully understood, as one needs to be flexible as to how, when, and where anti-racism strategies may best take place.

Another critical issue that needs to be understood is that negative effects of racism on Aboriginal and Torres Strait Islander peoples is substantial, and ongoing, and anti-racism research agendas rarely address this (Bodkin-Andrews & Carlson, 2016; Moodie et al., 2019; Moreton-Robinson, 2015). This was highlighted by Burrumurring who recalls when she, and a number of Aboriginal youth in a traineeship, faced a blatant incident of racial segregation when working for an environmental education organisation.

So anyway the kids were just absolutely devastated … They were just so devastated when they found that they couldn't sit with the visitors and talk with them … was what was most beautiful about the whole thing was when [the organisation] settled … The first time in three years I actually felt clean. I felt I am worthwhile and that's what racism does. It degrades you, yeah.

(Burrumurring the wedge-tailed eagle)

The resulting legal struggle to fight racism was exceptionally draining for her and the youth, but the eventual recognition that racism actually took place was a significant step towards healing.

Some research has realised that part of the fight against racism is in the need to identify how Aboriginal, Torres Strait Islander, and First Nations peoples can stay strong in the face of racism (Baez, Isaac, & Baez, 2016; Bodkin-Andrews & Craven 2013; Bodkin-Andrews et al., 2013; Campbell & Smalling, 2013). For example, research by Bodkin-Andrews and Craven (2013) found that Aboriginal Higher Degree Research students (often also respected Aboriginal community representatives), stressed a number of key steps to help Aboriginal youth heal from racism:

1. One must first see racism rather than to ignore its existence (acknowledge racism);
2. One must then realise that racism ultimately emanates from the racist individual and is not an accurate reflection of one's self (do not internalise racism);
3. One should try to remain positive, calm, and culturally strong in the face of racism (be careful of responding to racism with aggression);
4. One should seek the advice and support from trusted friends and family (talk about racism, do not let it fester within);
5. Recognise the inherent strengths within many Aboriginal communities that have resisted and fought colonisation and racism for many generations (stay proud and strong in one's Aboriginal identity and community); and
6. When possible, challenge racism by proving the racists wrong (fight to succeed and overcome racism itself).

The other one is I think schools are doing a great job of taking a zero tolerance policy towards racism… But I think they forget… a lot more care and understanding needs to be taken there. You need to help kids be proud of who they are and understand that racism is not just an attack on the kids, it's an attack on their culture, and if you take the culture away from them, the damage is irreparable… .

(Kannabi the 'storyteller')

Here Kannabi explores the strong role schools and teachers may play in fighting racism. However, students are aware of the forces of racism that move beyond verbal and physical interactions in the classroom and playground. They have knowledge of and lived experiences with racism that extends across the curriculum, wider communities, and the very governance structures within Australia. It is critical then to realise that customary anti-racist understandings and individual resiliency frameworks are not enough to help our students resist the insidious and perpetual forces of racism.

Gawaian Bodkin-Andrews et al.

Some international First Nations research has moved beyond individualist strategies and has sought to challenge the very institutions that may perpetuate racism and trauma. For example, within the American context, Campbell and Smalling (2013) identified the high rates of verbal and physical violence that Native American students (from 6th to 9th grade) are forced to endure and recommend promoting culturally specific and reinforcing activities. This includes the appointment of Native American teachers and facilitators for culturally grounded programs, ensuring that food is provided during these programs, being flexible to gender requirements, and having school administrators being outwardly supportive and involved in the programs.

In a similar vein, the *Sweetgrass Method* developed by Mowhawk/Caohuiltecan/Pawnee/Mexican scholar and psychologist, Mark Standing Eagle Baez (Baez & Isaac, 2013; Baez, Isaac, & Baez, 2016) was developed to help address intergenerational trauma that is too often exacerbated by bullying and racism within schools.

This method can be understood though three interrelated strands (*introspective, collaboration*, and *continuity*) that weave Indigenous and Western approaches together for healing. These strands target not only the healing of Indigenous youth, but also the cultural responsivity of all those who work in services to support them (e.g., clinicians, counsellors, teachers):

- *Introspective strand:* staff development meets cultural responsibility. Here educators look to achieve understanding, clarity, and preparedness to address and prevent the likes of bullying, racism, and colonial violence. This includes the educators addressing their own assumptions and biases, and developing knowledge of, and respect for, Indigenous protocols and ceremonies when engaging with Indigenous students and communities (see Chapter 2).
- *Collaboration strand:* earn respect from Indigenous families and communities and then develop meaningful partnerships with them. Prioritise earning the trust of Elders, Storytellers, and community representatives, and acknowledge the value of community knowledges and activities. When invited, respectfully engage with communities in activities and events that may fall outside any particular Western organisational role. From these trust building foundations, collaborations and partnerships between schools and communities become more viable and culturally centred for the students (see Chapter 7).
- *Continuous strand:* this strand does not focus on the end-product or outcome of any school/community partnership, but rather the potential for continuity of these relationships. That is schools must work towards sustainable partnerships with Indigenous communities, families, and students that will form a flexible and ongoing development for relationships that will serve both the community and the school (through strength-based exchanges of knowledges) (see Chapter 5).

It is essential that when educators and schools implement any strategy or method to fight racism and its potential negative effects on Aboriginal and Torres Strait Islander students, they commit to flexibility and diversity within their frameworks. This should not only include attempts to address individual attitudes of the perpetrators, but the complex web that racism has spun within and around the school itself. Once this is recognised, the ability to weave the potential strengths of Aboriginal and Torres Strait Islander students, families, and communities into a culturally responsive and productive school ethos will become more possible.

Conclusion

> ...right, I've got my grandkids now. I'm going to teach my oldest grandkid everything I know. That's not so much about the racism side or the bullying side, it's about the positives of what he needs to do to prepare himself. But, he needs to understand that he is a D'harawal person, and he needs to understand that plays a big part in his life... .
>
> (Wugan the raven)

Articles 14 and 15 within the United Nations Declaration of Indigenous Rights (2007) focus on both the education of Indigenous peoples and the education of the diverse values, knowledges, and practices of Indigenous peoples and communities. Importantly, these articles highlight an essential link between Indigenous education (the teaching of Aboriginal and Torres Strait Islander students) and Indigenous Studies (the teaching 'about' Indigenous peoples), that is "Indigenous peoples have the right to establish and control their educational systems and institutions" (Article 14.1). This quote emphasises the very sovereignty of Indigenous peoples and their intrinsic rights to define and control the Indigenous content with which Australia's education systems (and their teachers) should be engaging. Although teachers and curriculum developers may adhere to the Aboriginal and Torres Strait Islander focus areas within the Australian Professional Standards for Teaching (see Focus Areas 1.4 and 2.4, The Australian Institute for Teaching and School Leadership, 2011), strategies for the teaching of Indigenous histories, cultures, and languages (2.4), and the development of parent and community relationships to support Indigenous students (1.4) should not be solely derived from previous Western practices and values. Rather, for these standards to be truly effective, they must be approached from an Indigenous lens, they must respect, engage with, and defer to Indigenous voices, scholarship, and leadership – you may want to begin by familiarising yourself with Indigenous-led media like *IndigenousX* (https://indigenousx.com.au/), *Speaking Out* (https://www.abc.net.au/indigenous/speaking-out/9579350), and *Blacademia* (https://thebabyacademic.com/podcast/). As noted in the research of many of the Indigenous scholars cited within this chapter (Bodkin-Andrews et al., 2019; Bond et al., 2018; Brown, 2019; Moodie et al., 2019), we must resist the systemic racist silence that has for too long defined the racism (and whiteness) imbedded within Indigenous education and Indigenous studies.

From this chapter, we hope you have learned that it is essential to be aware of racism in all of its forms and that Aboriginal and Torres Strait Islander students do suffer from the impact of racism. Strategies need to be put in place to support our students, and work with our communities to help Aboriginal and Torres Strait Islander students to be even stronger. Education is not just limited to addressing the attitudes and ignorance of the perpetrators of racism, but also to help our Aboriginal and Torres Strait Islander students know that they are not alone.

> Well, education always is the key, and I've always thought that the best way to want somebody to accept and love something is to educate somebody on it and to give ownership to it, so it's our Aboriginal culture and people and everything that goes in with that… then that sense of ownership comes with protection and love, and I see that with little kids, very young, when you teach them something and you go, "This is, you know, our culture. This is our Australia…" .
>
> (Beela the yellow-tailed black cockatoo)

Reflective questions

1. What role do you think the media and political coverage of Aboriginal and Torres Strait Islander peoples play in perpetuating racism?
2. Do you think anti-racist practices may be harmful to Aboriginal and Torres Strait Islander students?
3. Can you describe a time you may have participated in, or perpetuated, racism (knowingly or unknowingly)? How would you act/think differently today?

References

Andersen, M. J., Williamson, A. B., Fernando, P., Eades, S., & Redman, S. (2018). "They took the land, now we're fighting for a house": Aboriginal perspectives about urban housing disadvantage. *Housing Studies*, 33(4), 635–660.

Augoustinos, M., & Rosewarne, D. L. (2001). Stereotype knowledge and prejudice in children. *British Journal of Developmental Psychology*, 19(1), 143–156.

The Australian Institute for Teaching and School Leadership. (2011). *Australian professional standards for teaching*. Education Services Australia. https://www.aitsl.edu.au/docs/default-source/national-policy-framework/australian-professional-standards-for-teachers.pdf?sfvrsn=5800f33c_64

Aveling, N. (2002). Student teachers' resistance to exploring racism: Reflections on "doing" border pedagogy. *Asia-Pacific Journal of Teacher Education*, 30(2), 119–130.

Aveling, N. (2006). "Hacking at our very roots": Rearticulating white racial identity within the context of teacher education. *Race Ethnicity and Education*, 9(3), 261–274.

Baez, M. S. E., & Isaac, P. (2013). A Sweetgrass Method of bullying prevention for Native American youth. *Journal of Indigenous Research*, 3(1), 1–13.

Baez, M. S. E., Isaac, P., & Baez, C. A. (2016). HOPE for Indigenous people battling intergenerational trauma: The Sweetgrass Method. *Journal of Indigenous Research*, 5(2), 1–15.

Behrendt, L., Porter, A. & Vivian, A. (2016). Factors affecting crime rates in six rural Indigenous communities. In J. F. Donnermeye (Ed.) *The Routledge international handbook of rural criminology*. London: Routledge, pp. 33–44.

Bessarab, D. (2017). Interrogating gender: What's race and class got to do with it? In P. Dugeon, J. Herbert, & D. Oxenham (Eds.) *Us women, our ways, our world*. Broome, Western Australia: Magabala Books Aboriginal Corporation, pp. 174–191.

Bessarab, D., & Ng'andu, B. (2010). Yarning about yarning as a legitimate method in Indigenous research. *International Journal of Critical Indigenous Studies*, 3(1), 37–50.

Beswick, D. G., & Hills, M. D. (1972). A survey of ethnocentrism in Australia. *Australian Journal of Psychology*, 24(2), 153–163.

Beyond Blue. (2014). *Discrimination against Indigenous Australians: A snapshot of the views of non-Indigenous people aged 25–44*. Published Online: Beyond Blue Pty Ltd. https://www.beyondblue.org.au/docs/default-source/research-project-files/bl1337-report---tns-discrimination-against-indigenous-australians.pdf?sfvrsn=2

Bin-Sallik, M. (2003). Cultural safety: Let's name it! *The Australian Journal of Indigenous Education*, 32, 21–28.

Bodkin-Andrews, G., & Carlson, B. (2016). The legacy of racism and Indigenous Australian identity within education. *Race Ethnicity and Education*, 19(4), 784–807.

Bodkin-Andrews, G., & Craven, R. G. (2013). Negotiating racism: The voices of Aboriginal Australian post-graduate students. In R. G. Craven & J. Monney (Eds.) *seeding success in indigenous Australian higher education*. Bingley, United Kingdom: Emerald Group Publishing Limited, pp. 157–185.

Bodkin-Andrews, G., Clark, T., & Foster, S. (2019). Aboriginal and Torres Strait Islander secondary students' experiences of racism. In S. Ratuva (Ed.) *The Palgrave handbook of ethnicity*. Singapore: Palgrave Macmillan, pp. 1–24.

Bodkin-Andrews, G., Newey, K., O'Rourke, V., & Craven, R. (2013). Promoting resiliency to counter racism: The lived wisdom within Aboriginal voices. *InPsych: The Bulletin of the Australian Psychological Society Ltd*, 34(4), 14–15.

Bond, C., Mukandi, B., & Coghill, S. (2018). "You cunts can do as you like": The obscenity and absurdity of free speech to Blackfullas. *Continuum*, 32(4), 415–428.

Bonilla-Silva, E. 2013. *Racism without racists: Color-blind racism and the persistence of racial inequality in America*. New York: Rowman & Littlefield.

Brown, L. (2019). Indigenous young people, disadvantage and the violence of settler colonial education policy and curriculum. *Journal of Sociology*, 55(1), 54–71.

Campbell, E. M. & Smalling, S. E. (2013). American Indians and bullying in schools. *Journal of Indigenous Social Development*, 2(1), 1–15.

Carlson, B. (2019). Love and hate at the cultural interface: Indigenous Australians and dating apps. *Journal of Sociology*. Advanced online publication. 10.1177/1440783319833181.

Carlson, B. L., Jones, L. V., Harris, M., Quezada, N., & Frazer, R. (2017). Trauma, shared recognition and Indigenous resistance on social media. *Australasian Journal of Information Systems*, 21. Online publication: 10.3127/ajis.v21i0.1570

De Maio, J. A., Zubrick, S. Silburn, S. R., Lawrence, D. M., Mitrou, F. G., Dalby, R. B., Blair, E. M., Griffin, J., Milroy, H., & Cox, A. (2005). *The Western Australian Aboriginal child health survey: Measuring the social and emotional wellbeing of Aboriginal children and intergenerational effects of forced separation*. Perth: Curtin University of Technology and Telethon Institute for Child Health Research.

Dunn, K. M. (2003). *Racism in Australia: Findings of a survey on racist attitudes and experiences of racism*. Presented at *The Challenges of Immigration and Integration in the European Union and Australia Conference (18-20 Feb)*, University of Sydney. https://openresearch-repository.anu.edu.au/bitstream/1885/41761/4/dunn_paper.pdf

Dunn, K. M. & White, A. (2008). Report on 2007 Australian Capital Territory Racism Survey. Published online: https://researchdirect.westernsydney.edu.au/islandora/object/uws:11587/datastream/PDF/view

Dunn, K. M., White, A. & Gandhi, V. (2010). Understanding racism and cultural diversity: 2007 South Australia Racism Survey. Published online at https://pdfs.semanticscholar.org/900a/a7af153f4b5b9631245bf4b78a4a395ef8a1.pdf

Feagin, J. R. (2006). *Systemic racism: A theory of oppression*. New York: Routledge.

Hogarth, M. (2017). Speaking back to the deficit discourses: A theoretical and methodological approach. *The Australian Educational Researcher*, 44(1), 21–34.

Jones, J. M. (1972). *Prejudice and racism*. Reading, MA: Addison-Wesley.

Kelly, L., & Oxley, E. (1999). A dingo in sheep's clothing?: The rhetoric of youth justice conferencing and the indigenous reality. *Indigenous Law Bulletin*, 4(18), 4–8.

Larson, A., Gillies, M., Howard, P. J., & Coffin, J. (2007). It's enough to make you sick: The impact of racism on the health of Aboriginal Australians. *Australian and New Zealand Journal of Public Health*, 31(4), 322–329.

Littlefield, A., Lieberman, L., Reynolds, L. T., Azevêdo, E. S., Beals, K. L., Brace, C. L., ... & Łaska-Mierzejewska, T. (1982). Redefining race: The potential demise of a concept in physical anthropology [and comments and reply]. *Current Anthropology*, 23(6), 641–655.

Mellor, D. (2003). Contemporary racism in Australia: The experiences of Aborigines. *Personality and Social Psychology Bulletin*, 29(4): 474–486.

Moodie, N., Maxwell, J., & Rudolph, S. (2019). The impact of racism on the schooling experiences of Aboriginal and Torres Strait Islander students: A systematic review. *The Australian Educational Researcher*, 46(2), 273–295.

Moreton-Robinson, A. (2015). *The white possessive: Property, power, and Indigenous Sovereignty*. Minneapolis: University of Minnesota Press.

Paradies, Y. (2017). Overcoming racism as a barrier to community development. In C. Kickett-Tucker, D. Bessarab, J. Coffin, & M. Wright (Eds.) *Mia Mia Aboriginal community development: Fostering cultural security*. Cambridge: Cambridge University Press, pp. 168–185.

Paradies, Y., Ben, J., Denson, N., Elias, A., Priest, N., Pieterse, A., ... & Gee, G. (2015). Racism as a determinant of health: A systematic review and meta-analysis. *PloS ONE*, 10(9), 1–48.

Pedersen, A., Walker, I., & Wise, M. (2005). "Talk does not cook rice": Beyond anti-racism rhetoric to strategies for social action. *Australian Psychologist*, 40(1), 20–31.

Pedersen, A., Walker, I., Paradies, Y., & Guerin, B. (2011). How to cook rice: A review of ingredients for teaching anti-prejudice. *Australian Psychologist*, 46(1), 55–63.

Porter, A. (2019). Aboriginal sovereignty, "crime" and criminology. *Current Issues in Criminal Justice*, 31(1), 122–142.

Price, D., & Price, B. (2013). Good culture – bad culture. Where do we go from here? In R. Craven, A. Dillon & N. Parbury (Eds.) *In black and white: Australians all at the crossroads*. Ballan, VIC: Connor Court Publishing, pp. 191–208.

Rigney, L. I. (1999). Internationalization of an Indigenous anticolonial cultural critique of research methodologies: A guide to Indigenist research methodology and its principles. *Wicazo SA Review*, 14(2), 109–121.

United Nations (2007). United Nations declaration on the rights of indigenous peoples, General Assembly, 13 September, 2007. Retrieved from: https://www.un.org/development/desa/indigenouspeoples/wp-content/uploads/sites/19/2018/11/UNDRIP_E_web.pdf

Walker, I. (1994). Attitudes to minorities: Survey evidence of Western Australians' attitudes to Aborigines, Asians, and women. *Australian Journal of Psychology*, 46, 137–143.

Walter, M., & Butler, K. (2013). Teaching race to teach Indigeneity. *Journal of Sociology*, 49(4), 397–410.

Walter, M., & Andersen, C. (2013). *Indigenous statistics: A quantitative research methodology*. Walnut Creek: Left Coast Press.

Western, J. S. (1969). The Australian Aboriginal: What white Australians know and think about him – A preliminary study. *Race and Class*, 10(4), 411–434.

Chapter 3

Critical self-reflection

A foundational skill

Aunty Denise Proud and Ann Morgan

Who we are

Aunty Denise Proud

My name is Denise Proud and I was born in Wakka Wakka country, Cherbourg Queensland. I have connections through my grandmother to the Koa people of the Winton area and through my grandfather to the Kuku-Yalanji people of North Queensland. My mother was a member of the stolen generation with connections to the Kamilaroi people. I have been involved in early childhood education since the 1960s; have worked as a cultural advisor in correction facilities and across the spectrum of community services including children, youth, men, women, and Aboriginal organisations. I grew up in Cherbourg under the control (so-called 'protection') of the Aboriginals Protection and Restriction of the Sale of Opium Act. I work as a consultant in early childhood education and am an Honorary Research Senior Fellow at the University of Queensland.

Ann Morgan

My name is Ann Morgan, my White Australian family are from Sydney with strong ties to Kurnell and the Northern beaches of Sydney. Our family name means 'lives by the sea'. My father's heritage is English, Irish, Scottish, and German, and from my mother's family I have Irish heritage. When I was a child we moved to Brisbane, and the bayside area of the Quandamooka peoples has become a strong place of belonging and connection for our family, even though many of us now live in other places. Since 2002, my family have lived in Inala, a community of diverse cultures, beautiful trees, parks, and birdlife. I am an educator and researcher in Flexi schools and continue to learn so much through my relationships with Aboriginal colleagues and friends, including Aunty Denise. We have known one another and worked together for almost a decade.

Introduction

Relationships are at the heart of who we are and how we work together. We start this chapter by introducing ourselves in the Aboriginal way – 'Who's your mob and where you from?'

Chapter overview

In this chapter we explore critical self-reflection and how it differs from reflective practice commonly adopted by teachers. Critical self-reflection challenges teachers to deeply explore and understand the underlying assumptions, values, and beliefs that shape their worldview and sociocultural standpoint (Gardner, 2014). When cultivating a strengths-based understanding of Aboriginal and Torres Strait Islander peoples, teachers need to critically self-reflect in three key ways. First, on their own cultural identity; second, on the wider social, cultural and historical context that has shaped their identity; and third, on the strengths, resilience, and richness of Aboriginal and Torres Strait Islander cultural identities of Australia. Readers will learn about critical self-reflection through three questions: Why does it matter? How do I do it? And what difference will it make? Through stories, research, and practical strategies, we as authors – one Aboriginal Elder, long-standing educator and researcher, and one non-Indigenous experienced educator and researcher – share our perspectives on critical self-reflection.

Educational outcomes for Aboriginal and Torres Strait Islander students

In the current Australian educational landscape, despite significant financial investment, Aboriginal and Torres Strait Islander students continue to be disadvantaged in terms of access and educational outcomes, and progress in this area is slow (Shay, 2017). Teachers have a significant role to play in creating change and equity for Aboriginal and Torres Strait Islander peoples. Critical reflection offers a way to address some of the stereotypes, bias (Eberhardt, 2019), and blind spots (Banaji & Greenwald, 2013) that exist within white Australian culture and, therefore, within those of us who are white Australians and have been shaped and influenced by our dominant culture. Whilst this may be challenging, the intention is not to create shame and guilt that lead to defensiveness. When looking at the big picture surrounding complex social issues, it can be easy to fall into feelings of confusion and a sense of being overwhelmed. A more solution-focused approach is to start making changes in ways where the most influence can be exercised – namely, starting with yourself. The professional responsibility of teachers is to be self-aware, which we suggest can be cultivated through critical reflection. We also suggest that by doing this there is opportunity for significantly improved educational outcomes for Aboriginal and Torres Strait Islander students. Further, developing greater self-awareness about personal values, beliefs, and assumptions has the potential to impact the status quo of inequity that continues to exist in Australian culture, especially for those not included in the dominant, white culture.

In the historical context of Australia, invasion, colonisation, institutional racism, and systemic violence have contributed to Aboriginal and Torres Strait Islander peoples being stigmatised and negatively stereotyped (Bodkin-Andrews & Carlson, 2016). This occurs within the media and within the social discourse about Aboriginal and Torres Strait Islander students. Over many generations, the impact of racism expressed in negative stereotypes, low expectations, and limited knowledge about the historical impact of invasion and colonisation (Cronin, 2017) have resulted in policies that directly and negatively affect Aboriginal and Torres Strait Islander peoples, especially in terms of unequal access and limited educational opportunities (Bodkin-Andrews & Carlson, 2016; Priest et al., 2018).

As outlined in the introduction, our lived experience, practice, and research, have identified the reasons why this kind of critical reflection matters. We are learning and practising ways of engaging in this type of critical reflection with ourselves and with teachers (Morgan, 2017). We are beginning to see how it can make a difference for Aboriginal and Torres Strait Islander students. So below we will outline three key ways to develop critical self-reflection to support teachers to become more effective in their teaching practice with all children and young people, and in particular with Aboriginal and Torres Strait Islander students.

The first way of critical self-reflection: know your own cultural identity

An invaluable insight from Aboriginal and Torres Strait Islander peoples is related to knowing your own cultural identity – who you are and where you are from. Before attempting to understand the cultural identity of another person, it is essential that teachers have a strong sense of their own cultural identity.

Why does it matter?

Learning to be critically self-reflective can cultivate greater self-awareness regarding who we are and what is important in our lives and work. Having a strong sense of the importance of our own cultural identity can make us more sensitive to the lived reality of others and the significance of culture for all people, including those whose cultural heritage is different to our own. Unless each person has a sense of knowing and valuing their own cultural identity, it is more difficult to have a deep understanding and appreciation of the significance and meaning of the cultural identity of others and why this knowledge is so important within many cultures. Therefore, knowing our own cultural identity and what has shaped who we are, is the first step in critical self-reflection.

How do I do it?

Engaging in critical self-reflection to consider the significance of our own cultural identity takes time. By doing this 'inner work' (Palmer, 2007) teachers may appreciate more fully the meaning and value of their cultural identity within their own lives. Some key questions to consider and reflect on may include:

- What is your relationship with yourself and your culture? Do you have a strong sense of your own cultural identity or is it something that you never consider?

- Who are your family, those who named you, your ancestors?
- Where did your family come from? Where is your special place?
- Have there been any challenges for you in relation to your cultural identity?
- What steps do you need to take to increase your appreciation of your own cultural identity? How might this be enriching? What might be challenging?

What are the implications for teaching practice of knowing your own cultural identity?

As teachers engage in critical reflection on their own cultural identity, they may experience being both challenged and enriched. Self-awareness highlights the social and cultural influences that have conditioned our ways of thinking and our ways of relating to others, all of which influence who we are as educators. Self-awareness can also complement and enhance a sense of appreciation for the richness of diverse cultures within Australia, especially those of Australia's First Nations peoples. Teachers who know and appreciate the value of their own cultural identity can challenge themselves to translate this knowledge and appreciation to the cultural identity of their students and the families of their students.

For us as authors, educators, and researchers, this awareness of our own cultural identity has led us to being relational practitioners. This way of being is the heart of who we are and how we work. It requires self-awareness and awareness of others. For instance, educational research has highlighted the importance of safe and supportive relationships between teacher and student (Pianta, Hamre, & Allen, 2012; Verschueren & Koomen, 2012). The social and emotional skills that engender relationships are increasingly seen as important for improving educational outcomes (Bingham & Sidorkin, 2004; Morgan, 2018; Morgan, Pendergast, Brown, & Heck, 2015). This is especially the case when teaching students from community-oriented cultures, such as the First Nations peoples of Australia (Shay, 2016). Whilst many teachers regularly engage in reflective practice directly related to curriculum, assessment, student engagement, behaviour management, and learner outcomes, all of which are important, they may not necessarily engage in critical self-reflection on cultural identity. Critical self-reflection is less commonly practised. Many Australians are unaware of the multiple and unique cultures, languages, lifestyles, ceremonies, and beliefs within First Nations peoples of Australia and, in particular, the centrality of relationships. One way of bridging the gap in teachers' knowledge and awareness of the culture of First Nations peoples, is to ensure that relationships between teachers and students are supported by respectful connections with families and communities (see Chapter 6).

Involving families, carers, and the wider community of Aboriginal and Torres Strait Islander students into educational spaces matters. It sends a clear message to children and young people that they are seen, valued, and appreciated not only for their cognitive capacity, but also for who they are as a human being in relationship with others and with their cultural identity. Unless teachers cultivate an authentic relationship and appreciation of the significance of knowing 'who am I?' and 'where am I from?' and modelling this self-awareness in the classroom, teachers may miss vital opportunities for connection and understanding of relational practice. When students feel safe, connected, and valued for who they are, the opportunities for learning and improved educational outcomes increase.

A story from practice: Multiple First Nations peoples of Australia (Aunty Denise Proud)

As I travel across Australia I am constantly astonished by how many people think Aboriginal people are all one nation; and come in one colour only.

Many people are not aware of the Torres Strait Islander people, nor the number of nations and language groups that exist across Australia. Just as there is a wide range of lifestyles in non-Indigenous people from central Melbourne to Coober Pedy, there is a wide or wider spread of lifestyles in the First Nations people in the mainland and islands of Australia.

The spectrum of the First Nations peoples can be appreciated by the fact that there are still more than 100 spoken languages. There are many different cultural practices, artforms, traditional stories, and dances across Australia. Aboriginal and Torres Strait Islander people very probably live in your suburb or area no matter where you live in Australia. There is a diversity of jobs and professions.

There are also common elements in the customs and beliefs of the First Nations people. There is the connection to kin, to family, and the place of our forebears and ancestors. There is very often a deep sense of spirituality, of connection to country, to animals, plants, and the land on which we live. Many will know their totem (our spiritual links), but some may not.

As educators of children and young people, we should always promote flexibility of thinking and avoid generalisations. As we ourselves should always judge the new people we meet on their individual merits, we should encourage students to think for themselves and avoid the stereotypes they may have previously heard.

The second way of critical reflection: Know the social, cultural, and historical influences on how you see the world

As human beings, we often see the world as we are, and feel connected to those who are like us, rather than seeing the world through the perspective of others. Our unconscious and hidden biases (Eberhardt, 2019), and our blindspots (Banaji & Greenwald, 2013) can limit our ability to see the world outside our own viewpoint and perspectives. Each individual can learn to be more self-aware and challenge their unconscious assumptions, values, and biases as they surface, sometimes in unexpected ways and sometimes in surprising and perhaps even embarrassing moments. Self-awareness includes consciousness of the social and cultural circumstances and situations that have shaped us and influenced who we are and how we function in our roles as teachers.

Why does it matter?

By engaging in critical self-reflection we can increase our consciousness of the social, cultural, and historical circumstances and situations that have shaped us and influenced who we are as teachers and how we see and understand the world. This extends to and includes how we see and understand the nature and purpose of education, and the nature and aspirations of the learners and colleagues with whom we engage. Research indicates that low expectations from teachers due to stereotyping and racism can result in limited educational outcomes, poorer health outcomes, and reduced socio-economic status (Priest et al., 2018). Alternatively, high expectations and positive relationships with teachers can make a difference to young people's learning and outcomes (Buckskin, 2012) (see Chapter 7).

How do I do it?

When faced with a challenging issue where you may feel uncertain regarding your knowledge and awareness of appropriate responses to students in your class, in particular those who identify as Aboriginal or Torres Strait Islander, take some time to reflect on your own reactions and consider how these might have contributed to the situation. Critically reflecting on your own practice and making changes to conditioned responses is always enhanced through collaboration and mentoring. Find others in your staff team who also wish to enhance their teaching practices with Aboriginal and Torres Strait Islander students.

Some of the following questions may be useful to consider as you critically reflect on practice.

Being a relational practitioner

- Do you have a positive relationship with your students? Do you know and understand them beyond your classroom? For example, are you aware of where they are from, what are their interests and goals?
- Is there anything in your teaching practice that would indicate to your students that you have a genuine interest and commitment to Aboriginal and Torres Strait Islander perspectives? For example, are you embedding Indigenous perspectives and relevant contemporary issues into your content, pedagogies, and resources? Are there any Aboriginal symbols, artwork, artefacts in your classroom or within your resources that would indicate an interest and commitment? In your teaching resources do you include materials written and created by First Nations peoples? Do you invite guest speakers who are First Nations people to present to your students?
- If you are aware that your students identify as Aboriginal or Torres Strait Islander, have you made any contact with their families, community, or Elders as a sign of interest and commitment to them as learners, prior to this situation arising?

Reframing deficit stereotypes

- If you identify any negativity or any stereotypical attitudes in yourself when facing challenges, consider whether these are the result of social conditioning. Could there be another perspective that you have not considered? Who might be an ally or mentor for you in this space on your staff team?

- Is there some deficit language or attitudes associated with your students that you have heard from other staff, within the local community, or in the media that might be affecting your perspective? Are there any assumptions you have made that need challenging?
- Are you aware of any biases you may have brought to the relationship or situation?

Collaborative problem solving (Ablon & Pollastri, 2018)

- Do you have certain expectations that were not met and that caused you frustration?
- Do you think you have communicated these clearly to your students and asked them about their expectations?
- Have you taken the time to listen and understand the perspective of your student/s?
- Have you made any assumptions that your students should understand your view or know better?
- Are you aware of any underlying needs that your student might have that have caused them to behave in a certain way that you found challenging?
- Were you imposing your will on a student without including their perspectives on how the situation or problem could be resolved?
- When faced with resistance, were you able to remain curious and ask clarifying questions?
- Are you conscious of ways that you could possibly compromise and find a shared solution? Who do you seek support from within your staff team or beyond?

What are the implications for teaching practice of knowing the social, cultural, and historical influences on how you see the world?

By becoming more deliberate in recognising and including a wider range of social and cultural perspectives in classroom conversations and activities, teachers can influence student learning outcomes. By having the courage to consider how conscious or unconscious bias influences the ways we perceive others and the ways we communicate our expectations of others, teachers can directly influence a young person's experience of success or otherwise, in their learning outcomes. The mindset of Australian teachers is shaped by their awareness (or lack of awareness) of Australian colonial history and how this has negatively affected Aboriginal and Torres Strait Islander peoples. Negative stereotypes and unconscious bias, high or low expectations of learners, and whether a teacher engages authentically in critical reflection and relational practice (Buckskin, 2012; Shay & Wickes, 2017), all have serious impact on learning experiences and outcomes for students. Therefore, teachers have a professional responsibility to grow their personal awareness and in their capacity to critically self-reflect on the impact they have on their students as they learn about the perspectives and experiences of Australia's First Nations peoples.

A story from practice: Understanding white Australian identity, culture and privilege (Ann Morgan)

As a teacher who has worked for over 35 years in a wide range of educational settings, I have learned and continue to learn the importance of being open to peeling back the layers of social, historical, and cultural conditioning that have shaped me. As a middle-class, white, well-educated Australian woman, it is possible and unfortunately probable, that I can be unaware and biased. I can assume that my experience and worldview is 'the norm' when that is clearly not the case in a pluralist, diverse country like Australia. Through engaging with diverse cultures and being challenged to critically reflect on the social, cultural, and historical privilege that I enjoy, I am now aware that many people do not experience the same access, opportunities, and privilege that I have experienced. The barriers to success and 'making it' are far more challenging for those who are not part of the dominant 'white norm' within Australian mainstream culture.

The message that hard work can achieve anything comes across loud and clear in our current social, cultural, historical, and political discourse. Fairness, however, is frequently not the outcome of 'having a go'. Many other hidden factors that lie beneath our collective unconscious are at play in terms of whether people experience fairness and equity. If the cultural, social, and historical context of my white Australian life were different, I would not necessarily have enjoyed the level of privilege that has come my way. When working with Aboriginal and Torres Strait Islander students and colleagues, I need to be critically reflective and challenge taken-for-granted assumptions. I need to be prepared to ask myself questions such as: How has my cultural and social conditioning influenced how I relate to students and colleagues? How might my own need to help, support and at times unconsciously rescue or save, disempower others by not recognising the resilience and agency of those with whom I work? Alternatively, can I be an ally and an advocate, working with, and guided by, those with whom I work, rather than only being a helper who may do more harm because I am not critically self-aware?

I have become more of a co-learner and a facilitator of learning rather than an expert, know-all, controller of learning. I now expect and work towards finding the collective wisdom of the group. By working collaboratively and recognising the agency of all participants in the learning group, outcomes are richer and deeper than one singular imposed perspective. Creating a culture of listening, dialogue, and collaborative problem solving (Ablon & Pollastri, 2018), has become a priority.

Learning to be critically self-reflective has opened my mind and heart to the lived reality of others, and assists me to recognise my own cultural biases. All teachers, particularly those who are part of the dominant white Australian culture, can learn to challenge and question their own assumptions, values, and biases to ensure they are acting for the best interests of all their students. By critically reflecting on practice, teachers can be conscious of acting inclusively. By doing so, they can be enriched by the cultures and worldviews of their students and colleagues who identify as First Nations Australians.

The third way of critical self-reflection: Know the strengths, resilience, and richness of Aboriginal and Torres Strait Islander cultural identities

Over time, stereotypes applied to particular marginalised groups of people in our society are often inflated and exaggerated. Entrenched, negative stereotypes are then perceived more broadly as being 'real' or 'true'. Such negativity influences the larger social discourse, by emphasising perceived deficits and problems, rather than the strengths, resilience, and richness within a group. Due to deficit discourses that continue to shape the stereotypical perceptions of Aboriginal and Torres Strait Islander peoples within Australia, teachers need to critically reflect upon their own stereotypes and biases. To achieve this, it is first necessary to be aware when they occur and then constantly challenge these stereotypical mindsets and the associated limiting beliefs. By re-affirming the strengths, resilience, and richness of Aboriginal and Torres Strait Islander cultural identities that have shaped and continue to shape our nation, unconscious biases and stereotypes can be reframed. Cultural conditioning is often imposed and learnt unconsciously and can be unlearnt and changed by making a conscious choice to change ingrained habits of thinking as they arise, without guilt or shame.

Why does it matter?

In the late 20th and early 21st century, First Nations peoples of Australia are exercising agency by reclaiming and telling their own stories, history, and experience in music, art, dance, literature, theatre, and film. For a long time, it has actually been white Australians who have defined what it means to be an Aboriginal or Torres Strait Islander person. Politicians creating government policies that directly affect Aboriginal and Torres Strait Islander peoples frequently have not taken enough time to genuinely and widely consult and work in partnership with the diverse range of First Nations peoples of this country and so their voices have not been heard. There remains resistance to really listening and understanding their lived experiences and perspectives. For example, the 2017 Uluru Statement from the Heart did not receive the level of attention by governments or non-Indigenous Australians that would enable a mature and genuine dialogue for change and self-determination to occur.

Given the diversity of cultures in Australia and, in particular, the richness of the cultures of our First Nations peoples, teachers have a personal and professional responsibility to become more conscious and aware of the ways that the dominant culture has shaped them and in turn, how this affects their students. By participating in ongoing professional learning, teachers can raise their level of awareness about the cultural heritage and identities of Aboriginal and Torres Strait Islander peoples. This commitment will also assist teachers to know more about the issues that impact and affect the degree of equity that Aboriginal and Torres Strait Islander students experience within the education system.

How do I do it?

By consciously engaging in critical self-reflection, teachers can learn to recognise how their social conditioning, unconscious beliefs, biases, and assumptions can impact negatively on Aboriginal and Torres Strait Islander peoples. For example, teachers can consider whether there is a lack of recognition and awareness of the richness of the cultures of the First Nations peoples of Australia within themselves, their colleagues, and in the general student body. As teachers become more self-aware, they can learn how to minimise and deconstruct expressions of cultural superiority that may be the result of ignorance and lack of awareness within themselves, or within the culture of their schools.

A significant way of appreciating the strengths, resilience, and richness of Aboriginal and Torres Strait Islander identities is to be proactive in learning about the First Nations peoples of Australia. The following suggestions for professional learning can be explored by teachers:

- Read books, view films, and become familiar with music, dance, and art works that are created by First Nations peoples. Understand the background stories and motivation for these works;
- Take responsibility for your own capacity to learn from reading, viewing, and engaging in cultural experiences;
- Attend cultural events in your local community;
- Take responsibility for your own education rather than only relying on Elders and other Aboriginal and Torres Strait Islander peoples to be your personal tutor;
- Develop authentic relationships and friendships with Aboriginal and Torres Strait Islander peoples through which you share, learn, collaborate, and become allies;
- Take seriously and become highly competent in the national Professional Standards for teachers relating to Aboriginal and Torres Strait Islander peoples (Australian Institute for Teaching and School Leadership (AITSL), 2019):
    - 1.4 Strategies for teaching Aboriginal and Torres Strait Islander students: Demonstrate broad knowledge and understanding of the impact of culture, cultural identity and linguistic background on the education of students from Aboriginal and Torres Strait Islander backgrounds;
    - 2.4 Understand and respect Aboriginal and Torres Strait Islander people to promote reconciliation between Indigenous and non-Indigenous Australians;
    - Demonstrate broad knowledge of, understanding of and respect for Aboriginal and Torres Strait Islander histories, cultures and languages.

What difference does it make?

Many Australians may not have met or know an Aboriginal person as a friend or colleague. Many Australians are not fully aware of the stories, experiences, and wisdom of the cultures of the First Nations peoples of Australia. These are rich and complex stories that raise complex issues that teachers can engage with and learn from. How do teachers, who have responsibility for educating young people, have conversations that are uncomfortable at times? Can teachers have the capacity and maturity to remain in the discomfort of complexity, in order to engage with the issues that must be addressed for First Nations peoples of this country?

A real challenge for teachers is to learn to listen, to ask, rather than tell or advise, or try to fix those who are perceived as 'the problem'. The difference this awareness will make will be felt by Aboriginal and Torres Strait Islander young people and their families (again, see Chapter 7 for examples of building such relationships). The valuing and respect that can be offered to the First Nations peoples of Australia open up the possibility of reconciliation, rather than stereotyping, and including rather than excluding or 'othering'. To be 'othered' implies being treated as inferior and 'less than', or being dismissed and excluded due to perceived negative differences. Knowing another person and appreciating their story and life experiences open up the possibility of inclusion by cultivating respect, empathy, and compassion. These capacities can be taught and modelled within classrooms, schools, and learning communities more generally. Synot (May 7, 2019) captured the potential transformation that is possible through respectful relationships between First Nations peoples and the wider Australian community when he stated:

> Australians have come to understand that First Nations peoples have a political and cultural right to be heard and to determine their own affairs. Many also understand that this power is key to addressing what the Uluru statement termed "the torment of our powerlessness". This means a new relationship between Indigenous and non-Indigenous peoples in Australia that establishes the foundations for a better future.

A story from practice: Cultivating empathy – thinking and being outside comfort zones (Aunty Denise Proud)

I remember that when I was young, my family would sometimes visit Brisbane from Cherbourg. This didn't happen very often as we were quite poor. Whenever we visited Brisbane, one of the first places we would go was Musgrave Park[1] in South Brisbane. Dad would walk around and find some of his old mates (who lived in the park and had nothing). We would be introduced to them and we would sit in a circle yarning, laughing, and reminiscing. One of my strongest memories is that dad would often take off a shirt, a coat or a pair of shoes; and hand it to one of his old friends without a word spoken. I look back fondly on those times and realise that this was one of the many ways that my sisters, brothers, and I learned to empathise and identify without judgement. My parents were always thinking of others, never forgetting them, treasuring the memories of their times spent together. I would sit quietly and watch the laughing, the natural interactions, and the feeling of being at ease with one other.

I suppose I absorbed my capacity to empathise from my parents, but it was only on later reflection that I realised that to empathise a person must truly think and be outside one's comfort zone, "to be in another's shoes".

[1]Aboriginal people have been meeting on these grounds for many generations.

Conclusion

Whilst there is no 'one size fits all' solution for meeting the diverse educational needs of the First Nations peoples of Australia, there are key concepts and practices that support the recognition and appreciation of the issues of concern for students from Aboriginal and Torres Strait Islander backgrounds. In the first instance, teachers can prioritise relational practice in their classrooms. This is not only beneficial for the education of students from Aboriginal and Torres Strait Islander backgrounds, but for all students.

Relational practice is a significant pedagogical approach that is strengthened and enhanced by critical self-reflection. In this chapter, readers have explored three key ways of engaging in critical self-reflection. First, know your own cultural identity; second, know the social, cultural, and historical influences on how you see the world; and finally, know the strengths, resilience, and richness of Aboriginal and Torres Strait Islander cultural identities. Within these three key ways of engaging in critical self-reflection, ideas and strategies have been outlined to explain: *Why does it matter? How do I do it? And, what difference does it make?*

In order to name and address the social and historical complexity within the relationships between First Nations peoples of Australia and the wider community, high levels of maturity, honesty, respect, and openness are required. Whilst this chapter focuses on teachers working in our schools, government representatives who create educational policies, and leaders of educational institutions who implement these policies, are also implicated. Without engaging in critical self-reflection, government representatives, educational leaders, and teachers will remain 'stuck' and unable to shift deeply held cultural biases and stereotypes that have been shaped and conditioned by our shared history and fuelled by the inherent oppression of invasion and colonisation. Australians must come to terms with the pervasive inequities related to educational outcomes, health, and wellbeing that continue to impact on the First Nations peoples of this country. These challenging issues will not significantly shift without commitment to increased knowledge, self-awareness, and engagement with critical self-reflection, by politicians, educational leaders, and teachers, all of whom influence and shape our precious children and young people. Students from Aboriginal and Torres Strait Islander backgrounds deserve better outcomes and a better future than what is currently happening.

Reflective questions

1. Within relationships in teaching and learning contexts, how might teachers make time and space to recognise and value the cultural identities of their students who identify as First Nations peoples? What practical steps need to be taken to enact critical self-reflection?
2. Whilst many teachers may not feel empowered to widely influence government policies and large institutions, what are three personal priorities and commitments to critical self-reflection that could support positive change within your classrooms and learning community?
3. After reading this chapter, how would you respond to the following three questions about critical self-reflection: Why does it matter? How do I do it? And, what difference does it make?

References

Ablon, J. S., & Pollastri, A. R. (2018). *The school discipline fix: Changing behavior using the collaborative problem solving approach*. New York: WW Norton & Company.

Australian Institute for Teaching and School Leadership (AITSL) (2019). Australian Professional Standards for Teachers. https://www.aitsl.edu.au/teach/standards

Banaji, M. R., & Greenwald, A. G. (2013). *Blindspot: Hidden biases of good people*. New York: Delacorte Press.

Bingham, C., & Sidorkin, A. M. (Eds.) (2004). *No education without relation*. New York: Peter Lang.

Bodkin-Andrews, G., & Carlson, B. (2016). The legacy of racism and Indigenous Australian identity within education. *Race Ethnicity and Education*, 19(4), 784–807. doi:10.1080/1 3613324.2014.969224

Buckskin, P. (2012). Engaging Indigenous students. In K. Price (Ed.) *Aboriginal and Torres Strait Islander education: An introduction for the teaching profession*. Cambridge: Cambridge University Press, pp. 164–180.

Cronin, D. (2017). Trapped by history: Democracy, human rights and justice for indigenous people in Australia. *Australian Journal of Human Rights*, 23(2), 220–241. doi:10.1080/1 323238X.2017.1373739

Eberhardt, J. L. (2019). *Biased: Uncovering the hidden prejudice that shapes what we see, think and do*. New York: Viking.

Gardner, F. (2014). *Being critically reflective: Engaging in holistic practice*. New York: Palgrave Macmillan.

Morgan, A. (2017). Cultivating critical reflection: Educators making sense and meaning of professional identity and relational dynamics in complex practice. *Teaching Education*, 28(1), 41–55. doi: 10.1080/10476210.2016.1219335

Morgan, A. (2018). *Different ways of being an educator: Relational practice*. Bloomington, IN: Balboa Press.

Morgan, A., Pendergast, D., Brown, R., & Heck, D. (2015). Relational ways of being an educator: Trauma-informed practice supporting disenfranchised young people. *International Journal of Inclusive Education*, 19(10), 1037–1051. doi:10.1080/13603116 .2015.1035344

Palmer, P. (2007). *The courage to teach: Exploring the inner landscape of a teacher's life*. San Francisco, CA: Wiley.

Pianta, R. C., Hamre, B. K., & Allen, J. P. (2012). Teacher-student relationships and engagement: Conceptualizing, measuring, and improving the capacity of classroom interactions. In S. L. Christenson, A. L. Reschly, & C. Wylie (Eds.) *Handbook of research on student engagement*. Boston, MA: Springer US, pp. 365–386.

Priest, N., Slopen, N., Woolford, S., Philip, J. T., Singer, D., Kauffman, A. D., ... Williams, D. (2018). Stereotyping across intersections of race and age: Racial stereotyping among white adults working with children. *PLoS ONE*, 13(10). doi:10.1371/journal. pone.0205614

Shay, M. (2016). Re-imagining Indigenous education through flexi schooling. In D. Bland (Ed.) *Imagination for inclusion*. Oxon: Routledge, pp. 116–127.

Shay, M. (2017). Emerging ideas for innovation in Indigenous education: A research synthesis of Indigenous educative roles in mainstream and flexi schools. *Teaching Education*, 28(1), 12–26. doi:10.1080/10476210.2016.1210594

Shay, M., & Wickes, J. (2017). Aboriginal identity in education settings: Privileging our stories as a way of deconstructing the past and re-imagining the future. *A Publication of the Australian Association for Research in Education*, 44(1), 107–122. doi:10.1007/ s13384-017-0232-0

Synot, E. (May 7, 2019). Constitutional reform made easy: How to achieve the Uluru statement and a First Nations voice. *The Conversation*. http://theconversation.com/constitutional-reform-made-easy-how-to-achieve-the-uluru-statement-and-a-first-nations-voice-116141

Verschueren, K., & Koomen, H. M. Y. (2012). Teacher–child relationships from an attachment perspective. *Attachment & Human Development*, 14(3), 205–211. doi:10.1080/146 16734.2012.672260

Chapter 4

Cultural learnings

Foundations for Aboriginal student wellbeing

Cheryl Kickett-Tucker

Who I am

Cheryl Kickett-Tucker

My name is Cheryl Kickett-Tucker and I am a Traditional Owner, academic and community development practitioner. I am a proud Wadjuk (Perth region) Noongar Aboriginal from the south-west of Western Australia (WA) with traditional ties to Ballardong and Yued Noongar people of the wheatbelt region of WA. I have worked with Australian Aboriginal people all my life in the fields of education, sport, and health and I am very passionate about using my research to make a real difference to the lives of Aboriginal children and their families. I was the chief editor of the award-winning text-book Mia Mia Aboriginal Community Development: Fostering Cultural Security (Kickett-Tucker et al., 2016) and I have also begun writing children's fiction. I am a very keen amateur photographer who likes to capture the strengths and positive elements of being Aboriginal. I am also a very active volunteer for Koya Aboriginal Corporation where I coach sport to many children and youth after school, on weekends, and during school holidays.

Introduction

Aboriginal culture is strength, and acts as a protective force for children and families (Lohoar, Butera, & Kennedy, 2014, p. 2). According to the English language, culture is defined as "the way of life of a people, including their attitudes, values, beliefs, arts, sciences, modes of perception, and habits of thought and activity…" (Oxford Reference Dictionary, 2020). However, for Australian Aboriginal people culture consists of protocols, identity, spirituality, food, languages, and lore (South West Aboriginal Land and Sea Council, 2020). Importantly though, culture is the very epicentre of an Aboriginal person's life, living, and sense of self. It is based on a different set of values and norms from 'mainstream' culture (Kickett-Tucker & Hanse, 2016) and has a direct link to wellbeing (Kickett-Tucker, 2009; Priest et al., 2013) and is important for identity development (Forrest, 1998). In schools, evidence suggests that a positive Aboriginal identity via culture combined with positive student identity increases the chances of successful school outcomes such as attendance, retention, and academic grades for Aboriginal children and youth (Purdie et al., 2000). However, how can teachers support a positive Aboriginal identity via culture in the school environment? (Also see Chapter 5.) I will present the need for decolonisation of teachers' perceptions, their teaching style, choice of teaching content, and the teaching environment by exploring Aboriginal culture, identity, and student wellbeing via the lens of an Aboriginal worldview.

Firstly though, I will define and justify the use of the terms Indigenous and Aboriginal in the Australian context. The term Indigenous is commonly used by Australian politicians and government departments to refer to the First Peoples of Australia and according to this definition it includes Aboriginal people and Torres Strait Islanders (Australian Bureau of Statistics, 2010). On Australia's eastern border, Indigenous is the preference, however, the term First Nations is starting to appear in the literature and in conversation. In Western Australia, however, my traditional lands, the term Aboriginal is a commonly accepted term among the First Peoples and I will use this term in this chapter.

Aboriginal worldview

Aboriginal worldviews are important in this chapter and are specifically related to pedagogy because they determine Aboriginal ontology (perspectives of reality) and Aboriginal epistemology (Aboriginal ways of thinking about or knowing reality). A worldview refers to the ideas and beliefs which a group of people hold about its world and the people and things in it (Arabena, 2008), providing a road map in which to live, learn, and survive and thrive (Martin & Mirraboopa, 2003). The tools needed to journey on the road of life are integral components of the Aboriginal worldview and include values, morals, and lore that guide and support behaviour, attitudes, and perceptions (Kickett-Tucker & Ife, 2018). The Aboriginal worldview works as a holistic lens that integrates, interconnects, and interrelates a set of principles of relationships, respect, connectedness, and meaning for how to learn, live, and be (Arabena, 2008).

Aboriginal perspectives of reality (ontology) and Aboriginal ways of thinking/ knowing of realities (epistemology) guide Aboriginal learning and, in the case of schools, it also must guide the teacher, the classroom environment, the content, and pedagogy. It is important that an Aboriginal lens is cast upon who teaches, what is taught and how it is taught. For instance, the Aboriginal worldview is communal and relational whereas the non-Aboriginal, Western worldview focuses on individualism and objectivity (Bessarab & Ng'andu, 2010; Tuhiwai Smith, 2003).

Aboriginal worldview shapes Aboriginal thinking and knowing within nine domains:

1. Life and living – continuous and circular with no finite end;
2. Capital – land, nature, animals, and plants are vital assets;
3. Environment – live in harmony with the environment (capital);
4. Time – no finite end with little relevance;
5. Land – custodianship that looks after the land;
6. Economies – land is the economy that must be respected and protected;
7. Self – kinship and reciprocity are central;
8. Society – oral in nature;
9. Religion/spirituality – everything and everyone is connected.

Cheryl Kickett-Tucker

Aboriginal ways of thinking (epistemology)

Theme	Western	Aboriginal Australian
Life and living	Based on a lineal understanding of the universe and life – a beginning and end.	Based on a non-lineal understanding of the cosmos and life – circular and continual
Capital	Money (particularly accumulation of wealth) as capital	Environment (nature) as capital
Environment	Dominance over environment	Living with nature
Time	Time and the measurement of time is a prevailing rigid element of society	Time and the measurement of time is less of an important element of society
Land	Land is owned by entities	We are custodians of the land
Economies	Land is an economic resource to be used to benefit society	Land (environment and nature) is viewed as our mother, the giver of life, and is protected to support life
Self	Individualism is a keystone	Kin-ism (kinship) and reciprocity is a keystone
Society	Literate societies	Oral societies
Religion/ spirituality	Afterlife, heaven and hell. Emphasis on regular daily prayer to God. Belief and acknowledgment in only one God (Just, 2017)	Dynamic, evolving, that connects past, present and future. Emphasis on relationships between and among every living and non-living thing. Is totemic (Kolig, 1988)

To further address this concept, Aboriginal ways of thinking (epistemology) compared to non-Aboriginal, Western ways of thinking are illustrated in Table 4.1.

Aboriginal ways of thinking influence behaviours and ways of doing. Table 4.2 shows a comparison of non-Aboriginal, Western ways of doing with Aboriginal ways.

Meaning for all experiences, perceptions, and attitudes is influenced by the values often reflected in Dreamtime stories. The Dreaming or in Noongar culture, Nyitting, refers to the spiritual worldview of Creation where the values for life and living are established. The Dreaming provides the "blueprint for life" because not only do Aboriginal people believe in the Dreaming, they live it:

> Not only is it the period of creation when the mythical ancestors roamed the earth, but it is also the life spirit which ties man, society and nature, both past and present, to the living now.
>
> (O'Keefe, 1984, p. 50)

Aboriginal people engage in an oral society and use storytelling to make sense of their reality. However, since the stories use cultural and archetypal metaphors to explain morals and values from the Dreaming, the results provide endless possibilities for one story or one reality. What this means is that there are multiple narratives to describe multiple realities in the Aboriginal worldview. Narratives are told by Aboriginal storytellers (teachers) within a spiritual and relational worldview. This is in direct contrast to the non-Aboriginal, Western worldview where stories are told from a rational and material lens (Kickett-Tucker & Ife, 2018).

Ways of doing (ontology)

Theme	Western	Aboriginal Australian
Society	Non-Spiritual	Spiritual
	scientific proof determines existence and truth	evidence is not always needed to explain the unseen
Identity	In relation	Relationships
	to material objects, particularly one's job and/or title	comprised of intricate, related networks of individual, family, nuclear, kinship, and community relations
		formed with connection with others and with "Country"
Lifestyle	"Do-ers"	"Be-ers"
	care about progressing their livelihoods by using their environment	content with what they have, including where they live
	look to the future to see where they can move forward	
Time	Linear	Cyclical
	finite and has a start and end	comes, goes, and returns again
Lore	Hierarchical	Customs
	people are assigned roles and consequently relationships are formed	authority is given to others based on relationships, age, and importantly cultural wisdom.
Wellness	An outcome	A journey
	based on successes of meeting their individual goals	quality of relationship with others

A story from home

In 2005, Cheryl's own child came home from primary school with year 6 homework. It was an English assignment and the question was "Write about when your family first arrived in Australia?" The author's child immediately said: "But Mum, we have always been here since the Dreaming." This is a classic example of an Aboriginal student worldview supported at home and which questioned a Western worldview at school.

Today, some 15 years later, Cheryl's youngest child brought home HASS worksheets about Aboriginal people. The activity was titled: "The Battle of Pinjarra." The child asked what it was about and Cheryl responded by describing the Aboriginal version of history regarding Pinjarra and re-labelled the event accordingly the Pinjarra Massacre. The child immediately told the teacher and we are looking forward to the author visiting the classroom to provide the Aboriginal lens to this history lesson. This example shows that time has moved on, but there are still challenges for teachers to gather up-to-date and culturally appropriate information/worksheets about Aboriginal people and culture.

Aboriginal culture

Culture is grounded in the Aboriginal worldview and structured by Aboriginal ontology and epistemology. It is made up of protocols, identity, spirituality, food, languages, and lore (South West Aboriginal Land and Sea Council, 2020) and according to Turner (2010), spirituality and a sense of sacredness is essential to Aboriginal culture and must be respected. Aboriginal culture is transmitted within

Cheryl Kickett-Tucker

a social order led by Elders and shared in a kinship system whereby family are central:

> Family is at the heart of Noongar culture. Our family trees are vast. Noongar ancestral connections are like an intricate system of roots, reaching back to the Dreaming or Nyitting. Our people are connected by kinships, the way stars in the sky form intricate constellations, connecting points together to form a unique shape.
>
> (South West Aboriginal Land and Sea Council, 2016)

The importance of culture is defined by the actions of Elders who share cultural learnings as early as the birth of a koorlong (child):

> Because children represented the future of the Dreaming, their education and development were very important. The process of imparting their complex responsibilities began at birth. Dreaming stories as told to children, stressed Aboriginal values such as respect for old people, sharing of food and duties to kin and the land.
>
> (Parbury, 1991, p. 24)

Connection to identity

Identity is formed by the knowledge and feelings attached to family, kin, culture, and country (Forrest 1998). Specifically, identity is "a part of an individual's self-concept that derives from his or her knowledge of membership in a social group (or groups) together with the value and emotional significance attached to that membership" (Phinney, 1992, p. 159).

Identity is a process that occurs over time. Culture is also taught over time in which customs, values and beliefs are shared (Kickett-Tucker & Ife, 2018). Identity and culture come together during the cultural process because it is a shared phenomenon between social groups and culture which helps connect individuals to their Aboriginal identity (Victorian Indigenous Youth Affairs Council, n.d; Kickett-Tucker, 2009). For young people, the identity process and connection to culture is a focus because:

> A strong racial identity gives our children and youth hope for a future, to be proud of who they are and where they belong, to be connected to something bigger than themselves, to be connected to a circle of strength, love and support.
>
> (Kickett-Tucker, 2009, p. 131)

It is important to understand the connection of identity with culture because children, and particularly youth, begin to interpret their social worlds in order to bring meaning to their sense of self. Specifically, culture is an important component of identity development which may have an impact on the demands of the dominant society (Gfellner & Armstrong, 2012; Phinney, 1992). When non-Aboriginal education is the dominant environment, then culture and identity will come into play because it has been shown that regular school attendance is one of the most significant factors of Aboriginal school success (Hancock et al., 2013), but it is the cultural disconnection experienced by Aboriginal children that is most threatening (Partington & McCudden, 1992).

Healthy and culturally sound Aboriginal identity is vital for Aboriginal children as it allows them to feel "no shame to be yourself … secure … safe and part of the community … self-confident … comfortable" (Kickett-Tucker & Coffin, 2011, p. 159). Culture provides a pathway for the future:

> When they have culture first, they have the very thing that will hold them strong throughout their lives, no matter what they choose to do or where they choose to do it.
>
> (Elder Eustice Tipiloura, 2014, p. 13)

These are highly valued feelings and morals that strengthen Aboriginal wellbeing. In this way cultural connection is critical to identity and wellbeing. For Aboriginal children to engage successfully in school, their culture, language, and identity must be recognised, valued, and taught so that their self-esteem and wellbeing have a strong platform from which to grow and strengthen their school engagement.

A story from experience

An Aboriginal male reflected on his education and shares the following about teacher engagement:

"I went to co-educational state high school and then I transferred to an Aboriginal school. When I look back at my teachers, this is what I know… The best teachers were those who sought a long-term relationship with Aboriginal people. They were actively committed to individual students and they were in it for the long term. In my case, when I relocated to the Aboriginal school, I was fortunate to have male teachers who treated me like a friend. This started because we shared our love of music. They knew when to engage and when not to engage because we developed a bond with mutual respect. I am still connected with my teachers even though the school bell rang long ago." The student graduated year 12 in 1984.

Connection to wellbeing

Aboriginal identity and related self-esteem are intrinsically linked to Aboriginal wellbeing (Kickett-Tucker, 2009; Priest et al., 2013). This is because the strength of an individual's Aboriginal identity is important in the self-evaluation process needed to arrive at a level of self-esteem (Umaña-Taylor & Fine, 2004; Umaña-Taylor et al., 2002). The connection between Aboriginal identity and self-esteem is vital, because an individual will create an image about themselves and, in turn, these mind maps will set the parameters for their subsequent behaviour.

When culture is strong and identity is celebrated, then the wellbeing of individuals, families, and communities are strengthened. In the Northern Territory for example, Balunu is a children and young person's program reconnecting children to culture. According to Balunu founder, David Cole, culture is the focus because:

...it's about building self-identity, and with that as the foundation we move to self-worth, self-belief, getting the kids to understand who they are and be able to walk in two worlds.

(in Davidson, 2014, p. 1)

Research from other Indigenous peoples from around the world has shown that cultural continuation protects lives and guards against suicide and self-harm. This is also the case for Indigenous Sami and Canadian youth (Chandler & Lalonde, 2008; Silviken & Kvernmo, 2007).

Similarly, other studies have shown that a strong sense of one's identity, and pride is positively associated with psychological wellbeing and the ability to develop strengthening strategies for dealing with discrimination and the challenges of daily life (Chandler & Lalonde, 2008; Kvernmo & Heyerdahl, 2004; Umaña-Taylor, Yazedijian, & Bamaca-Gomez, 2004). In sum, racial identity helps to develop resilience so that skills and knowledge are developed to assist the individual to overcome and cope with life's challenges (Jackson & Sellers, 1996; Niles, 1999).

For Aboriginal children, a healthy and culturally sound Aboriginal identity is vital because it supports security through being part of the community and encourages self-confidence. Furthermore, culture and identity help equip Aboriginal children and youth with the skills required to manage adversity and positively influence their self-esteem (Kickett-Tucker, 2009).

Time for reflection

Culture is not just about learning heritage, Dreamtime stories, flora, fauna, dance, music and protocols ... it is also about the shared values of being Aboriginal. In the school setting, culture is also demonstrated by the respect and care Aboriginal children give to others. It is the reciprocity and connection of belonging and the bond experienced between kin. These values are shared at birth when kinship is determined. This is the Aboriginal strength. How does this strength translate at school, in the playground and in the classroom? What can you do to re-focus your lens to see Aboriginal students' strengths and how will you build their strengths into your teaching content and methods?

But what happens at school? Implications for pedagogy

While school is a primary agent for social change, it is also a place that is predominantly non-Aboriginal which may alienate Aboriginal children, causing them to have a difficult time adjusting and in turn may lead to them experiencing confusion and conflict in regard to their racial identity (Partington & McCudden 1992).

So how can a non-Aboriginal teacher influence their classrooms so that Aboriginal students' worldview and identity are acknowledged, respected, and affirmed? Using the Aboriginal worldview that says everything in the Aboriginal world is created and connected by relationships, then the first change must begin with the non-Aboriginal teacher's own relationship with themselves (see Chapter 3). White privilege and the worldviews of teachers need to be acknowledged in the everyday life of these professionals because it permeates their actions, reactions, and expectations toward Aboriginal people and particularly Aboriginal students. To start with, it must be acknowledged that colonisation has and continues to grant privileges to certain groups based on their ethnicity. Colonisation is a severe imposition of Western knowledge systems, which do not recognise, respect, or value the knowledge systems of the original inhabitants of the land (Burchill, Higgins, Ramsey, & Taylor, 2006; Ife, 2013). An outcome of colonisation is the privilege that is afforded to some and not others. Privileges such as wealth, land, status, and opportunities are distributed to select groups. Yet many Aboriginal people have not experienced such opportunities because they simply don't have that privilege.

First, to begin the journey of decolonisation in the school environment, the teacher must be critically self-aware to identify and recognise his/her own position of privilege and understand his/her position as part of the dominant colonist population and recognise and re-focus his/her thinking and behaviours (again see Chapter 3). To do this, the teacher needs to acknowledge that he/she is teaching Aboriginal students and then must shift his/her view and intent accordingly. In regard to view, the teacher must recognise that Aboriginal people have their own worldview which will determine Aboriginal student values, perceptions, and attitudes, which ultimately will impact behaviour. To actively recognise Aboriginal student worldviews, the teacher needs to stop, reflect, and alter their 'privileged' judgements, expectations, attitudes, and behaviours toward Aboriginal students, the curriculum, and how it is taught. Teachers must not impose their privileged views and agenda within the classroom. Teachers must view Aboriginal children as unique individuals who hold and share a worldview from the world's oldest living culture.

Second, the teacher must be aware and up to date with the Aboriginal version of history (national and locally based events), particularly critical topics of invasion, dispossession, and colonisation, and how these events have impacted individuals, families, kin, locally based communities, and the wider Aboriginal population. The teacher must reflect on how historical events manifest in contemporary Aboriginal Australia and think about the intergenerational trauma which has impacted the thoughts, attitudes, and behaviours of Aboriginal people, their wellbeing, and livelihoods. The teacher needs to acknowledge that Aboriginal students endure the impacts of history in their everyday lives and are forced to navigate such trauma when in a white-dominated social environment such as school.

Third, the teacher must develop genuine, respectful and reciprocal relationships with Aboriginal students, their carers, and Elders in the school community (see Chapter 7). The relationship needs to journey to a genuine partnership and one in which the teacher assumes a humble position whereby he/she actively listens and acts according to the wisdom shared with them from Aboriginal people, especially their own students.

Lastly, teachers must acknowledge that while they are teaching Aboriginal children, they may feel pain, anger, and frustration with the struggles experienced by their students. They may share compassion and empathy and are, thereby, part of the healing processes, but the struggle itself is an Aboriginal struggle and teachers should walk alongside their students and Aboriginal community. Self-determination for Aboriginal people is demonstrated when we control our lives, our reactions, and our legacy and the most appropriate response from compassionate teachers is to walk beside not in front or behind. To do this, teachers needs to consult Aboriginal carers and particularly Elders who will mark the space in which to share in our journey.

This journey of discovery will only happen with active and sustained connection to Aboriginal people who will guide the way. Every journey requires preparation and in order to arrive at a destination, teachers must be patient in building a genuine heart toward Aboriginal people.

Conclusion

In Australian schools, Aboriginal worldviews are central to learning, living, and thriving Aboriginal culture which positively impacts Aboriginal identity and wellbeing. Considering the time spent by Aboriginal students in non-Aboriginal, Western social systems such as schools, it is imperative the connection with Aboriginal students, their families, and communities is strong and sustainable, because we know that a positive racial identity combined with positive student identity increases the chances of successful school outcomes such as attendance, retention, and good academic grades for Aboriginal children and youth (Crooks et al., 2008; Purdie et al., 2000). At the coal face, non-Aboriginal teachers are school social agents who must partake in a lifelong journey to identify and acknowledge their privilege and worldview and how it impacts their work with Aboriginal students. Unless this journey is undertaken, then schools will only know one way of working with one worldview.

Reflective questions

1. A worldview is defined as ideas and beliefs which a group of people hold about its world and the people and things in it. What are your ideas and beliefs about Aboriginal people? Where did you learn this? Compare your ideas and beliefs with the Aboriginal worldview tables in this chapter. How will you make amends to your thinking and teaching?
2. Reflect on Aboriginal culture and the current curriculum and resources used at your school. How will you incorporate the local Aboriginal identity, language, and culture in what you teach? Who can help you?
3. Decolonisation is the first step to Aboriginal cultural security. Reflect on your own perceptions and judgements of Aboriginal people and how you will adjust so can you begin the journey toward decolonisation.

References

Arabena, K. (2008). Indigenous epistemology and wellbeing: Universe referent citizenship. (AIATSIS Research Discussion Paper 22). https://aiatsis.gov.au/sites/default/files/research_pub/arabena-dp22-indigenous-epistmology-wellbeing-universe-referent-citizenship_0_3.pdf

Australian Bureau of Statistics. (2010). Indigenous statistics for schools: About Aboriginal and Torres Strait Islander statistics. https://www.abs.gov.au/aUSStatS/abs@.nsf/2f762 f95845417aeca25706c00834efa/e9edc3c77168a3d2ca2570ec000af328!OpenDocument

Bessarab, D., & Forrest, S. (2017). Nginap natj katiny. Anggaba jina nimoonggoon: Whose knowledge it that? Aboriginal perspectives of community development. In C.S. Kickett-Tucker, D. Bessarab, J. Coffin, & M. Wright (Eds.) *Mia Mia: Aboriginal community development: Fostering cultural security*. Cambridge: Cambridge University Press, pp. 1–16.

Bessarab, D., & Ng'andu, B. (2010). Yarning about yarning as a legitimate method in Indigenous research. *International Journal of Critical Indigenous Studies*, 3(1), 37–50.

Burchill, M., Higgins, D., Ramsey, L., & Taylor, S. (2006). Working together: Indigenous perspectives on community development. *Family Matters. Australian Institute of Family Studiese*, 75, 50–59.

Chandler, M. J., & Lalonde, C. E. (2008). Cultural continuity as a protective factor against suicide in First Nations youth. *Horizons*, 10(1), 68–72.

Crooks, C. V., Wolfe, D. A., Hughes, R., Jaffe, P. G., & Chiodo, D. (2008). Development, evaluation and national implementation of a school-based program to reduce violence and related risk behaviors. *Institute for the Prevention of Crime Review*, 2, 109–135.

Davidson, H. (2014). Indigenous suicide: "Prevention should focus on cultural reconnection", *The Guardian*. https://www.theguardian.com/australia-news/2014/nov/17/indigenous-suicide-prevention-should-focus-on-cultural-reconnection

Forrest, S. (1998). That's my mob: Aboriginal identity. In G. Partington (Ed.), *Perspectives on Aboriginal and Torres Strait Islander education*. Katoomba, New South Wales: Social Science, pp. 96–105.

Gfellner, B. M., & Armstrong, H. D. (2012). Racial-ethnic identity and adjustment in Canadian Indigenous adolescents. *Journal of Early Adolescence*, 33(5), 635–662. 10.1177/0272431612458036

Grieves, V. (2014). Culture, not colour, is the heart of Aboriginal identity. http://theconversation.com/culture-not-colour-is-the-heart-of-aboriginal-identity-30102

Hallett, D., Chandler, M. J., & Lalonde, C. E. (2007). Aboriginal language knowledge and youth suicide. *Cognitive Development*, 22(3), 392–399. 10.1016/j.cogdev.2007.02.001

Hancock, K. J., Carrington, C. J., Lawrence, D., & Zubrick, S. R. (2013). *Student attendance and educational outcomes: Every day counts.* Report for the Department of Education, Employment and Workplace Relations, Canberra.

Ife, J. (2013). *Community development in an uncertain world: Vision, analysis and practice*. Melbourne: Cambridge University Press

Jackson, J. S., & Sellers, S. L. (1996). African–American health over the life course: A multidimensional framework. In P. Kato, & T. Mann (Eds.) *Handbook of diversity issues in health psychology*. New York: Plenum Press, pp. 301–317.

Just, F. (2017). An introduction to the three major "Western religions". https://catholic-resources.org/Courses/Intro-WesternReligions.htm

Kickett-Tucker, C. S. (2009). Moorn (Black)? Djardak (White)? How come I don't fit in Mum? Exploring the racial identity of Australian Aboriginal children and youths. *Health Sociology Review*, 18(1), 119–136.

Kickett-Tucker, C. S., & Coffin, J. (2011). Aboriginal self-concept and racial identity: Practical solutions for teachers. In N. Purdie, G. Milgate, & H. R. Bell (Eds.) *Two way teaching and learning: Toward culturally reflective and relevant education*. Camberwell, Victoria: Australian Council for Educational Research, pp. 155–172.

Kickett-Tucker, C., & Hanse, J. (2016). Ngalang moort: Family as the building block of community development. In C.S. Kickett-Tucker, D. Bessarab, J. Coffin, & M. Wright (Eds.)

Mia Mia: Aboriginal community development: Fostering cultural security. Cambridge: Cambridge University Press, pp. 199–216.

Kickett-Tucker, C. S., & Ife, J. (2018). Identity in Australian Aboriginal communities: Koordoormitj in the essence of life. In S. Kenny, B. McGrath, & R. Phillips (Eds.) *The Routledge handbook of community development*. Routledge: New York, pp. 310–322.

Kickett-Tucker, C. S., Bessarab, D., Coffin, J., & Wright, M. (Eds). (2016). *Mia Mia: Aboriginal community development: Fostering cultural security*. Cambridge: Cambridge University Press.

Kolig, E. (1988). Australian Aboriginal totemic systems: Structures of power. *Oceania*, 58(3), 212–230.

Kvernmo, S., & Heyerdahl, S. (2004). Ethnic identity and acculturation attitudes among indigenous Norwegian Sami and ethnocultural Kven adolescents. *Journal of Adolescent Research*, 19, 512–532.

Lohoar, S., Butera, N., & Kennedy, E. (2014). Strengths of Australian Aboriginal cultural practices in family life and child rearing. *Child Family Community Australia Information Exchange*, 25, 1–20. https://aifs.gov.au/cfca/sites/default/files/publication-documents/cfca25.pdf

Martin, K. L., & Mirraboopa, B. (2003) Ways of knowing, being and doing: A theoretical framework and methods for indigenous and indigenist re-search. *Journal of Australian Studies*, 27(76), 203–214.

Mead, A. (2020). Six differences between Aboriginal and Western world views. http://www.donpugh.com/Psych%20Interests/ABORIGINES/SIX%20DIFFERENCES%20BETWEEN%20ABORIGINAL%20and%20%60WESTERN'%20WORLD%20VIEWS-,.pdf

Niles, S. (1999). Stress, coping and mental health among immigrants to Australia. In WJ Lonner, DL Dinne, DK Forgays, & SA Hayes (Eds.) *Merging past, present and future in cross-cultural psychology*. Selected readings from the 14th International Congress of the International Association of Cross-Cultural Psychology. Lisse, Netherlands: Swets and Zeitlinger, pp. 293–307.

O'Keefe, E. A. (1984). Towards an understanding of the significance of "The Dreamtime" to Aboriginal people. *The Australian Journal of Indigenous Education*, 12(4), 50–56.

Oxford Reference Dictionary. (2020). Overview: Culture. https://www.oxfordreference.com/view/10.1093/oi/authority.20110901080526139

Parbury, N. (1991). *Survival: A history of Aboriginal life in New South Wales*. New South Wales: NSW Department of Aboriginal Affairs.

Partington, G., & McCudden, V. (1992). *Ethnicity and education*. Wentworth Falls: Social Science.

Phinney, J. S. (1992). The Multigroup Ethnic Identity Measure: A new scale for use with diverse groups. *Journal of Adolescent Research*, 7(2), 156–176.

Priest, N., Paradies, Y., Trenerry, B., Truong, M., Karlsen, S., & Kelly, Y. (2013). A systematic review of studies examining the relationship between reported racism and health and wellbeing for children and young people. *Social Science and Medicine*, 95, 115–127.

Purdie, N., Tripcony, P., Boulton-Lewis, G., Gunstone, A., & Fanshawe, J. (2000). *Positive self-identity for Indigenous students and its relationship to school outcomes*. Canberra: Commonwealth Department of Education, Training and Youth Affairs.

People Culture Environment. (2014). *The Elders' report into preventing Indigenous self-harm and youth suicide*. Melbourne: People Culture Environment.

Silviken, A., & Kvernmo, S. (2007). 'Suicide attempts among indigenous Sami adolescents and majority peers in Arctic Norway: Prevalence and associated risk factors.' *Journal of Adolescence*, 30, 613–626.

South West Aboriginal Land and Sea Council. (2016). Family. http://www.noongarculture.org.au/family/

South West Aboriginal Land and Sea Council. (2020). Kaartdijin Noongar-Noongar Knowledge: Sharing Noongar Culture. https://www.noongarculture.org.au/

Tajfel, H. (1981). *Human groups and social categories*. Cambridge: Cambridge University Press.

Tipiloura, E. (2014). Eustice Tipiloura Meliville Island (Tiwi), NT. In M. Gooda, & P. Dudgeon (Eds.) *The Elders' Report into Preventing Indigenous Self-harm & Youth Suicide* (p. 25). https://www.cultureislife.org/wp-content/uploads/2018/12/Elders-Report-CultureIsLife.pdf

Tuhiwai Smith, L. (2003). *Decolonising methodologies: Research and Indigenous people*. Dunedin, New Zealand: University of Otago Press.

Turner, M. (2010). *Iwenhe Tyerrtye: What it means to be an Aboriginal person*. Alice Springs, NT: IAD Press.

Umaña-Taylor, A. J., & Fine, M. A. (2004). Examining a model of ethnic identity development among Mexican-origin adolescents living in the U.S. *Hispanic Journal of Behavioral Sciences*, 26, 36–59.

Umaña-Taylor, A. J., Diversi, M., & Fine, M. A. (2002). Ethnic identity and self-esteem of Latino adolescents: Distinctions among the Latino populations. *Journal of Adolescent Research*, 17, 303–327. doi:10.1177/0743558402173005

Umaña-Taylor, A. J., Yazedijian, A., & Bamaca-Gomez, M. (2004). Developing the ethnic identity scale using Erikonian and social identity perspectives. *Identity: An International Journal of Theory and Research*, 4 (1), 9–38.

Victorian Indigenous Youth Affairs Council. (2020). Voices telling it like it is: Young Aboriginal Victorians on culture, identity and racism. https://www.yacvic.org.au/assets/Documents/Indigenous-Telling-it-how-it-is.pdf

Chapter 5

Strong identities, strong futures

Indigenous identities and wellbeing in schools

Marnee Shay, Grace Sarra and Annette Woods

Who we are

Marnee Shay

My mob are from Daly River, Northern Territory (Wagiman) through my mother and grandmother (we identify culturally on our maternal side) and I have English and Scottish heritage through my father. My sister and I grew up around South East Queensland. We were raised by my mother who always wanted us to know about our culture and to be proud of our Aboriginality because she was born in an era where racism and discrimination towards Aboriginal people was endemic and she wanted something different for my sister and me. I was lucky to be able to study through an Indigenous college in the late 90s / early 2000s when I started my first degree as an undergraduate student. I had the unique experience of having mostly Indigenous lecturers teach me about our histories, the systems that perpetuate racism and disparities across the board and, remarkably, it was the first time in a formal education setting where messages, both explicit and implicit, were given to me about the strengths and resilience of our people. Looking back now I reflect on my experience at university and school and see how absent our people were in the curriculum and the school environment – and when we were present it was reinforcing stereotypes and myths that my mother, grandmother, and generations before had to endure. Now I work with many pre-service teachers who care about these issues and want to do the right thing, and that keeps me motivated to keep fighting for change.

Grace Sarra

It is important as an Aboriginal and Torres Strait Islander woman to provide an understanding of my cultural postioning in relation to my identity and the importance of connection to family, country/place, spirituality and Indigenous knowledges, which are at the core of who I am and what it means to me to have a strong Aboriginal identity and a strong Torres Strait Islander identity. My family heritage acknowledges my mother's family lineage of Aboriginal heritage from the Birrigubba and Kalkadoon nations. My father's family lineage is of Torres Strait Islander heritage from the Torres Strait Islands from the Eastern and Central Islands. Growing up in Townsville in the late 60s, I was the eldest child of five biological siblings in the Western sense, however, my mother is the matriarch of her family and the eldest of 19 brothers and sisters which entails growing up in an extended family, so we grew up with many brothers and sisters where our cousins were known as our brothers and sisters as well. This gave me a strong identity that has instilled cultural knowledge which includes traditional healing and spirituality, providing me with a formidable foundation in my cultural position to exist and be able to interact and communicate between the Western world and an Indigenous world.

Annette Woods

My Mum and Dad's heritage was Scottish, Irish and English and both the families can map their arrival in Australia to early colonial times. My mother and father grew up in the Eora Nation on Durug Lands, and growing up in these working-class parts of Sydney continued to impact on their ways of being till they passed, despite having lives of rich experience. Their education, lifestyle, sense of family and belonging, and their approach to work, money, and helping others was always tied to growing up in large families where money was sparse, but life pretty good. They instilled in their three children – of whom I was the youngest by seven years – a sense of social justice, fairness, and an unstated rule of never getting ahead of yourself and your background no matter what you achieved. I was born near where they grew up, but we spent my early childhood years moving regularly and it was only once Mum and I settled in a beach-side town after my Dad had passed that I realised what feeling like you were home in a place entailed. Currarong is a small beach-side community surrounded by Dharawal Dhurga Lands and remains significant to the Jerrinja and Wreck Bay Aboriginal Communities, and many other Aboriginal people. The large public high school I attended in a nearby town had large numbers of Aboriginal students, and was a shining example of how systemic education practices – such as streaming, uniform policies, and behaviour regimes – embedded in underlying and unrecognised racism, classism, and sexism in 1970s Australia ensured the success of some and not others. I may not have been able to articulate what I saw or felt then, but I think it was those years that set the foundation of future university studies and eventually teaching work and research focused on supporting socially just ways to provide equitable access for all students to quality education.

Introduction

The concept of identity is complex and diverse. As a construct, identity is widely understood through Western ideologies and theoretical frameworks, and as a result Indigenous experiences and ways of being, knowing, and doing are often excluded and marginalised. But we do know, from many studies in the field of education and other disciplines, that identity as an element of youth development plays a fundamental part in how young people perceive themselves now and into the future (Stokes, Aaltonen, & Coffey, 2015). It is, therefore, vital that educators in Australian schools are equipped to provide opportunities to all young people to explore the concept of identities, but we believe this is particularly important for Indigenous young people due to the impact of colonial histories and the implications of racism connected to these histories (Shay, 2018).

Identities can be viewed or represented in many ways. Different disciplines and ways of knowing influence how we might construct our own identities and how we might perceive the identities of others. In education contexts, identities are often thought of from a developmental frame, whereby educators have used theorists such as Erikson (1968) to understand how children and young people develop their identities and behave in accordance with various stages of development. Such stages of development have not been theorised for Indigenous young people. This is not to say that Indigenous young people are inherently different from other groups of young people, rather that issues have been identified by Indigenous scholars suggesting that many theories, including those related to identity, are now recognised as not being culturally benign. Since the earliest colonial times Indigenous ways of being, knowing, and doing (see Chapter 4) have been not been sufficiently well recognised (if at all!) in educational policies, research, and teaching practice. This has resulted in a lack of understanding of the lived realities of Indigenous peoples. This chapter recognises distinct Indigenous ways of being, knowing, and doing as fundamental in understanding Indigenous identities.

In this chapter, we will discuss how Indigenous and Australian identities have been constructed and influenced by Australia's colonial history. We will critically explore the role of the media, in particular, in influencing these constructs politically and socially. We will then provide counter narratives through vignettes based on Indigenous young people's and Indigenous researchers' experiences of exploring Indigenous identities in school settings. We emphasise the importance of strengths-based approaches to positive identity development for Indigenous young people, and indeed more widely in classroom practices to ensure everyone in Australian classrooms is provided with a diverse and authentic curriculum and messages in relation to stong Indigenous identities. We also offer some practical strategies for educators to use in their classroom practices to work towards a model of explicit identity-affirming practices and do so over other approaches such as inclusion, which we suggest often take up deficit understandings about Indigenous peoples.

Background – Indigenous identities in Australia

As First Nations peoples, Aboriginal peoples have been living in Australia for approximately 65,000 years and are considered the oldest surviving culture in the world (Walter, Martin, & Bodkin-Andrews, 2017). Aboriginal and Torres Strait Islander peoples in Australia have been subject to identity categorisation from the time of invasion in 1788, when the British claimed Australia was 'Terra Nullius', or a land belonging to no one. Terra Nullius, although a legal fiction overturned by the high court of Australia in 1992 in the famous Mabo Case, has impacted on how Indigenous peoples have been categorised, subjugated, and constructed over the past 230 years or so. The ideology of Terra Nullius persisted when the White Australia Policy (1901) overtly stated that the future of Australia was 'white'.

In 1901, Attorney General Alfred Deakin stated on 12 September: "that end, put in plain and unequivocal terms … means the prohibition of all alien coloured immigration, and more, it means at the earliest time, by reasonable and just means, the deportation or reduction of the number of aliens now in our midst. The two things go hand in hand, and are the necessary complement of a singly policy – the policy of securing a 'white Australia'" (National Museum Australia, 2019). There was no reference to the Blackness of the First peoples, Indigenous Australians, within the White Australian Policy, exemplifying how Terra Nullius was operationalised in the colonisation and nation building of this country. Furthermore, legal historian John McCorquodale has reported that since colonisation, there have been no less than 67 categorisations, definitions, or descriptions to determine who is identified as an Aboriginal person (Carlson, 2016).

Legislative conditions throughout colonisation for Indigenous Australians centred around identity; the idea that Aboriginal and Torres Strait Islander peoples were non-existent moved to a focus on blood quantum in the early 1900s, resulting in use of terms such as 'half caste' in political, media, and everyday communications. Such terms are now recognised as being highly offensive, however, the work that such language has done in the past to *other* Blackness, and to marginalise Aboriginality or Indigenous heritage as somehow *less* than caucasion cultural or racial heritage remains a legacy. The use and legitimisation of language that is founded on racist ideological understandings and the ways of thinking and framing that this use enables are one part of the colonial system that has ensured inequity and social injustice for Aboriginal and Torres Strait Islander people within our society.

These ways of talking about and, as such, thinking about, Aboriginal and Torres Strait Islander peoples are evident in policy and political decision making in Australia as well. As just one example of many, it was this thinking that resulted in what is widely recognised as the 'Stolen Generation'. This is a term used to describe the impacts of a policy where babies and children of Indigenous parents with mixed heritage were forcibly removed from their parents under the guise of welfare (Wilkie, 2007). The aim was to remove all ties to their identity as Indigenous peoples, with children not permitted to stay connected to their families. Unable to speak their language and unable to practise their cultures the consequences for children and their families were traumatic, and the impacts continue today (Williams-Mozley, 2012). Further, the establishment of reserves and missions, where Indigenous peoples were able to be moved forceably into government managed facilities and away from their home Lands, again under the guise of providing welfare, had traumatic consequences and was a policy that aimed to break ties to culture and worked to destroy languages and cultural practices (Wilkie, 2007). All aspects of Indigenous peoples' lives were controlled in these conditions, and the only opportunity for freedom and access to similar rights to the rest of the Australian community was to relinquish their identities through the 'Certificate of Exemption' (Shay & Wickes, 2017). The impacts of the Certificate of Exemption remain today, and many Aboriginal and Torres Strait Islander peoples are now reclaiming their identities and relearning their cultures and connections that they were forbidden to practise.

The implications of the legacy of colonialism continue in current Australian society where there is evidence of ongoing disposition and marginalisation of Indigenous peoples. A diverse range of statistics and the lived experiences of Aboriginal and Torres Strait Islander peoples attest to this continuing legacy. In relation to education, Indigenous peoples continue to be under-represented as teachers in Australian classrooms, as academics in Australian universities and as elected members of the Australian Government. This lack of representation in positions of power within these institutions overtly and covertly sends messages to all, including Indigenous and non-Indigenous educators and students in Australian classrooms. As Indigenous peoples have persistently experienced educational disadvantage, despite some progress through equity programmes toward addressing historical disadvantages caused by colonisation, there has been very little emphasis in policy and practice about the role schools play in identity development and affirming the strength of Indigenous young people.

Racism and the role of identity construction within the media

One of the resilient modes of representation of race and culture as well as gender, age, and other demographic categories used to define and disadvantage or advantage people in our modern society is the media. It is the case that new channels of communication and alternative media, including social media and other digital outlets, have provided a platform for dissenting voices to critique policy or other systemic and institutional regimes. The implications of increased access to spaces to voice opinions has been researched quite extensively, both generally and in relation to politics and events that involve Aboriginal and Torres Strait Islander peoples (McCallum, 2013; McCallum, Waller, & Dreher, 2016). Indigenous communities and their advocates have increasingly used these channels to provide alternative accounts and to take a position on representations of Aboriginal and Torres Strait Islander peoples, cultures, and authority. In a media study which investigated the mediatisation and policy disruption evident in the 'Recognise' campaign launched by then Prime Minister Abbott in 2015, McCallum, Waller and Dreher (2016) found that alternative and new media did amplify a wider range of perspectives and voices in the debate, including Indigenous voices. However, in general these alternatives to the traditional media have a select audience – more likely to be supporters of the same or similar views as put forward in the alternative news, or those who will vilify the same, and as such have less reach in re-presenting the identities of Indigenous peoples made available. Algorithms run what we see and are exposed to on social media platforms, selecting the content that we are offered based on previous indications of 'liking' something, and the alternative news media, while gaining audience numbers, continues to have a smaller reach than traditional news media. So while these new channels provide access to media spaces for a broader population to voice opinions and concerns, this does not necessarily translate to being heard in ways that can be influential (McCallum, 2013).

There is a large body of research in the fields of Indigenous politics, policy, and media studies that demonstrates that Australian media amplifies representations of Aboriginal and Torres Strait Islander peoples that are negative and perpetuate racism within society (Fforde et al., 2013; McCallum, Waller, & Dreher, 2016). As white Australia is centred and normalised via the traditional press and television media, minority cultures are often under-represented. However, in relation to Aboriginal and Torres Strait Islander representations, "the media has a less than admirable record of representing Indigenous peoples, when they are represented at all in Australia" (Parker, 2011, p. 54). The impact of these representations has been catastrophic, not only in relation to the perpetuation of racial stereotypes and myths. Little (2012, p. 43) outlines the impact of the media as having a "direct link to the disparities between mainstream social and economic comfort and Indigenous peoples' exclusions from those experiences".

It is possible to understand a little about how the media works to portray Aboriginal and Torres Strait Islander peoples and their lives, issues, and daily concerns in a negative light by thinking about some of the language used in current media. In an article published by the *Sun Herald* (Bolt, 2019), the headline 'Blame boos on race politics' sets the tone of the article, the basic premise of which is that football fans selecting Aboriginal players to be the target of mob behaviour in the form of booing should not be explained though a racial lens. Chronicling the events that played out in the final seasons of AFL player Adam Goodes' football career, the article goes on to attribute the booing not to racism, but rather to the player's growing unpopularity for bad playing tactics as "he got older and slower". In this way the article suggests that the booing could not be a response based in racism – rather that the player's character or ability should be seen as the catalyst.

Our interest here is not to unpack the event that initiated this booing as this has been done elsewhere, but to consider how the language of this article – and others like it - achieves its aim of representing the ensuing booing as 'not racist'. The article frames Goodes and other un-named men using adjectives such as "powerful" and discusses how they were involved in the "public shaming of a scared 13-year old girl". Such language plays on notions of power coming from size and strength, ensuring stereotypes are brought to the fore and suggest fear is warranted. The piece uses three other textual moves to shape the football player as a bully and not the victim of racism, and the booing as expected treatment from fans and not based in racism. The first is to accuse the opposition side in order to rob victim status and thus inauthenticate any charge of racism by the perpetrators. In this case Goodes is described as being engaged in bullying. In a second move the text prevails on readers to consider themselves in this position when they are asked to "imagine your own child thrown to the wolves like that". This emotive language seeks sympathy and encourages readers to connect with the non-Indigenous fans who of course would be driven to behave in this way in protest of such an unjust situation. Thirdly the article claims to not support the booing behaviour, but in the next phrase to do just that with the statement "I don't like fans abusing players, but…". Beginning a statement where you are going to say something against someone or something in this way can be seen to inoculate the speaker or writer from critique (Augoustinos, Lecouteur, & Soyland, 2002). Another common example of this that may be heard in everyday talk is 'I'm not a racist, but…'.

The overall effect of an article like this is to reframe an event with new characters, the powerful Indigenous man wielding fear, and the 'ordinary' sports fans who should have no blame for taking the only means they have at their disposal to protest what is framed as a terrible wrong. This vilifies the AFL player who was victim of the booing behaviours, and removes any logic to consider the booing behaviour as founded in racist ideologies. But this type of media reporting also serves to centre white, non-Indigenous issues as 'normal' and clearly *others* Aboriginal and Torres Strait Islander peoples. This move is achieved without any subtlety in phrases such as "But he identifies as Aboriginal, which means up-ending normal moral calculations". Note what is marked as *normal* in this sentence. Taken as a singular media report this article could be closely analysed to demonstrate how the language represents Indigenous and non-Indigenous peoples in stereotypical ways. However, our point here is to uncover how some of the media reports use certain representations and block others in their portrayals. And we should also rememember that this article is just one layer in a continuous narrative, played 'on repeat' within media in societies like Australia, and also remember that this narrative remains rarely interrupted in the traditional media. Consider the representations that this never-ending narrative offers to all young people as they form their identities and come to see their worth.

Voices of Indigenous young people on identity – counter narratives

We recently completed a research project[1] where we worked to privilege the voices of Aboriginal and Torres Strait Islander young people on their perspectives about their identities. We worked with a diverse group of Indigenous young people from urban, regional, and remote communities. Below are some examples of what Indigenous young people are articulating identity as being:

> "understanding where you come from"
> "representing who you are"
> "how you see yourself"
> "being different"
> "you don't choose your identity"
> "skin colour – bloodline connection"
> "staying true to your culture"
> "respect for Elders"
> "family"

Earlier in the chapter, we discussed the imposition of colonial constructs of Indigenous identities and the ways in which the media reinforces these constructs, which are highly racialised and often bound with prevailing myths and stereotypes such as other, inferior, primitive etc. Privileging the voices of Indigenous young people can allow us to listen to how they navigate these representations and their constraints. This can allow for understandings of how such representations are often at odds with their lived experiences, and may demonstrate to teachers why identity is an important dimension for them to consider in their work as teachers interacting with Indigenous young people everyday in classrooms and schools.

For some Indigenous students, having positive experiences of what it means to be Aboriginal or what it means to be Torres Strait Islander may differ. Some young people may have been raised within their cultural context with their Indigenous family members, and others may be impacted by their families' experiences of disruption through the inter-generational effects of colonisation on Indigenous people, or through the loss of culture or from being a member of the Stolen Generation. Because of the diversity of experiences of Indigenous peoples in Australia, it is critical that teachers provide space for young people to talk and explore their identities. For Indigenous students this is particularly critical, due to the misrepresentations and the impact of these within education settings; for all young people who are often exploring where they fit, where they belong, and how they see themselves these types of activities are also important.

How can teachers affirm identities of Indigenous young people?

There are a number of ways that teachers can contribute to the identity affirming of Indigenous students in their classrooms. Some of these practical suggestions for teachers are unpacked in more depth in other chapters in this book, but what we need to reinforce here is that identity work must always be an inherently strengths-based endeavour. Furthermore, some of our suggested approaches below have been emphasised as important in Indigenous education broadly for many years – our aim here is to highlight the importance of these in contributing to identity-affirming practices of teachers.

Strengths-based approaches and high-expectations relationships

Strengths-based approaches have been used for some time, particularly in professional frameworks for social workers and human services workers. A strengths-based approach is fundamentally about looking at the strengths of a person, and their communities, first and foremost – what are they good at, what is good in their lives, what resources and capital they have access to – and then taking a collaborative approach in working with the person (McCashen, 2010). The role of a teacher should be to encompass all of these principles. However, as schools and classrooms are not racially or culturally neutral places, the colonial constructs of Indigenous identities and the current policy approaches that reinforce gaps, deficits, and failure impact on the ways that teachers can sometimes perceive Indigenous students as not possessing capital or strengths. This is of course not reality.

Strengths-based approaches and high-expectations relationships go hand in hand. If teachers are not using a strengths-based approach, they are at risk of developing low expectations for all their students, including their Indigenous students (i.e., based on the idea that Indigenous students are without strengths and assets and therefore not capable or able learners in their classrooms). Chris Sarra (2011a) developed what he termed a 'stronger smarter philosophy', which honours a positive sense of Aboriginal and Torres Strait Islander cultural identity through acknowledging and embracing Indigenous leadership and empowering strengths-based approaches and processes that are anchored in high-expectations relationships (Sarra et al., 2020). High-expectations relationships mean that teachers will:

- Challenge their beliefs and assumptions of Indigenous students that can impact on how they teach;
- Think critically about what assets Indigenous students bring to the classroom rather than what they don't bring;
- Ensure that rigour and quality are applied to classroom practices and curriculum for all students in their classrooms;
- Get to know their students, their strengths, abilities, and interests.

Critically reflect on your identity

In doing identity work as teachers, it is vital that teachers know about and reflect on their own identities and lived experiences. This is critical in order to understand identities and cultural realities outside of their own experiences. The three Rs (Respect, Relationships, Reconciliation) is a resource developed for preservice teachers in response to the inclusion of professional teacher standards 1.4 and 2.4, both focused on Indigenous education practices of teachers. Of the three modules, one is entitled 'know yourself' (www.rrr.edu.au). There are many ways to do this work, and it should always be considered as an ongoing process of thinking critically about the assumptions and biases we have as teachers. This opens possibilities to locate the social, cultural, and historical experiences we have had and how these develop certain stereotypes and assumptions; and then challenge ourselves with information and resources that challenge these ideas or provide a perspective outside of our own. (See Chapter 3 for more practical ideas on how to engage with critical self reflection.)

Embed Indigenous perspectives/knowledges across all areas of the curriculum

Embedding Indigenous knowledges and perpsectives plays an important part in how identities are constructed – Indigenous identities and the many other cultures and identities in Australia, including white Australians. As Phillips outlines,

> Teaching and learning is not merely about the acquisition of knowledge through information. Schools contribute to the ways in which we see ourselves and our connections to others. What we experience in the classrooms assists in developing ideas about our role in Australian society. The images that were constituted to support Indigenous dispossession many years ago are the same images passing into the minds of young non-Indigenous *and* Indigenous children as they sit in their classrooms today.
>
> (2012, p. 21)

To date, the curriculum in Australia has focused on Eurocentric beliefs, values, and practices (Hart, Whatman, McLaughlin, & Sharma-Brymer, 2012), resulting in very little accurate knowledge or understanding of Indigenous peoples, cultures, and histories being included. In order to rebalance this knowledge and re-present Indigenous knowledges and views that reflect the identities of Indigenous young people, embedding Indigenous knowledges and perspectives into the curriculum is an important aspect of identity-affirming work teachers can do in classrooms (Sarra, 2011b).

Working with community

Aboriginal and Torres Strait Islander communities are experts in their communities. The knowledge and expertise that exists can sometimes be overlooked by teachers when they are undertaking their roles as classroom teachers. To truly understand the culture and identities of Indigenous young people, teachers will need to build relationships and collaborate with the local community (see Chapters 7 and 14). There are many resources now available for teachers who want to know how to engage with community; here is a summary of some ways to develop these relationships:

- Do some research before you meet with community – know who the local traditional owners are, know what country you are on, find out what the relationship between community and the school has been in the past;
- Connect with Indigenous staff at the school, introduce yourself and ask for some advice as well as offering your support in their role. Strong relationships must be reciprocal;
- Understand there are local protocols for each community, find out as much as you can about your community. Ask positive and informed questions;
- Meet people in the community, don't expect community to always come to the school;
- If there are community events on, attend these events and introduce yourself informally;
- If you invite local people in to work with you, make sure there are funds to pay them for their time and expertise.

Role models

Role models are important for all young people. In working with a large group of Indigenous young people in our recent project, Indigenous young people would say consistently how important role models are for them. The young people recognised the importance of role models for creating a positive sense of identities. Having access to a range of Indigenous role models where young people can see ways to aspire to similar ways of being is also a role that schools can play in identity affirming. There is an abundance of Indigenous sports role models – Jonathon Thurston, Ash Bartey, Adam Goodes, Cathy Freeman, and so many more; but it is important that schools do not stop with sport – we must not forget the many fields in which Indigenous people excel, including the arts, community, science, politics, medicine, research, maths, literature, and so many more. As the media has assisted in creating the notion that successful Indigenous people are usually sports people, classroom teachers have the opportunity to ensure that many other examples are provided in their classrooms. You can include specific activities on role models within your curriculum, or if you are in a specific discipline, highlight the work and contributions of Indigenous peoples within these varying fields.

Providing activities and spaces for young people to talk about and express their identities safely

Our project on Indigenous youth identity, wellbeing, and schooling provided explicit space for Indigenous young people to think and reflect on what identity means to them and the significance of this to their wellbeing and learning. In undertaking the research, we developed a series of creative-based research

Marnee Shay, Grace Sarra and Annette Woods

workshops to support young people to think and reflect. We worked with a diverse cohort of Indigenous young people, including young people who would be labelled 'disengaged' from schooling, but we found across the project Indigenous young people were more than happy to share their interests and views, and that they had strong views on education, cultural identity, and wellbeing. This came as a surprise to some of the teachers who were working with the same young people in other dimensions of their schooling lives. One example of an activity to get young people thinking about identity and the things that make them 'who they are' was to create a 'me map'. We asked young people to draw a map of the things that shaped them, that made them who they are and the information that they provided was in-depth and complex. An activity like this would not only support teachers to get to know their students, to know more about who they are and what is important to them, but it also allows young people to express their identities in a supportive space.

A story from practice: Indigenous young people – why talk about identity?

"I've been told messed up shit about being black."
The quote above was from an Indigenous young person on our project and exemplifies the importance of the role of teachers in identity affirming in schools. In asking Indigenous young people about what they think is important if schools are to talk about identity, particularly for Indigenous young people, they said they need:

- Support
- Dignity
- Need to know why things are
- Confidence
- Help
- Know how to be a leader not a follower
- Role models
- Advice
- Experience
- Support to accomplish goals in life.

In addition to what Indigenous young people had to say, local Indigenous researchers on the project who worked to support young people across the project also shared their views from their communities' perspectives on why a focus on identity is important:

- Elders were proud of students
- Children and community were proud
- Helped to form better relations with children and community members
- More young people came out and identified as Indigenous
- Created a sense of self-worth among students. Sense of pride and belonging. Friendships that may not have otherwise connected
- Positive role models within community were identified
- A number of students spoke up.

Conclusion/summary

Identity-affirming work of teachers in schools has the potential to be transformative in engaging Indigenous learners and also in correcting the untruths, myths, and stereotypes that prevail for all young people in Australian classrooms. It is a sad reflection on Australian history that in current times we would need to make such a suggestion, however, through listening to the voices of Indigenous young people and looking at educational outcome data it is clear that these are discussions that need to continue in teacher education programmes and beyond. While some of the constructs about Indigenous identities permeate politically, socially, and through the media, teachers can play an important role in countering these negative representations by:

- Utilising strengths-based approaches and entering into high-expectations relationships with Indigenous students;
- Knowing themselves and their own identities;
- Engaging with local Indigenous communities;
- Incorporating diverse Indigenous role models into curriculum and classrooms; and
- Providing safe spaces for young people to explore and express their identities.

Many ideas from this chapter will connect with other chapters in this book – that is because doing Indigenous education successfully is multidimensional and requires consideration of factors in and outside of the school environment. Wellness and positively engaging Indigenous learners requires a considerable shift in current foci of practices in schools. An emphasis on simple, quantifiable notions of success, for example NAPLAN scores and attendance data in Indigenous education policy has resulted in schoolbased educators mirroring this narrow focus in their practices. We propose identity-affirming work has a role to play in any shift toward a more successful education experience for all, and encourage classroom teachers to embed this within their professional practices.

Reflective questions

1. How has Australia's colonial history shaped your identity?
2. How has Australia's colonial history shaped your understanding of Indigenous identities?
3. In what ways has the media impacted on your understanding and perceptions about Indigenous identities?
4. In what ways has the media impacted on your understanding of your own identity?
5. What are some further ideas for identity-affirming practices relevant to the young people in your class?

Note

1. The 'Cultural Identity, Health and Wellbeing of Indigenous Young People in Schools' project was a three-year project funded by the Lowitja Insititute. We acknowledge and thank all of the young people, local researchers, and the schools who participated in the study.

References

Augoustinos, M., Lecouteur, A., & Soyland, J. (2002). Self-sufficient arguments in political rhetoric: Constructing reconciliation and apologizing to the Stolen Generations. *Discourse and Society*, 13(1), 105–149.

Bolt, A. (2019). Blame boos on race politics. *Sun Herald*, 20 June, 2019, p. 11.

Carlson, B. (2016). *The politics of identity: Who counts as Aboriginal today?* Canberra, Australia: Aboriginal Studies Press.

Erikson, E. (1968). *Identity: Youth and crisis*. New York: Norton.

Fforde, C., Bamblett, L., Lovett, R., Gorringe S., & Fogarty, W. (2013). Discourse, deficit and identity: Aboriginality, the race paradigm and the language of representation in contemporary Australia. *Media International Australia*, (149), 162–173.

Hart, V., Whatman, S., McLaughlin, J., & Sharma-Brymer, V. (2012). Pre-service teachers' pedagogical relationships and experiences of embedding Indigenous Australian knowledge in teaching practicum. *Compare: A Journal of Comparative and International Education*, 42(5), 703–723. doi:10.1080/03057925.2012.706480

Little, J. (2012). "Enraged Aborigines" at the embassy ball. In J. Phillips & J. Lampert (Eds.) *Introductory Indigenous Studies in Education* (2nd). Frenches Forest NSW: Pearson, pp. 40–55.

McCallum, K. (2013). Distant and intimate conversations: Media and Indigenous health policy in Australia. *Critical Arts*, 27(3), 332–351.

McCallum, K., Waller, L, & Dreher, T. (2016). Mediatisation, marginalisation and disruption in Australian Indigenous affairs. *Media and Communication*, 4(4), 30–42.

McCashen, W. (2010). *The strengths approach: A strengths based approach to creating change*. Bedingo: St Luke's Innovative Resources.

National Museum Australia. (2019). *Defining moments: White Australia policy*. www.nma. gov.au/defining-moments/resources/white-australia-policy

Parker, K. (2011). Indigenous people in the media: Telling it like it is and how it could be. In S. Maddison & M. Brigg (Eds.) *Unsettling the settler state: Creativity and resistance in Indigenous settler-state governance*. Leichardt, NSW: Federation Press, pp. 51–67.

Phillips, J. (2012). Indigenous knowledge perspectives: Making space in the Australian centre. In J. Phillips & J. Lampert (Eds). *Introductory indigenous studies in education* (2nd). Frenches Forest NSW: Pearson.

Sarra, C. (2011a). *Strong and smart – Towards a pedagogy for emancipation for First Peoples*. Oxon: Routledge.

Sarra, Grace (2011b). Indigenous studies in all schools. *International Journal of Inclusive Education*, 15(6), 611–625.

Sarra, C., Spillman, D., Jackson, C., Davis, J., & Bray, J. (2020). High-expectations relationships: A foundation for enacting high expectations in all Australian schools. *The Australian Journal of Indigenous Education*, 49(1), 32–45. doi:10.1017/jie.2018.10

Shay, M. (2018). More than cultural celebrations: Indigenous identities in school settings. In Tania Ferfolja, Criss Jones Diaz and Jacqueline Ullman (Eds.) *Understanding sociological theory for educational research* (2nd). Singapore: Cambridge University Press, pp. 102–115. doi:10.1017/9781108378482.008

Shay, M. & Wickes, J. (2017). Aboriginal identity in education settings: Privileging our stories as a way of deconstructing the past and re-imagining the future. *Australian Educational Researcher*, 44(1), 107–122. doi:10.1007/s13384-017-0232-0

Stokes, H., Aaltonen, S., & Coffey, J. (2015). Young people, identity, class, and the family. In J. Wyn & H. Cahill (Eds.) *Handbook of children and youth studies*. Singapore: Springer, pp. 259–278.

Walter, M., Martin, K. L., & Bodkin-Andrews, G. (2017). *Indigenous children growing up strong: A longitudinal study of Aboriginal and Torres Strait Islander families*. London: Palgrave Macmillan.

Wilkie, M. (2007). *Bringing them home: Report of the national inquiry into the separation of Aboriginal and Torres Strait Islander children from their families*. Human Rights and Equal Opportunity Commission. https://humanrights.gov.au/sites/default/files/content/pdf/social_justice/bringing_them_home_report.pdf

Williams-Mozley, J. (2012). The Stolen generations: What does this mean for Aboriginal and Torres Strait Islander children and young people today? In K. Price (Ed.) *Aboriginal and Torres Strait Islander Education*. New York: Cambridge University Press, pp. 21–34.

Chapter 6

Weaving Torres Strait Islander language and culture into education

Robyn Ober, Noressa Bulsey, Norah Pearson and Claire Bartlett

Who we are

Robyn Ober

I am a Mamu/Djirribal woman from the rainforest region of North Queensland. I am currently employed as a research fellow with Batchelor Institute in the Northern Territory and have recently completed my PhD studies focusing on 'Aboriginal English as a Social and Cultural Identity Marker in an Indigenous Tertiary Educational Context'. I have an extensive educational background, teaching in early childhood, primary, and tertiary sectors in remote, rural, and urban contexts. I have a strong interest in both-ways education, educational leadership, and Indigenous Australian languages and, in particular, Aboriginal English. I have undertaken several research projects focusing on these topics and have published papers in educational and linguistic journals, both nationally and internationally.

Noressa Bulsey

I am a Torres Strait Islander woman with cultural connections to the Top Western and Eastern Islands of the Torres Strait. After completing my secondary education at Thursday Island, I moved to the Northern Territory for work before commencing teacher education studies at Batchelor Institute in 1983. I have an extensive primary and tertiary teaching experience in Northern Territory remote contexts. In recent years, I have been instrumental in developing cross-cultural awareness programs and relevant resources for staff and students at Batchelor Institute.

Norah Pearson

I am a Torres Strait Islander woman from Masig (Yorke) Island and I speak Kala Lagaw Ya. I am an experienced early childhood educator who completed a Bachelor of Education Early Childhood degree through the Batchelor Institute/Charles Darwin University partnership. I am currently a classroom teacher in the Torres Strait.

Claire Bartlett

I am the Academic Director of Professional Experience at Charles Darwin University. Prior to this, I was a senior lecturer in the Initial Teacher Education program at Batchelor Institute of Indigenous Tertiary Education. I teach English Language and Literacy, English as an Additional Language and/or Dialect (EAL/D) and Professional Experience. I research and publish about the implementation of English literacy reform for Aboriginal and Torres Strait Islander students learning EAL/D. I am a registered primary teacher and I have had teaching posts in Far North Queensland and remote Western Australia.

This chapter focuses on Torres Strait Islander culture, teaching, and learning. We are a diverse group of authors. We are practitioners, researchers, and teacher educators. In this chapter we aim to provide an overview of culture, histories, and education that are unique to the Torres Straits and Torres Strait Islander peoples and provide some practical tips for teachers in embedding Torres Strait Islander perspectives into the curriculum or who might be considering a teaching post in the Torres Straits. First, however, let us introduce ourselves.

Introduction

Indigenous Australian people are made up of two distinct groups – Torres Strait Islander people who mostly inhabit the islands of the same name and Aboriginal people who live on the mainland. Both groups share similar ways of being, doing, and knowing in shared learning environments, but there are also differences that set each group uniquely apart. Torres Strait Islander students come to school with their own ways of being, doing, and knowing that are similar to, but also different from Aboriginal students. This chapter focuses on the importance of language, culture, and identity to Torres Strait Islander students and shines a light on their unique ways. It also examines those issues associated with teaching and learning in a both-ways educational context. It does so from the perspective of two experienced practitioners through their social and cultural lens as Torres Strait Islander educators (Noressa and Norah).

The Torres Strait Islands are situated between the mainland of Papua New Guinea and the tip of Cape York Peninsula in North Queensland. There are 18 inhabited islands that make up the Torres Strait. There are also two mainland communities. Torres Strait Islander people can be grouped as coming from five main regions: Eastern, Central, Western, North/Top Western and the Northern Peninsula Area, which includes Bamaga and Seisa on the mainland (Synott & Whatman, 1998). The administration centre for the Torres Strait Islands is based on Thursday Island – what is affectionately known to the locals as 'TI'. There are over 8,000 people living in the Torres Strait with a further 21,000 people living on the mainland of Australia (Synott & Whatman, 1998, p. 56).

Torres Strait Islander culture is complex and is shaped by aspects of Australian, Papuan, and Austronesian cultures (Torres Strait Islander Regional Council [TRIRC], n.d.). Torres Strait Islander culture also differs within each community. Through a history of colonisation, Christianity, and maritime trade Torres Strait Islander languages, societies, and cultures have evolved, shaped by a history of colonisation, Christianity, and maritime trade (Angelo & Carter, 2015). According to the Australian Institute of Aboriginal and Torres Strait Islander Studies (AIATSIS) two languages are currently spoken in the Torres Strait, each with several distinct dialects: Meriam Mir, which has two dialect groups and Kala Lagaw with four dialects. Torres Strait Islanders also commonly speak creoles – English-based languages shared between different language and dialect groups (AIATSIS, 2005) (see Chapter 8 for a discussion of languages, creoles, and dialects). The Arts are a fundamental part of Torres Strait Islander culture and

Torres Strait Islanders have a long history of creating music, instruments, dances, costumes, and crafts. Through the Arts, Torres Strait Islanders pass on important knowledge of society and culture.

Schooling in the Torres Strait

In the Torres Strait, public schooling is provided by Tagai State College which comprises 18 community-based campuses that cater for students in pre-primary, primary, and secondary school. These campuses are located on the following Islands: Badu, Dauan, Erub (Darnley), Horn, Moa (Kubin and St Pauls), Mabuiag, Malu Kiwai (Boigu), Mer, Poruma, Thursday (primary and secondary), Ugar (Stephen), Warraber and Yam. Education in Tagai State College is underpinned by the concept of YUMI, a Torres Strait Creole term that "identifies a collective of people, united by a common purpose" and describes a "unique fusion of academic rigour, identity, culture, history and community" (Tagai State College, n.d.). This is evident in the school's vision – one that is focused on "Navigating YUMI to a successful future, by embracing our unique Torres Strait Island identity, to achieve a world class standard of education" (Tagai State College, n.d.). A key part of this is the 'both-ways' approach to teaching and learning.

Both-ways learning

The principles of both-ways learning means the bringing together of learning Western and Indigenous languages and ways of doing, being, and knowing. It means that linguistic and cultural knowledge are reflected in the curriculum, learning and teaching approaches, and in the culture of the educational setting. It is also when teaching and learning are built on respectful relationships and partnerships between Indigenous and non-Indigenous peoples (Ober & Bat, 2007).

It has long been acknowledged that effective teaching is vital to ensure children develop skills, knowledge, and understandings and to achieve positive outcomes in school (Darling-Hammond, 1999; Hattie, 2003). Teachers in cross-cultural settings are effective if they are socially, culturally, and linguistically connected to their students. Effective teachers of Aboriginal and Torres Strait school students achieve this by using approaches underpinned by a both-ways philosophy. Moreton-Robinson, Singh, Kolopenuk, & Robinson (2012) strongly suggest that pedagogy that reflected Aboriginal and Torres Strait Islander ways of knowing, being, and doing was necessary for success.

Both-ways is a philosophy that has at its core three fundamental principles:

1. Respectful relationships and partnerships between Indigenous and non-Indigenous peoples;
2. Learning from each other (Western and Indigenous languages and ways of doing and being and knowing);
3. Strengthening Indigenous identity by incorporating Indigenous knowledge in our work.

(Ober & Bat, 2007)

Robyn Ober et al.

While a both-ways approach underpins the provision of public schooling in the Torres Strait, it hasn't always been that way. Public schooling in the Torres Strait is shaped by a history of colonisation and assimilation that resulted in racist and oppressive policies and practices that privileged Western ways of knowing, doing, and being. These were gradually replaced by policies of self-determination that gave rise to practices that called for Torres Strait Islander languages, cultures, and identities to be harnessed for teaching and learning. Brought about by the leadership of Torres Strait Islander councillors, the local Elders, teachers, and school staff – and their participation in educational decision-making and governance – both-ways learning is now practised in all public schools in Torres Strait Island communities.

In this chapter, two experienced Torres Strait Islander educators and both-ways practitioners share their learning journey, describing their own education experiences. They describe how this has influenced and impacted upon their teaching practice, philosophy, and pedagogy in the school classroom. Their stories highlight the importance of weaving together language, society, and culture for successful teaching and learning for Torres Strait Islander learners.

A story from practice: Noressa's story

My cultural heritage is of Torres Strait Islander with family coming from both Top Western and Eastern Islands. Both of my grandmothers on my mother and father's side were island women. They came from the top-western island – Boigu and eastern islands – Murray Island of the Torres Strait. They married my grandfathers who came from Indonesia to work in the pearling industry in the Torres Straits.

I grew up on Thursday Island and completed my education at the local primary and secondary school during the 1960s and 70s. Education during this era was very different to the current situation. Due to the policies of the day I was classified a coloured person, because of my mixed cultural heritage. I had to attend Thursday Island State School; the decision of where I had to do my schooling during 1961–1964 was not in our control. As the main hub of the Torres Strait Islands and the multicultural make-up of the community, Thursday Island has an interesting educational history:

The Thursday Island State School was opened on 13 July 1885. Mr F. W Rayment was the first Principal. The State School for Coloured Children was opened in 1913 under the Protector of Aboriginals. Miss Richards was appointed School Teacher. It became a State School under the Department of Public Instruction on 5 February 1940. On 9 September 1954 it was renamed the Wai-Ben State School. In 1964 the Thursday Island State School was amalgamated with the Wai-Ben State School, and a Secondary section was established. In 1985 the School commemorated 100 years of operation.
(https://aiatsis.gov.au/sites/default/files/catalogue_resources/CDThursday.htm)

In 1971, I completed my year 10 at Thursday Island State School. Year 10 was the highest level that students could achieve during this era. The following year, I moved to Darwin, where I worked for several years until Cyclone Tracy struck in 1974. My family then moved to Batchelor, where I firstly worked as a domestic servant, but was so inspired and encouraged by students that I met there, that I made the decision to enrol in the Teacher Education course. This is my story:

I began my teacher education studies in 1983. I enjoyed my teacher education studies especially the D-BATE (Deakin-Batchelor Aboriginal Teacher Education) program which was jointly run by Deakin University and

Batchelor College. It encouraged me to weave my culture into my teaching practices through a both-ways philosophy which I believe is fundamental to the teaching and learning process. This teaching program provides opportunities for Aboriginal and Torres Strait Islander students and the communities to achieve the learning outcomes through a negotiated curriculum. For example, I remember one day in class when I was studying to be a teacher, the lecturer had us doing some conceptual maths activities about volume, area, and capacity. This involved such things as seeing how many students could fit under a classroom table, then packing as many students into a car and a telephone booth. The last activity had us running around in the courtyard outside the classroom. As I ran a round holding my skirt, I thought to myself, what would my family say if they could only see me now? But then I remembered I ran around like this when I was a kid trying to knock down wongai or almond fruits or getting the fish into the nets. But for goodness sake, I thought, why did I wear a wraparound skirt today? I also thought – Oh, so this is how you interpret space in a Western maths concept. The training encouraged me to look through my cultural lens first before linking it into a Western way of learning.

So when I began teaching at a school in the Territory, I drew from the knowledge that I gained during the teacher education program and also from my own culture. This is because first, and foremost, my culture is my life-jacket and it is with me everywhere I go. So when teaching I use a both-ways philosophy, where students' cultural knowledge, languages, and ways of being, doing, and knowing are valued and celebrated. I weave my own cultural knowledge including teaching and learning strategies into the school curriculum just like I had been taught to weave the different strands together into an island mat. Both-ways is not hard, because we are doing it without even thinking about it.

As you can see from Noressa's description, both-ways education is important. As a teacher you can be informed by the curriculum and use it for your teaching, but do so in ways that suit the needs of your students (see Chapter 13 for a description of a Strengths Analysis which can be done). You can do this by being innovative and creative, keeping a clear sight of your own culture, but at the same time not limiting the students. You can achieve this by explicitly recognising what they bring to the teaching and learning space. You can also achieve this by providing opportunities for students' contribution to their learning.

By doing these things you can create a common ground in education, regardless of where the teaching and learning is taking place. This common ground is both a supportive teaching environment and one that is rich with new learning opportunities. In the next section, Noressa describes how she achieved this when she began teaching in a new context.

A story from practice: The cultural lens

My cultural lens went into overdrive the first day at my new teaching post. This school was an Independent secondary school with predominantly Aboriginal and Torres Strait Islander students.

I knew that when planning a teaching program, it is important to always start by building and establishing relationships. To help establish a relationship with my new students and for them to connect and re-connect with each other, I decided to allow the students to set up the classroom themselves on the first day. So I left the tables and stacks of chairs in the position they were left after the room was cleaned at the end of the previous school term.

I was being guided by my cultural lens, our ways of working, being, and doing. I was preparing the learning space for relationship building and community engagement and for this to occur naturally. This was culturally appropriate and culturally safe for the students that I was about to meet in the classroom for the first time. It was going to make a statement about Aboriginal and Torres Strait Islander students' cultural knowledges and cultural activities, about their ontologies, epistemologies, and axiologies and how these go beyond the curriculum requirements. It was also about my providing a space for Aboriginal and Torres Strait Islander students to have the freedom to contribute to their own teaching and learning environment.

The school day started and when the students arrived, I asked the students to position themselves where they thought best in the classroom. This freedom to arrange and position themselves helped me to learn about the student's relationship with each other and this information was helpful not only for me, but for the students and other staff members within the school. When the students were finally positioned, and seated accordingly, I asked the question "Is everyone sitting where they are supposed to be?" and their response was a definitive "Yes". What a picture it was to see the students having the freedom to culturally place themselves in a Western learning space. You see, the students placed themselves according to their kinship systems which are very important in terms of cultural rules, protocols, and social connection. The older students automatically positioned themselves where they thought appropriate, even when the seating was set up according to how the teacher had placed the furniture. Most of these students come with the cultural knowledge of their complex kinship system taught to them from birth and reinforced throughout their childhood and now as young men and women.

It was only after this activity that I placed the students' names on their desks according to their seating arrangements. By doing these things in this way the students knew that the space was theirs and they took ownership over it.

Noressa not only demonstrates how to provide opportunities for students to contribute and have ownership of their own learning, she also showed how teachers need to be learners, too. The way she encouraged her students to draw on their ways of doing things (e.g., positioning themselves in the classroom according to their kinship system) allowed her to learn about the values of the community in which she was teaching, their beliefs, and knowledges. Of course, if she was teaching in her own community, she would be related to most of the children through kinship and would have an already established social connection. She would have the background knowledge of families, communities, outer islands, kinship systems, cultural rules, protocols etc. However, because this was not the case, she needed to learn these things. By doing things in the way she did, she was able to create a stronger relationship with her students and for them, with each other. She provides further advice about building relationships:

> In island way we say you must be a 'good pasin', (good person) always be respectful and kind no matter whether you are a teacher, family member, friend or visitor. This is integral to our ontology, our ways of being. It is embedded in our cultural identity. It is an important step towards building good relationships with one another.

Aboriginal and Torres Strait Islander people have our own ways of knowing, 'epistemologies', our own ways of being, 'ontologies', and our own ways of doing, 'axiologies' (Moreton-Robinson & Walter, 2009). Our ways of being, doing, and knowing are embedded in all aspects of our daily lives, making visible what is meaning and logical in our understanding of ourselves and the world that surrounds us (Porsanger, 2004).

There are cultural protocols in place throughout the Torres Strait Islands that teachers need to be aware of, but firstly relationships with the people must be established and strengthened. Relationship takes time and by creating a good rapport with their students, teachers will begin to establish and strengthen relationships built on trust, respect, honesty, and integrity. This will then have ripple effects onto the parents and community just like the ebb and flow of a tide that continues to bring about change and make that critical difference in students' lives. However, this is not a one-way street; there is also the opportunity for teachers to be personally enriched as they learn about the Torres Strait Islander culture, languages, songs, dances, and celebrations. This is Torres Strait Islander peoples' 'ways of being, doing, and knowing' and teachers will be surrounded by their rich cultural traditions, but it is up to them to engage and learn from the local people

Talk in the classroom

Aboriginal and Torres Strait Island students are used to communicating with each other through their mother tongue, Kriol, Aboriginal English, and/or English. They need to be encouraged to use their different languages because it helps them to think about the curriculum content and to be able to discuss these concepts. That is, it supports their learning. As Noressa explains:

> You shouldn't say to students "you cannot speak like that", as it is their way of communicating in the education space. If students are encouraged to communicate through their first language including Kriols and Aboriginal English, then it brings a different dynamic to the learning that is taking place. One student I taught had previously never gone to school, but after six months in my class he flourished in his schoolwork. This is because he was given the opportunity to learn new content through his language and culture. If he didn't understand then others in the class could support him and explain, not through long English conversations, but by short and simple explanations in his language. This helped him to achieve good results. Students should be encouraged and allowed to speak their languages to support their learning.
>
> It is not just language, either, it is the connection between language and understanding that is important. And this also has important implications for assessment. When Aboriginal and Torres Strait Islander students are assessed only in Western ways, this does not take into consideration their being, knowing, and doing. Aboriginal and Torres Strait Islander students have a wealth of knowledge before they enter school, but to take advantage of this, teachers need to provide students with opportunities and freedom to bring their language and culture into the school environment. However, this does require strong leadership and support to ensure Aboriginal and Torres Strait Islander students gain quality education through a strengths-based approach, drawing on students' social, cultural, and linguistic knowledge systems. There are cultural protocols in place throughout TSI and building relationships are very important. Relationship takes time and by building a rapport with their students will have a ripple effect like the ebb and flow of a tide that will develop and strengthen student, parent, and teacher relationships.

How these things can be brought together successfully is highlighted by Norah, especially in her early days at school, but her experience in high school shows how when this is not done, there can be negative consequences.

A story from practice: Norah's story

In my early years I went to school on Masig Island in the Torres Strait. It wasn't like now. The principal was non-Indigenous, but all of the teachers were Torres Strait Islanders. Then they were called community teachers. I felt I belonged. It was just normal – our language and culture were just a normal part of being at school. We moved between our languages all the time without noticing because we were mostly all Indigenous and all spoke the same.

We knew at the end of year 7 that we would have to go away to high school. In year 8 I went to boarding school on Thursday Island. My parents then sent me to Cairns where I completed year 9. In year 10 I went to Townsville. Boarding school was a very big step to take. It was hard because most of the teachers and students were non-Indigenous and the lessons were purely in English. There was no-one who spoke like me, so it was a struggle.

The shift impacted on me academically as I found it hard to understand what was being taught at school because of the language. I dropped out part way through year 11 and went back home. I did this because it was too hard for me and I felt that I didn't belong because back then they didn't respect us. I don't remember NAIDOC (celebrations) nor being identified as a Torres Strait Islander. It was like I was out there on my own. Leaving home, I would always cry. I felt like I was going into a whole new place of learning by myself. The curriculum back then didn't value my culture and perspectives. Now in some schools Torres Strait Islander students are performing well and being valued and respected for who they are, and they are part of a group. But when I went to school none of that was happening, so I didn't have that security. Even though I had family around, it was like there was something missing. The thing that was missing was belonging.

Context matters

To be a good teacher in the Torres Strait (in fact, anywhere) it is important to know the people you are teaching and how they live. Each school is in a different community and language is different everywhere, including in the Torres Strait where every island is different. Also, don't assume that because a person is a Torres Islander that they will know and understand the children on all the different islands – as with Aboriginal students, it is important to understand the diversity within groups and their particular context.

To be an effective teacher in the Torres Strait, as in other parts of the country, take the time to find information about your students and their community. Talk to expert teachers and seek out local knowledge, and then apply it in your classroom. Undertake professional development, especially courses in cultural awareness so you can learn about Torres Strait Islander people, their culture, and protocols. Seek out local resources in schools including local people, and the information they have about local knowledge. As we can see in Chapters 9 and 14, it is important to go into the community and speak to Elders and to respectfully find out how they can support you. It is particularly important that teachers new to the Islands work with Elders and teacher assistants – they are valuable sources of information as they understand the students' language and culture. In this way, the students will feel like they belong.

Conclusion

As we saw in Noressa's and Norah's stories language, society, and culture shaped their learning experiences and teaching practices. When harnessed for teaching and learning, their educational experiences were positive, and they experienced success. In contrast, when these aspects were ignored or poorly woven into their education, their experiences were negative. Norah's success in primary school happened because she was taught by Torres Strait Islander teachers who used her language, and their teaching practices reflected Torres Straits Islander ways of knowing, being, and doing. As Oliver, Grote, Rochecouste, & Exell (2013) suggest, recognising Aboriginal and Torres Strait Islander students' language, culture, and identity are vital for success.

Therefore, it is vital as teachers that we all recognise what is stated in the Queensland Studies and Assessment Authority Aboriginal and Torres Strait Islander Languages Syllabus (QSAA, 2019): "Indigenous languages are infused with Indigenous knowledge and a specific way of viewing the world that interlinks people, place and culture in a living pattern of relationships" (p. 1). Acknowledging this in our classrooms creates culturally safe spaces where people feel they belong and this is vital for educational success for Aboriginal and Torres Strait Islander learners (Frawley, Ober, Oclay, & Smith, 2017). Unfortunately, as Larkin (2011) reported, Aboriginal and Torres Strait Islander people continue to be excluded and marginalised in education settings, including at university.

Therefore, it is important to recognise the role of language, culture, and identity in order to create successful opportunities for all students, and as shown in this chapter, particularly for the teaching and learning of Torres Strait Islander children. Although Noressa's and Norah's stories come from different times and places, they demonstrate the vital importance of weaving these aspects together and doing so using a both-ways learning approach. As Torres Strait Islander educators and both-ways practitioners they have strengthened their pedagogies, drawing on their own ways of knowing, being, and doing. Noressa and Norah are both strong in their cultural identity and have harnessed that strength, confidence, and pride into their teaching practice. For teachers who will be working in the Torres Straits, remember to look around and observe the strength of the local people who have occupied these islands for generations and acknowledge their intellectual capacity and learn to build relationships with them. This is a step forward in helping you to become a better teacher within Indigenous intercultural contexts.

Reflective questions

1. How could you learn about the values, beliefs, and knowledges of the Torres Strait Islander students and community in which you are teaching?
2. How would you provide Torres Strait Islander students with opportunities to learn new content through language and culture?
3. How would you ensure your curriculum valued Torres Strait Islander students' culture and perspectives?

References

Angelo, D., & Carter, N. (2015). Schooling within shifting landscapes: Educational responses in complex Indigenous language contact ecologies. In Androula Yiakoumetti (Eds.) *Multilingualism and language in education: Sociolinguistic and pedagogical perspectives from Commonwealth countries*. Cambridge: CUP, pp. 119–140.

Australian Institute of Aboriginal and Torres Strait Islander Studies (AIATSIS) and the Federation of Aboriginal and Torres Strait Islander Languages and Culture (FATSILC). (2005). *National Indigenous Languages Survey*. Canberra: Australian Government Department of Communications, Information Technology and the Arts. https://aiatsis. gov.au/sites/default/files/research_pub/nils-report-2005.pdf

Darling-Hammond, L. (1999). *Doing what matters most: Investing in quality teaching*. Kutztown, PA: National Commission on Teaching & America's Future.

Frawley, J., Ober, R., Oclay, M., & Smith, J. (2017). *Indigenous achievement in higher education and the role of self-efficacy: Rippling stories of success*. Perth, Western Australia: National Centre for Student Equity in Higher Education (NCSEHE). https://www. ncsehe.edu.au/publications/indigenous-achievement-in-higher-education-and-the-role-of-self-efficacy-rippling-stories-of-success/

Hattie, J. (2003). *Teachers make a difference. What is the research evidence?* Paper presented at *Australian Council for Educational Research Conference*, Melbourne, Vic. https:// research.acer.edu.au/research_conference_2003/4

Larkin, S. (2011) Indigenous perspectives: Enriching scholarship and practice. *Australian Social Work*, 64(1), 2–5. 10.1080/0312407X.2011.542610

Moreton-Robinson, A., Singh, D., Kolopenuk, J., & Robinson, A. (2012). Learning the lessons? Pre-service teacher preparation for teaching Aboriginal and Torres Strait Islander students. https://www.aitsl.edu.au/docs/default-source/default-document-library/learning-the-lessons-pre-service-teacher-preparation-for-teaching-aboriginal-and-torres-strait-islander-studentsfb0e8891b1e86477b58fff00006709da.pdf?sfvrsn=bbe6ec3c_0

Moreton-Robinson, A., & Walter, M. (2009). Indigenous methodologies in social research. In Walter, M. (Ed.) *Social research methods: An Australian perspective* (2nd edn). Melbourne: Oxford University Press, pp. 1–18.

Oliver, R., Grote, E., Rochecouste, J. & Exell, M. (2013). A task-based needs analysis for Australian Aboriginal students: Going beyond the target situation to address cultural issues. *International Journal of Training Research*, 11(3), 246–259.

Ober, R., & Bat, M. (2007). Paper 1: Both-ways: the philosophy. *Ngoonjook: Journal of Australian Indigenous Issues*, 31, 64–86.

Porsanger, J. (2004). An essay about indigenous methodology. http://www.ub.uit.no/munin/ handle/10037/906

Queensland Studies and Assessment Authority. (2019). P-10 Aboriginal and Torres Strait Islander languages syllabus. https://www.qcaa.qld.edu.au/p-10/qld-curriculum/ p-10-aboriginal-torres-strait-islander-languages

Synott, J. & Whatman, S. (1998). United to the sea and land: Cultures, histories and education in the Torres Strait. In G. Partington (Ed.), *Perspectives on Aboriginal and Torres Strait Islander education*. Katoomba, NSW: Social Science Press, pp. 55–74.

Tagai State College. (n.d.). Mission and values. https://tagaisc.eq.edu.au/Ourschool/ Missionandvalues/Pages/Missionandvalues.aspx

Torres Strait Island Regional Council. (n.d.). Our Communities. http://www.tsirc.qld.gov. au/

Chapter 7

Developing strong relationships with Aboriginal students, families, and communities

Mike Exell and Graeme Gower

Who we are

Mike Exell

I am a non-Aboriginal man from Celtic and Germanic origins. I grew up in Perth and worked as a volunteer basketball coach and research assistant collecting data from Aboriginal high school and university students whilst studying at university. I then worked as a journalist in regional Western Australia before I began work-ing with the Clontarf Foundation, which I have done for the past five years across regional and remote Western Australia. As part of my role I work at academies based at host schools where I help run a program designed to attract Indigenous boys to attend school, complete Year 12, and transition into the workforce.

Graeme Gower

I am a descendent of the Yawuru people of Broome and spent my initial school years growing up in the town before attending secondary school in Perth. I later graduated as a primary school teacher and taught in Kimberley and Pilbara schools for eight years before joining Edith Cowan University. I have been involved in a number of roles at the university, including being Coordinator of Aboriginal external programs, Head of School (School of Indigenous Australian Studies), lecturing in Aboriginal teacher education, Indigenous cultural competency, the Masters' program, and research involving Aboriginal education. I'm now the lead of Curtin University's 'On Country' program – helping Aboriginal teaching assistants to become teachers.

Introduction

This chapter is concerned with the importance of developing relationships with Aboriginal students. This is because the level of success and engagement Indigenous students have in their education can often depend on the relationships they form with their teachers. Throughout this chapter, we will look at some real-life examples Mike has observed during his time working in schools in regional and remote Western Australia and Graeme has experienced as a classroom teacher and university educator. This will include an outline of strategies that have been observed as successful in relationship building and examples of how teachers, including Graeme, have achieved these in their classrooms. Later in the chapter this will include a specific and extended case study of a highly successful high school English teacher, 'Miss Alice', and the strategies she has used across a range of contexts.

The role of family and impact on schooling

Extended family members can have a much different role in the upbringing of an Indigenous child than may be experienced by a non-Aboriginal Australian child. Indigenous families often take a community-based approach to the raising of a child, with all family members, from the parents, grandparents, cousins, uncles, aunties, and older siblings all playing an important part in the child's upbringing. For instance, this is highlighted by the terms 'Uncle' and 'Aunty' that have much different connotations in Australian Indigenous culture than in non-Aboriginal society. This not only highlights the importance of their roles in the upbringing of a child, it is also a very important way to signal respect (see Chapter 8). While these terms signify a parent's sibling in Western culture, it can be applied to many extended family members in the Aboriginal context. The community-based approach towards raising a child is key in explaining why respect for elders is a core value in Australian Indigenous culture.

With this in mind, it is important to reflect on how this community-based approach to child raising can carry over into a child's education. It can often be the case for Indigenous children that their teacher is the first adult with whom they will have a close, long-term relationship, but who they are not related to. This can be challenging, as this will almost always be with someone from outside their culture and, not surprisingly, the students and their family may be cautious about this relationship. Therefore, teachers will need to find ways to demonstrate to families that they are receptive to forming mutual and respectful relationships with parents and extended family members. Opportunities to create and develop these relationships can be achieved through inviting families to attend sausage sizzles, and/or movie nights at the school. In addition, some principals have established designated spaces at school for parents and teachers to meet informally over a cup of tea as a means of establishing and strengthening relationships. The forming of these relationships is likely to develop over time and will require a level of patience and understanding by the teacher in efforts to build mutual trust and respect. A newly appointed teacher for example, may not be aware of and/or have a good understanding of the impact of transgenerational trauma which continues to affect many Aboriginal families today. Examples include the long-term effects of child removal, the marginalisation of Aboriginal people as a result of past government policies, poor health and education, racism, the high frequency of deaths among family and extended family members, and the rate of suicides by young Aboriginal children, to name a few (Beresford, 2012). These traumatic experiences, therefore, are likely to play a significant role in shaping the formation of relationships with teachers, and the engagement of families in school activities.

Yet, as we indicate, there are considerable benefits of developing such a close relationship with family, as is described next.

One example of this comes from when Mike was working in regional Western Australia with a group of male, Year 12 students to help them achieve their best possible educational and employment outcomes. While building a close relationship with the students was imperative to his role, the level of outcomes achieved would not have been possible without support from their families. Open communication with them, asking for their advice and opinions, and showing that he was willing to go the extra mile for their sons, led to a very trusting relationship and, ultimately, great outcomes for the students.

A story from practice: The importance of relationships

One student Mike worked with in WA's regional east was severely affected by Foetal Alcohol Syndrome. Despite his limited learning capacity, he was very well supported by his carer and achieved 100 per cent school attendance during Years 11 and 12. With support of his carer, Mike was able to secure him work at the local K-Mart store, where he and the other students had previously done a worksite tour. He was successfully able to transition into the workplace and, in fact, his carer telephoned Mike 12 months after the ex-student finished school to let him know he had won employee of the month. Despite no longer working with the student, the relationship Mike built was valued so much by the family they wanted to share this success with him.

It is important to understand that to emulate a community-based approach, extending it from the family to school, also means that the child's education cannot be created to exist just during school hours – it must also extend well beyond that time. Here we do not mean teaching outside of school hours, but rather becoming a part of the student's life, showing an interest in their lives, and in doing so, building a strong relationship with his or her family. Opportunities to build relationships with students and their families after school hours will vary between remote community, regional town, and city school settings. There may be opportunities for teachers to be involved or attend community events and/or Aboriginal and Torres Strait Islander days of celebration, such as NAIDOC week or sporting carnivals. Attendance or participation at these events by teachers will be noticed by parents and community members and this, in turn, can open up the lines for communicating and for getting to know one another, in an informal way.

In the classroom

As we have indicated, building positive relationships with students helps them to attain positive outcomes. It is important to be aware of this because as teachers you may be faced with helping students who, for various reasons, are below the national standard in reading, writing, and numeracy. It also can be quite challenging when their students do not appear to have the requisite skills necessary to cover what is in the curriculum. However, this does not mean that students cannot achieve well nor that they will not enjoy the class, as this can happen when appropriate methods are used and when a culturally inclusive curriculum is employed. Furthermore, if students feel safe and comfortable within a classroom

Mike Exell and Graeme Gower

environment, they are much more inclined to engage with their learning, which in turn leads to greater success.

There are many published resources and guidelines available to assist teachers and school leaders to modify the curriculum and teach in culturally appropriate ways. Many of these publications have been developed by school systems, educational authorities, and by Aboriginal and Torres Strait academics in attempts to achieve equitable schooling in Australia for Aboriginal and Torres Strait Islander students (Lloyd, Lewthwaite, Osborne, & Boon, 2015). While many of these resources provide useful strategies and guidelines on 'what' to do, what is often missing is 'how' to go about doing it. For the beginning teacher or for the teacher who is working with Aboriginal and Torres Strait Islander students for the first time, this may be a daunting task. However, this situation can be alleviated by approaching colleagues who have been teaching at the school in previous years to discuss effective teaching strategies and resources that have worked for them. Collegial support and advice can also be drawn from Aboriginal and Torres Strait Islander Workers and/or Officers who are employed in schools with Indigenous enrolments to assist the teacher on Indigenous matters, and who also may have the role in forming a link between the school and the community. In assisting teachers, these Aboriginal and Torres Strait Islander Workers and/or Officers can also provide helpful insights in curriculum development and they can also assist in the teaching of Aboriginal and Torres Strait Islander perspectives in the classroom. For example, in Western Australia, the teaching of the local Aboriginal language provides a great opportunity for Aboriginal and Islander Officers (AIEOs) and Aboriginal Teacher Assistants (ATAs) and/or members of the Aboriginal community to be directly involved in teaching activities at the school and offers a strong foundation for building and sustaining effective school and community relationships. Graeme has observed AIEOs and ATAs being involved in the successful teaching of Aboriginal languages and the Standard Australian English equivalent across a variety of school settings.

Aboriginal culture is rich in diversity and history, and this must be taken into account when interacting and building relationships with Aboriginal people and students, as the experience will differ from region to region. As a teacher, it is crucial that you get to know each of your Aboriginal students and how they learn. It is also important for the students to get to know and trust you as a person and as their teacher. Secondly, knowing and understanding Aboriginal culture and history of the local area will provide a strong foundation for the development of culturally appropriate teaching skills, curriculum content, and learning styles (see Chapter 14).

Many Aboriginal students will be able to successfully embrace Western knowledge and learning styles, however, this may not always be the case for others. To a large extent, the culturally appropriate teaching and learning styles that are being referred to, will develop with experience and in time as you interact and engage with students, AIEOs, and the Aboriginal community.

Aboriginal students are often group learners and dislike being singled out for individual success as this often leads to 'shaming' of the person by the other members of the group. This reflects traditional practices where responsibilities are shared as a group, rather than being controlled by recognised leaders. The notion of shared learning also reflects the practices of an oral culture where the exchange of knowledge is communicated through narratives, linking content to the local and surrounding environment and problem solving through real-life examples and existing understandings (Yunkaporta, 2009). Aboriginal students are 'relational' and 'place-based' learners, so it is important to incorporate these understandings in pedagogical practice. The immediate school environment can provide many teaching and learning resources for a range of subject areas to achieve these ends. The following provides examples of how these various needs could be addressed (and again see Chapter 14 for discussions of how this can be done).

Graeme recalls incorporating these learning styles in a primary class that he taught in the Kimberley region of Western Australia. He would often draw upon existing knowledge and use local examples when teaching new content or concepts to his students. His Science and Humanities and Social Sciences lessons incorporated Aboriginal knowledge and understandings, and reference to the local language in naming some plants, animals, places, and objects. The AIEO also assisted Graeme in providing appropriate cultural examples in the teaching and learning process. Aboriginal culture and way of life provides a range of examples in teaching science, for example, the six seasons and the relationship that each season had to certain foods being available.

In addition, Graeme would also schedule a quiz activity at the end of each week based on subject content that was taught during the week, including some from previous weeks, and these were combined with some general knowledge facts. He approached the manual arts teacher to make five buzzers with lights to add a competition aspect to the activity, but being mindful that the competitive aspect was conducted in the spirit of fun. Graeme found that this activity increased the retention of knowledge among Aboriginal students and provided a social or group learning experience that supported a level of competitiveness in a friendly manner. The activity also helped to strengthen the relationship that he had established with the students as evidenced by the level of mutual respect that was demonstrated not only in this activity, but across a range of classroom behaviours and interactions.

The following describes how another teacher, Miss Alice, also worked to achieve outstanding results by building a positive relationship with her students. Miss Alice grew up in Tamworth, a regional town in New South Wales, about 400km inland from Sydney. After studying in regional NSW, where she did a double degree in secondary teaching (English) and a bachelor social science (Psychology), she and her husband moved to Egypt to take up teaching roles at international schools. They have also taught in Vietnam and Qatar, and then in NSW and in the Kimberley region, Western Australia:

While 'Miss Alice' faced challenges when teaching her Indigenous EALD students (again see Chapter 8 for information), she made sure she created a very welcoming environment in her classroom. She did this by using the extra time in her classrooms to learn more about her students, taking genuine interest in their hobbies and showing a sincere level of care. She was fluid in her teaching style, adapting what she did according to their needs and interests. She also did not hold the students to unreasonable behavioral expectations, although, like their elders, she always expected the students to respect her rules. As a result her students always appeared to look forward to her class, even though it was a subject (English) that can often be a negative experience for students from an EALD background.

Mutual respect is one key to a strong student–teacher relationship and when this is not in place it can have negative consequences both for the students and the teacher. For example, where Mike has worked in regional and remote schools, he has observed that many Indigenous high school students have reservations about subjects such as Maths, Science, and Humanities & Social Sciences (HASS) and has seen negative behaviours emanating from students, ranging from work refusal to physical and verbal outbursts.

One HASS teacher indicated to Mike that he believed that students refuse to come to his class due to their dislike of the subject area, however, Mike noticed that it is often due to the students (with whom he had a lot of contact) not feeling welcomed within that classroom. For example, it was clear that the teacher concerned had not done much in terms of building any sort of relationship with his Aboriginal students. Also his classroom teaching style was very traditional, being quite didactic in how he approached his lessons (in stark contrast to the way Graeme made it a fun and interactive experience) and was not culturally inclusive. As a result his students struggled to relate to the subject matter. Yet despite the resultant outbursts and even when students refused to enter his class (e.g., one student did not go to his class for over six months and referred to him as "Stupid Teacher" saying "He talks cheeky" – disrespectfully – to his students), he did not reflect on his practices, and never changed what he did.

Self-identity

A challenge faced by some teachers, no matter their experience, is engaging Indigenous students in the classroom. As described above, a student's level of engagement is often linked to the relationship they have with their teacher and how comfortable they feel within the classroom environment. In many cases, this is also related to the student's self-identity in how they perceive themselves academically. It is often heard, particularly in regional and remote locations, students saying things such as "I'm not smart" or "I'm dumb, I don't get it". As a consequence, they are often unwilling to try and to risk failure, and so put up barriers so they will not feel like they have failed.

It is important to note how this negative academic self-identity contrasts with the positive one often related to their sporting achievements. This is noted by Kickett-Tucker (2009), who observed how much pride students carried because of their sporting success. In the school setting, students will not only talk with pride about their achievements during organised club or school sport, but even during lunch time football and basketball games. When they next have those students in their classroom, teachers who are on duty during these times will be peppered with questions such as "did you see me take that climb?" (i.e., when taking a football mark) or "did you see me break his ankles" (i.e., when dribbling during a basketball game). It is important at these times to build upon such positive self-identity statements, as there is not only the potential to carry over such positive affirmations into the classroom, but also it can enhance the relationship between teacher and student in the classroom environment. Encouraging appropriate risk-taking and using open-ended questioning are further strategies that teachers can use to promote positive self-identity and strong relationships in classroom settings.

In turn, teachers building good relationships can foster better student engagement within their classrooms. As noted by Halse & Robinson (2011), engagement is behavioural, cognitive and, of relevance to this chapter, affective (which includes such things as self-identity and relationship with teachers and peers). For students to achieve positive educational outcomes, it is vital that they engage in the learning process. Clearly strong relationships have much to contribute to the education of Indigenous students. The question then remains how to build such relationships.

Relationship building

As Sarra (2011) suggests, all good teachers share a number of qualities, and in various ways these demonstrate good relationships and/or suggest ways that we can develop these. Specifically, he indicates that good teachers:

- Are genuinely interested in their students;
- Make time for their students out of class;
- Ask their students what they did on the weekend;
- Go watch their students play sport;
- Make time to meet with students' families;
- Are passionate about their teaching.

Sarra not only outlines what makes a good teacher, but he also describes ones that will leave lasting impressions and influence on their students.

As an exercise, think back to when you were in school, either in primary or secondary school, and think about which teachers stood out to you, and who has had the most impact on your life. Which of the six points that Sarra (2011) has suggested did they fulfil? Now which of the six points do you think are the most important?

Next we will consider the points Sarra (2011) has noted, but examine these three in further detail: 'They are genuinely interested in their students', 'They make time for their students out of class' and 'They are passionate about their teaching'.

Undoubtedly being genuinely interested in your student is a key quality to being a successful teacher. A student–teacher relationship can offer a unique opportunity to shape a young person's life. However, it is still a relationship, and no one enjoys being part of a one-way relationship. If a teacher does not show interest in their students, then the students will probably not show an interest in the teacher and the content and skills they are trying to teach. On the other hand, if interest is shown, students are much more receptive to the content the teacher is teaching. This can be achieved quite simply in the way Sarra suggested, by asking about the student's weekend as they enter the classroom, or sitting with students during any free time and taking the time to allow them to share their interests.

These can be particularly important steps to take, especially with students who may be shy and reluctant to share their thoughts and ideas. Miss Alice talks about how this can be achieved:

> For those kids who do take that little bit longer to build that relationship, you've just got to sit down with them one-on-one and spend time with them. So you've just got to find time within the class.... to sit with them and just chat to them, and [ask]... what did you do on the weekend? Or what's your favourite movie? And from there you gradually build that relationship with them, and they start to feel more comfortable with you as well. That's the case whether it's (teaching) overseas, regional or remote, I just feel like all teenagers are similar....

Making time for students outside of class is another way to build relationships. As discussed earlier, the classroom for some students can be a quite uncomfortable and intimidating setting. Students may also see the classroom as a place which is not theirs, rather that it is the domain of the teacher. By making time for students outside the classroom, whether it be sharing a joke in the corridors or having a kick of football at lunchtime, the relationship continues to grow in a neutral setting where the student has a more positive sense of self. One deputy principal with whom Mike worked was often required to deal with most major behavioural issues of the school in his office and so this place was seen by students as a place where they would get into trouble. To counteract this the deputy prioritised the activity of spending time in an environment where students would feel comfortable (in the playground, on the football oval and outside of school), and was able to maintain strong relationships, despite being seen as the disciplinarian.

Sarra describes a good teacher as being passionate about their teaching. Passion is the key to delivering any message with success, whether it is a teacher, a salesman, or a talk show guest telling a story. The more passionate they are when delivering their message, often the more engaged the audience. This is also true when teaching, and becomes of utmost importance when teaching Indigenous students, especially in regional and remote settings. Students feed off the energy of the teacher; if you present the subject matter in a boring way, then of course the students will be bored. However, if it presented in a stimulating and engaging way, the lesson will be more enjoyable and there will be a greater chance of reaching the students. Whilst students may not be able to say what makes, and does not make, a good teacher, they all know which classes they are looking forward to in their timetable.

Making time to meet with students' families is also very important. Many students may come from families whose parents did not finish school, or who did not necessarily have a good experience within the education system. As such the prospect of meeting a teacher can be quite confronting and can make the family feel ill at ease. Therefore, it is important teachers make sure they have positive interactions with not only their students, but also their families. This has the potential to contribute in positive ways not only to the individual student's learning, but to the school community more generally. Making parents feel welcome and taking the trouble to engage with them are ways to achieve this.

In rural locations one way to achieve this is by teachers watching their students play sport on the weekend. In the regional areas, teachers also often play for the senior team, while the students play in the associated junior levels. Interacting around weekend sport creates an extra bond with the students, and provides excellent opportunities for teachers to meet the families in a setting away from the school. And it does not only have to be sport; finding activities or providing support for community events are other ways that teachers can develop stronger relationships both with their students and their families.

Practical teaching examples

A unique challenge faced by teachers of Indigenous students can be low attendance at school. Low level attendance can occur for a number of reasons – social, cultural, and familial – and this can make it hard for teachers to cover the curriculum and teach the content they need to cover, yet at the same time make the classroom a welcoming environment for the students. Again Miss Alice explains her strategy for engaging low attending students:

> I make a point of going up to them and speaking to them one-on-one. I'll say "where have you been, how have you been going, it's good to see you back", and it's really important in how you frame that. Even if they're are coming in, and I've only seen them once that whole month, I'll give so much positive praise like (saying) "it's so good to see you here" or "I know you've only written a sentence but that's really awesome". I'll also ask questions like "will you be back in tomorrow?" The students feel that positive energy and then they feel more positive about being in the classroom.

Combined with the low attendance, many remote schools also often have smaller class sizes, sometimes much smaller than many teachers would have experienced previously. Such small class sizes can be a challenge for any teacher, however, as Miss Alice explains, an important way to tackle this challenge is having the right mindset.

> The small class size and the low attendance was a big challenge when I first moved here (a remote location). The question I had to ask myself was "How am I going to deal with that in my class?" … Now I actually quite like small class sizes now because it's a lot easier, so I don't really feel like that's a negative anymore, that's a good thing. It was a gradual thing coming around to it, because when I worked in regional WA, I had classes with 32 to 33 kids … So it took me a while to get into the mindset that having four kids is totally fine and you can still work with them one-on-one, even more so than if you have 33 children.

Having a positive mindset is very important to setting goals and achieving outcomes for the students and for building relationships and creating positive experiences, as Miss Alice explains:

> The priority is to get your kids into your classroom, get them into school and then from there you can hopefully teach them something. You want to make school a positive place … So you need to come up here being open to the idea that this, even though we are in Australia and at a school, is not how it would be anywhere else in the country. It is totally like back to basics about building relationships and having strong, but positive behaviour management.

Improving pedagogy

Improving educational outcomes and learning experiences for Aboriginal and Torres Strait Islander students continues to be a key priority for governments, educational systems, and educators. Different ways have been undertaken to address this priority. In Western Australia, for instance, the Department of Education's 'Aboriginal Cultural Standards Framework' outlines a set of expected standards for educators with an aim of developing culturally responsive schools (Department of Education, 2015).

The document outlines five standards: relationships, leadership, teaching, learning environment, and resources. Each standard provides a number of key indicators to guide educators in developing a range of knowledge and skills, and various developmental stages in progressing from being culturally aware to becoming culturally proficient. The Framework's Teaching Standard provides specific guidelines for teachers to plan and implement effective teaching practices for Aboriginal students, including the preferred learning style of each student (Department of Education, 2015). As a teacher, do investigate this or similar documents to support your teaching, particularly with regard to building relationships.

One way that Graeme found effective was to build on the fact that many of his Aboriginal students became highly engaged in activities that involved an enquiring and practical approach to learning. He would conduct lessons outside the classroom on several occasions each week to provide practical examples that were familiar to the students. For example, in maths, the basketball and netball ball courts provided a practical means for learning area, perimeter, and units of measurement. He would also ask the students to apply these understandings to their knowledge of the local environment. In this way, both the learning and experience was positive, and both the students and Graeme were able to demonstrate mutual respect, which in turn further supported building a strong relationship.

Conclusion

The ability to build strong relationships with students is key to achieving positive outcomes, in terms of both academic results and personal development. Successful relationships are built on mutual trust, respect, and understanding, and this will take time and persistent efforts to develop and strengthen. The development of strong relationships will also be aided by being positive, including in situations where the student could be seen to be at fault, and by showing genuine interest and care for all students. At times this will require you as a person and classroom teacher, to suspend your own cultural paradigms and think 'outside the box' in understanding and applying Aboriginal ways of 'knowing' and 'doing'.

In this chapter we discussed the importance of developing relationships with Aboriginal and Torres Strait Islander students and provided suggestions on how to modify the curriculum and teach in culturally appropriate ways to improve their learning experiences and educational outcomes. We hope that his chapter has given you some insights on becoming a successful teacher in Aboriginal and Torres Strait Islander school settings, and importantly, given you the opportunity the make a difference in their lives.

Reflective questions

1. Outline ways in which you could make your classroom welcoming to Aboriginal students. Think about including aspects that incorporate their worldview or knowledge system.
2. Why is it important for teachers to obtain feedback and/or confirmation from a local Aboriginal person prior to their teaching of Aboriginal perspectives?
3. Provide classroom teaching examples to support the following Aboriginal learning styles: Yarning/story-telling, deconstructive and reconstructive learning (e.g., teaching from the known to the unknown), place-based learning or teaching examples that include the local environment).

References

Beresford, Q. (2012). Separate and equal: An outline of Aboriginal education, 1900-1996. In Q. Beresford, G. Partington, & G. Gower (Eds.) *Reform and resistance in Aboriginal education*. Perth: University of Western Australia Press, pp. 85–119.

Department of Education WA (2015). Aboriginal cultural standards framework. http://det. wa.edu.au/aboriginaleducation/detcms/navigation/aboriginal-education/

Halse, C., & Robinson, M. (2011). Working with Aboriginal students. In R. Craven (Ed.) *Teaching Aboriginal studies*. Sydney: Allen & Unwin, pp. 257–272.

Kickett-Tucker, C. (2009). Moorn (Black)? Djardak (White)? How come I don't fit in Mum? Exploring the racial identity of Australian Aboriginal children and youths. *Health Sociology Review*, 18(1), 119–136.

Lloyd, N. J., Lewthwaite, B. E., Osborne, B., & Boon, H. J. (2015). Effective teaching practices for Aboriginal and Torres Strait Islander students: A review of the literature. *Australian Journal of Teacher Education*, 40(11). DOI: 10.14221/ajte.2015v40n11.1

Sarra, C. (2011) Transforming Indigenous education. In N. Purdie, G. Milgate, & H. R. Bell (Eds.) *Two-way teaching and learning: Toward culturally reflective and relevant education*. Victoria, Australia: ACER Press, pp. 107–118.

Yunkaporta, T. (2009). Aboriginal pedagogies at the cultural interface. PhD thesis, James Cook University. http://eprints.jcu.edu.au/10974

Chapter 8

Supporting the diverse language background of Aboriginal and Torres Strait Islander students

Rhonda Oliver and Simon Forrest

Who we are

Rhonda Oliver

My mother was raised mostly by her Irish grandmother as a second generation Australian in Perth, but my father's family (the Olivers) have been in Australia since at least the beginning of colonisation with my father being born in a small country town called Cunderdin, Western Australia and his mother (a Starr) was born in Kalgoorlie. As a young man my father travelled to many remote communities servicing lighthouses along the coast – I grew up with Aboriginal artefacts on our mantelpiece, gifts he had received in return for making spearheads. Unbeknown to me until quite recently, as someone who could 'fix anything', he also provided help at an Aboriginal boarding school where I have had a decade-long research relationship. Although I grew up in suburban Perth, I did go to school with some Aboriginal students – ironically some of my school friends are the aunties of one of my now colleagues. As I tell the many teachers I work with, I didn't choose Aboriginal Education – it chose me. In fact, I began my career as an 'English as a Second Language' teacher working with newly arrived migrant children. It was through my research into child second language acquisition that I was drawn into working in this area.

Simon Forrest

I was born and raised in Wajuk boodjar. My mother is Nyungar and my father Yamaji/Wongi. I have kin connections to people and country at Goomalling, Swan Valley, Mt Magnet and Leonora/Laverton. I trained as a primary school teacher and worked in schools in Aboriginal communities and rural towns. My most influential teaching experience impacting on me personally, professionally, and culturally was teaching in a remote community school. This experience influenced me in my future direction as an educator (for nearly 40 years), and in my philosophy, methodology, and practice, especially in Aboriginal contexts. I have also worked in the public sector in senior managerial positions in education and Indigenous affairs policy and implementation, while continuing my university teaching of undergraduate students in the regional city of Geraldton. In 1983 I was the second only Aboriginal person appointed to an academic position in Western Australia at the Western Australian College of Advanced Education, later Edith Cowan University. In 1995 I was successful in being appointed as the Inaugural Head of School Kurongkurl Katitjin at Edith Cowan University. In 2010 I was appointed as Director of the Centre for Aboriginal Studies at Curtin University and in 2014 as the inaugural Curtin University Elder in Residence. In 2017 I became the first Aboriginal person employed at Curtin University to proceed through the promotion process to be promoted to a Professorial position.

Introduction

Many Aboriginal and Torres Strait Islander students speak Aboriginal English (AE) – a dialect of English, a creole, or a traditional Indigenous language as their home language. This is important, not only for day-to-day communication, but also as a way of maintaining cultural self-identity. However, once they begin school the rich linguistic repertoire of Indigenous young people can be a disadvantage, especially when teachers are unaware of their students' language backgrounds and the ways these may differ significantly from Standard Australian English (SAE) – the dialect of English that is most often used for instruction in Australian classrooms. This chapter discusses the language background of Aboriginal and Torres Strait Islander students and the impact this may have for their learning, and the implications it has for schools and teachers. It should be noted that the examples used for illustrative purposes in this chapter come from Western Australian data because this is where Rhonda and Simon have done the majority of their teaching and research. As we note later in the chapter, Aboriginal and Torres Strait Islander languages vary across the nation.

To begin this chapter we will first describe the ways language use varies and particularly how it is interconnected with the context in which it is used. This includes the cultural environment of the speakers, which can vary considerably from one population to another. We do this because it is important to understand that we do not all communicate in the same way – something that it is vital to be aware of if we are to create contexts for success when teaching Aboriginal and Torres Strait Islander students in our classrooms. It is also imperative to understand the consequence of this in the current environment of national curricular and testing regimes. We will then go on to describe the language backgrounds of Aboriginal and Torres Strait Islander students starting with traditional languages, then creoles, and finally AE, a dialect of English (if you are not sure of the difference between language and dialect, don't worry, as we will describe this in detail later in this chapter). Finally, we will consider the pedagogical implications and make some suggestions for classroom practice.

We are sure you know that we communicate with each other using language, and that you know different cultural groups may use different language(s). It is also important to understand that language involves more than just the sounds we make, the words we use, and how we put the words together. That is, it is more than just the linguistic features we use when we communicate. Communication involves creating and sharing our meanings – and sometimes these cannot be translated easily from one language to another or even from one dialect to another. This is because of the way cultural understandings underpin language and these understandings (e.g., knowledge, concepts, ideas, beliefs, etc.) differ from one cultural group to another. Because of these differences it is not surprising that there is potential for confusion when speakers from different backgrounds come together. One simple example to illustrate this is the way the words used for family relationships can vary from one dialect or language to another. In SAE we use the same word for grandmother regardless of whether the person we are referring to is our paternal or maternal grandmother. In some languages, two distinct words are used. Even for different dialect speakers of the same language, in this case English, family relationship words can be very different. For AE speakers, for instance, the word 'cousin' is used for what SAE speakers would call second, third or even fourth cousins and the words 'brothers and sisters' in AE may be used for the term 'cousins' in SAE.

Communication can also involve non-linguistic features such as the use of facial expressions, gestures, and other signs. Across different languages, these can also vary not only in how they are made, but also how often they are used. For example, in northern parts of Australia amongst Aboriginal people gestures are used frequently in day-to-day communication. Raising your index finger can serve as a greeting, whereas lips and eyebrows, rather than fingers, are often used for the purpose of pointing.

These examples highlight the fact that how we communicate depends very much on who we are, the context in which the interaction occurs and on the audience. Consider, for instance, the way people talk (including their use of non-linguistic features) when they are teaching in a classroom – this will be very different from the way they communicate when playing sport, doing their shopping or catching up with friends. These differences occur because context both shapes and is shaped by the language we use and how we communicate in different settings. It is even more complex when different languages and dialects are involved.

As we have noted above, our language also reflects differences in our culture. This is because language and culture are inextricably entwined. Think about the words we use in our everyday lives and think about how they would be different if we lived in a different place, eating different food and living in a different way. One famous example that is often used to illustrate this point is the various words for snow used by the Inuit people – the First Nations people living in the arctic region of Canada, Alaska, and Greenland. Similarly there is a wide range of words for rice in the Bahasa Malay language reflecting the importance of that food to Malaysian society. You can imagine the range of words that are used by Aboriginal and Torres Strait Islander children, being such a culturally diverse group. This is because culture shapes and is reflected in the language they use, just as our own culture and environment shapes how we communicate. However, you might also find there are words that are commonly used many people (e.g., taxi, email, huh?), including by both non-Aboriginal Australians and also by most Aboriginal and Torres Strait Islander people. However, you might also find that when the same words are used cross-culturally, they have different meanings.

For teachers, the influence of culture on language and vice versa is particularly important to understand. This is because culture creates the framework by which meanings are conveyed to and interpreted by students in our classrooms. Another way to say this is that what we are teaching our students will be filtered through our own and our students' cultural understandings and these may not necessarily align. So Aboriginal and Torres Strait Islander students might have specific words and local meanings for what we are talking about in class, but these might not be known by the teacher. Conversely the students may have a great deal of knowledge about the local environment, customs, beliefs etc, but this may not be well understood by the teacher because of a lack of shared language used to describe these things. This may create a situation where misunderstandings occur or where students become confused by the mismatch and withdraw from participating in class. During his teaching, for example, Simon saw first-hand how the collectiveness nature and sharing within Aboriginal communities was a source of conflict:

> Once when Simon was teaching, a non-Aboriginal boy in his class, Tom, came up to tell him that Johnny, who was Aboriginal, had stolen his pencil, and he was quite upset. Simon told Tom not to worry, he'd talk to Johnny at recess and try and sort out the problem. At recess Simon told Johnny that Tom was upset because he'd stolen his pen. At this Johnny became quite indignant – "No!" he said, he hadn't stolen the pen. Simon then pointed to the pen on Johnny's desk and said, "but that's Tom's pen." "Yes," said Johnny "I took his pen to use it, but I haven't stolen it".

Sometimes because of the mismatch between language and understandings teachers will judge Aboriginal students' knowledge and abilities less favourably. In fact, this has been reported to be the case for our national Australian testing regime (NAPLAN) where it has been shown in various research studies that Aboriginal students are culturally and linguistically disadvantaged by the way the test items are created because they do not take into account Aboriginal communication styles and cultural knowledge. These types of assessments also fail to recognise that SAE is not the first language of many Aboriginal students (e.g., Nguyen, Oliver, & Rochecouste, 2015; Wigglesworth, Simpson, & Loakes, 2011). As you can imagine, the consequences of these issues are quite profound.

One key focus in schools, especially in the primary schools, is the development of literacy skills. Once more, cross-cultural and linguistic differences have a potential impact on Aboriginal and Torres Strait Islander (and other linguistically and culturally diverse background) students' understanding of both spoken and written texts and the way they create their own. For example, those of us who are monolingual and who only have access to a standard dialect tend to think that, regardless of the language that is used, all genres (e.g., reports, arguments, narratives etc) are created in similar ways – but this is not true. Culture will influence what is valued and what is considered appropriate in terms of the way things are said or written down and because of this, there are cultural differences in the way things are sequenced in an oral or written text. SAE speakers, for instance, when telling or writing a narrative text follow a very linear course, however, for Aboriginal English (AE) speakers (and speakers of a variety of other languages), this is not necessarily the case. This has the potential to create misunderstandings because what is expected to happen in spoken language or in written texts, does not happen, and this can lead to confusion. It can also inhibit the development of student literacy skills if appropriate accommodations are not made for the students. We will talk about what these may look like later in this chapter. Clearly, there is a strong need to understand the language background of Aboriginal and Torres Strait Islander students so we are in a better position to teach them in ways that are linguistically and culturally appropriate, and in ways that create contexts for success.

Aboriginal and Torres Strait Islander students' language backgrounds

To help you understand how we as teachers can accommodate Aboriginal and Torres Strait Islander language and literacy needs in the classroom, we will begin by providing a description of these languages and dialects. So far, we have mostly used AE examples, but a range of different languages are spoken by Aboriginal and Torres Strait Islander people including traditional languages, creoles, as well as the dialect AE. In the next section we will then discuss aspects of these languages and dialects that need to be considered when teaching students. We then go on to make suggestions of things you might do in your classroom to support their success. Please note this is not a comprehensive list, but hopefully, as a teacher, you will be able to use the information we provide to modify what you do in appropriate ways to suit your particular students and will continue to explore ways to adapt your teaching to support learning success.

Traditional languages

Australian Aboriginal and Torres Strait Islander people make up about 3% of the Australian population. Of these, it is predicted that currently only 11% speak a language that was traditionally spoken in their community. Some examples of Australian traditional languages include Martu, Kija, Jaru, Arenthe, and Noongar, and Meriam Mer and Kala Lagaw Ya in the Torres Strait Islands. Today it is predicted that there are only about 70 traditional languages still being spoken. This is a considerable reduction from the 250 or so that were believed to exist in the 18th century. Although there has been a resurgence in the support for reviving and learning traditional languages – with programs being put into place in different parts of Australia – all Aboriginal languages remain highly endangered. In fact, McConvell and Thieberger (2001) predicted that by 2050 no traditional languages may be spoken in Australia. Given how important home language is to sustaining culture,

School rules across languages

Language	Be RESPECTFUL	Be RESPONSIBLE	Be a LEARNER
Arrernte (Central & Eastern)	Antarnte-arrerrtyeke	Mwarre anetyeke	Akaltye-irretyeke
Western Aranda	Ntarnte-arrerrtyeke	Marre netyeke	Kaltye-irretyeke
Luritja	Antani tjukaru	Palya nyinantjaku	Nintirrku tjaku
Warlpiri	Warra-warra kanyi	Ngurrjurlu nyinaya	Pinarrijarriya

From Yipirinya school rules (used with permission)

supporting positive cultural identity, and, in turn, how this contributes to well-being, we hope this is not the case!

Like all languages, traditional Aboriginal and Torres Strait Islander languages differ at all levels – at the sound, word, grammar, and pragmatic (i.e., how language is used) level. These traditional languages are as different to English as are languages such as Japanese, Swedish, or Afrikaans. Furthermore, although traditional languages spoken in communities that are located near to each other have some similarities, those that exist some distance from each other geographically are also linguistically distant (i.e., distinctly different). See the example in Table 8.1 taken from a set a school rules.

The languages shown in Table 8.1 are located geographically near to each other – so you can see some similarities, but you will also notice differences. If you look carefully, you can also see that it is not just the words that are different, but also how these words are combined and, if you look very carefully, you can also see how the grammar appears different (in this case how the tense, specifically the word 'be', is created). Teachers working in locations where traditional languages are spoken, including remote communities, but also other urban locations and regional towns, need to find out which one this is and, where appropriate and with the support of bilingual aids, refer to this language in their classroom (e.g., if they are willing, asking students how to say things in their language, putting bilingual labels on objects in classrooms and around the school etc).

Creoles

Although creoles are not traditional languages, they are languages in their own right. They have emerged from contact between two groups of language speakers. This has occurred throughout the history of mankind and in many different places around the world. For example, on Mauritius you will find French creole speakers. These speakers communicate using a language that has emerged from contact between the French who colonialised the island and those who were living there already. It includes words from other languages spoken on the island including English, African and South Asian languages and it has its own rules about how the words are combined and what meanings are conveyed. In Australia, the language of Aboriginal creole speakers has emerged from contact between traditional language speakers and those speaking another language, particularly English. In the first stage of contact a pidgin developed to enable better communication between the two distinct cultural groups (i.e., the Aboriginal and non-Aboriginal people). When this pidgin was used by successive generations it became what is called a creole. To add confusion to this situation, in northern Australia the creole that is most often spoken is called 'Kriol'. It is predicted that there are up to about 20,000 speakers of this particular creole.

Kriol, like other languages, has its own sound system, words, and grammar. See below and see if you can work out what it means:

Det preya weya Jisas bin titjim im wekinmen olabat

At first you might it hard to work out, but if we tell you it is the title of prayer, you will begin to see that there are parts of this that look a bit like English, however, there are other aspects that shows its roots come from traditional language(s). Like other languages there are also regional differences and words and expression will vary from place to place. Fortunately, there are a number of Kriol resources that teachers can access to develop their own understanding and also as way to support their students.

Aboriginal English

AE is a dialect of English rather than another language. There are various definitions of what a dialect is, but put simply it is the form of a language spoken in a particular region or by a particular group of people. When people sound different they are said to have an accent, but when they have different words, meanings and sentence structures, then it is a dialect. Standard American English, Scottish English, SAE, and AE are all examples of different dialects. It is very important to note that no dialect is superior or worse than another. As Trudgill (2012, p. 2) says "Dialects are not good or bad, nice or nasty, right or wrong – they are just different from one another". They all have peculiarities unique to them, but they are as rule governed as each other. Interestingly, when dialects are formed because of geographical separation, such as British English versus SAE, the differences between the two are tolerated. When dialects form in other ways, such as when a more powerful group imposes their language on an existing population, then dialects are less tolerated and those who speak it may experience linguistic discrimination.

You will have seen that some dialects, such as SAE, are called 'standard'. The reason for this is not because they are the 'correct form' or the benchmark against which all other dialects should be measured, but rather because they are the form that is closest to the how the language is written. However, in Australia, as in many other countries, SAE is the language of power – being the form of language used for government and professional purposes, in the court of law, and, of most relevance to this chapter, for education.

You can imagine if the way you speak is close to the way the language is used in school, then the transition to schooling is an easier task than if the form of your home language is different. Similarly, learning to read and write – which can be quite a challenging task even for the brightest students – can be that much more difficult when the form of your spoken language is some distance from the written form. And in this respect you don't have to be an AE speaker to find Australian schools challenging, as the following example shows:

> As with a lot of 'working class' people, Rhonda grew up speaking a non-standard form of English and she also has a very broad Australian, but non-Aboriginal accent. She did well at school and enjoyed reading and writing from a young age. However, one experience in her early years at school caused her considerable confusion – clearly it has had a big impact as she still remembers it very clearly, despite it happening a long time ago. She had been asked to write a story about what she did on the weekend. Duly she set to work beginning with the introduction "On Satday I went to see me aunty and cousins" and then she went on to describe in detail what she did. Very proud of her long and very neatly written story, she presented it to the teacher whose response was along the lines of "It is a very nice story, but you need to write it again properly". Rhonda returned to her seat and wrote it again, trying very hard to be even neater. On completion of this second attempt she again presented it to the teacher who once again said she needed to "write it properly". With increasing frustration she returned to her seat, but it was only after the third attempt the teacher said "you've spelled some words wrong, go and write them as they sound". This only added to Rhonda's confusion and frustration – she had already written her story according to how the words sounded – well at least the way they sounded when she (and her family) spoke. Because the teacher did not make explicit to Rhonda the difference between how the words sounded and how they are written, she simply remained confused.

For many Aboriginal students they also experience some distance between their home dialect and school and this can present them with challenges when appropriate attention is not drawn to the differences in the form of written and spoken English.

Rhonda grew up speaking a non-standard form of English. Aboriginal English is yet another example of non-standard English. It is not 'incorrect'; it is simply another dialect of English – one that is spoken by most Aboriginal people. Because it is used so pervasively by the Aboriginal population for their day-to-day communication, we will provide some detail about it here.

Aboriginal English is a way of speaking that differs from Standard Australian English at all levels of use and structure. As described above, it is as rule governed as SAE – and it is definitely not 'rubbish talk' as some Aboriginal people have sadly learned to describe their own language. Because it reflects a particularly cultural context, it has its own concepts, functions, uses, and forms. In fact, with the loss of so many traditional languages, it is a vehicle for handing on cultural knowledge to new generations. For instance, it is used to describe relationships with the land, shared places, and shared knowledge. As we have described above, it can be used to signify family relationships, to show respect (e.g., the use of the labels 'aunty' and 'uncle' for older people) and also to acknowledge the obligations and responsibilities of these relationships. In this way, it can be used to express identification with a particular Aboriginal community, but also it can be used to exclude others.

A story from practice: Simon's story

Simon describes growing up and regularly visiting the non-Aboriginal family that his mother lived and worked for as a 'domestic' when she was a young woman. She was very close to the family, even calling one of her own children after the daughter in the family. As a sign of respect, during their visits she'd have her children, including Simon, call them 'Aunty' and 'Uncle' despite not being blood relations. In later years, however, it did puzzle Simon that their children did not have to call his mother 'Aunty'. He wondered if it is a cultural difference, or if it was because their mother had been their 'domestic'.

Like all languages and dialects, AE also has regional differences, so words can be pronounced differently or mean different things in different regions of Australia. The dialect can even differ just a few hundred kilometres apart. As teachers of Aboriginal and Torres Strait Islander students, it is important to understand these differences and make an effort to find out what the local words and structures are.

Below we provide a description and some examples and rules that apply to AE (note, however, it is not comprehensive), and remember there are regional dialectal differences in the way that AE is spoken and so these examples are quite generic – you might find things are said or done differently with the AE speakers you teach. We are using different levels of linguistic features to present these examples, but be aware that there can be an overlap with some features occurring in a number of categories.

PHONOLOGICAL

It is not unusual for dialects to sound different. One common marker that shows AE is the language being spoken by individuals is when they pronounce the word 'ask' saying it as 'aks'. Again we need to reinforce the idea that this is not wrong, it is just how it is said in AE.

Other AE differences, and especially those that may impact upon development of literacy success in SAE include the fact that sounds such as:

/p/ and /b/ (e.g., *cup* and cub);
/t/ and /d/ (e.g., *but* and *bud*);
/k/ and /g/ (e.g., *luck* and *lug*);
/th/ and /t/ (e.g., *thin* and *tin*);
/th/ and /d/ (e.g., *then* and *den, that* and *dat*);
f/ and /v/, e.g., *riber* instead of *river*,

are not necessarily differentiated in AE and can be used interchangeably when spoken.

The 'ing' sound is another which is often pronounced differently in AE than SAE. It is often pronounced as 'in' so that words such *hunting and crying* are said as *huntin, cryin*. Vowel sounds may also be hard for AE speakers to differentiate. Like those sounds described above, this occurs because they are not considered different in AE. For example, *been* and *bin* and *had* and *head* may be heard and said the same way by AE speakers. Other SAE sounds that may be pronounced differently by SAE and AE speakers occur when consonants are joined together. So an AE speaker will say *firs* for *first* and *nex* for *next*. This also means for AE speakers verb forms such as *eats* the 's' will be dropped and said as *he eat* for *he eats* and plurals can sometimes lose their 's' ending, such as *snake* for *snakes*.

And it is not just the dropping of sounds that can occur. Sometimes sounds can also be added in the language of AE speakers. For example, the sound /h/ made be used with English words beginning with a vowel such as *h'Aboriginals* and *h'alright*. As we have indicated, these phonological variations occur because of the inherent differences between AE and SAE, and not because Aboriginal people who use AE can't speak 'properly'. However, it is important to be aware of these differences as they have the potential to impact on AE speakers' development of SAE literacy skills.

Lexical

We all have family or community words that are shared and understood amongst ourselves. For example, think of the many 'Australian' words and expression that lose their meaning or might be wrongly interpreted when used elsewhere (e.g., thongs, tinnies, bring a plate). These words have developed over time and, as with all languages, are loaded with cultural understanding. Similarly, AE includes vocabulary that carries cultural significance – such as the family relationships we described previously. Other words have developed because of historical reasons – such as borrowing from other languages, including traditional languages, and applying words in new or novel ways (e.g., deadly for good, grannies – for grandchildren and great-nieces and -nephews).

Some AE has evolved because of the way the original English word was heard and then the associations made between these words. For example, non-Aboriginal people in the north of Western Australia are referred to as *gardia*, sometimes said as *kartia* (possibly because contact with guards or police – who were *white people* – and this was then applied to all). As we mentioned before there are regional differences, so while *gardia* is used in the north of the state, in the south of the state the word *wadjella* is used (some suggest this is a traditional word, others that it emerged from *white fella*). Other examples include *Modiga* (for car, coming from motor car), *Riber* (for river). In addition, English would have been adopted and then adapted to express Aboriginal meanings such as:

> *Ole girl* – an elderly woman
> *Camp* – one's home

For liar/you lie – not serious/just pretending
Mob – for a group of people, often with whom you are connected, such as your extended family.

Other words have developed through the innovative use of English, including:

Combining words – *cousinbrother, ownlation, womanhead*
Reduplication – *piggy piggy*
Affixation – *quickway, longway, onetime, darktime, fat-one*
Words like sounds – *smash.*

At the same time, Aboriginal words with Aboriginal meanings may be used without an awareness that these words are anything but that needed to convey the speaker's meaning and not actually SAE. Rhonda and all the children she grew up with, including some Aboriginal kids, used the word 'boondi' as in 'chucking a boondi' (throwing a rock at someone) without knowing this was an AE term. Interesting things are also done to Aboriginal words in AE, such as adding English endings on to Aboriginal words (e.g., *yorga* → *yorgas* meaning woman/women, *jirrupin* → being happy, *Kangarooin/rooin* → going hunting for kangaroos).

Once more it is important to recognise that these lexical differences are simply ways that AE differs from SAE. Their use is not incorrect, particularly in conversational language and, in fact, they allow Aboriginal students to show their identity in positive and overt ways enabling them, through their language use, to signify their cultural membership. However, to access the literacy practices of school – which is mostly conducted in SAE – they need support to be made aware of these differences.

Syntactical

AE and SAE also differ in the ways that words are combined when used. This means that there are different grammatical rules or, as we say, the syntax of AE and SAE varies from each other.

For example, in AE it is possible to:

- Have double subjects e.g., *Carly she's goin'*;
- Use unmarked gender e.g., *e's a cheeky one*;
- Use double negatives (that are still negative) e.g., *They don't have nothing*;
- Use of *unna?* or *inni?* as tag questions, e.g., *It's good, inni?* (rather than SAE isn't it?);
- Create wh- questions in a slightly different way e.g., *What you do that for? What for you do that? What kine that thing?*;
- Not use articles (a, an, the) before a noun e.g., *We bin go Perth for holiday*;
- Mark possession with using apostrophe 's' e.g., *Kath dog, Rhonda office*;
- Use of 'for' instead of using apostrophe 's' e.g., *Dis Simon for hat*;
- Quantify in things vague ways e.g., a big mob, *little bit long way, close up, jus'ere*;

- Not to have to use 'am/is/are/was/were' e.g., *Dey teenagers, we comin*;
- Signify past tense with 'bin/been' e.g., *We **bin go** Broome*.

Here again it is vital that as teachers we recognise how AE differs from SAE and support our students to move between their various linguistic codes in successful ways. This can be achieved by drawing attention to how the codes are distinct (note: not right or wrong) and then using this to explicitly develop the type of knowledge students can use to transverse their language and literacy development.

Pragmatics

Finally, as we described at the beginning of this chapter, language involves more than just the sounds we make, the words we use, and how we put the words together – it also involves how we engage with the context in which we communicate. Contextual appropriacy relates very strongly to the concept of pragmatics – or the social rules around language use. Again, for those of us who are not multilingual we tend to think these rules of communication are the same, but they are not. Silence, for example, can be a big part of an AE conversation. In her various travels working with Aboriginal students and their family members, Rhonda has never laughed more – laughter is such an important part of these conversations. As we've mentioned, body language and gestures also figure prominently and these are not necessarily the same as those used by non-Aboriginal or Torres Strait Islander people. For instance, looking at someone in the eye, especially when they are being reprimanded, is often not appropriate. For non-Aboriginal teachers, the volume of their Aboriginal or Torres Strait Islander students' voices may seem different – sometimes much quieter and sometimes much louder. As students get older, teachers may find that it is inappropriate for different gender, but also different family members, to talk to each other, for example, in some communities a son-in-law cannot talk directly to his mother-in-law. Even on the level of taking turns during conversations things can be different – who can and who can't have the next turn being governed by strict rules. All this has consequences when undertaking class discussion, or pair and group work in class.

Together we have described how the dialect of AE differs from SAE. Before that we talked about the form of traditional languages and creoles. Next, we consider how understanding the language background of Aboriginal and Torres Strait Islander students can support a strengths-based education, but also may present challenges that teachers need to carefully consider.

Implications for pedagogy

Some people living in Australia are surprised to learn that there are Aboriginal students attending school who do not have English (be this SAE or AE) as their first language, and although the proportion is small, it is indeed the case for some students, particularly those who have close connections to remote communities.

For this cohort of students it is important to teach them in similar ways you would to any others who are learning English as an Additional Language (EAL). While this might seem obvious, it is common to find students who have a traditional language or a creole as one of their first languages being taught in the same way as students who have English as their first language and few, if any, modifications are made to the mainstream curriculum to accommodate their language background. That is why it is important to understand the differences that exist so that as teachers we can accommodate their needs (also see Chapter 13 about Strengths Analysis) by adapting our methods and approaches in ways that make them more accessible and appropriate, and so enhancing their opportunities for success.

Another extremely important point to make here is that it is vital as teachers that we support and value our students' home languages. This is important not only for their cultural identity and wellbeing (imagine how you would feel if someone denigrated a key part of who you are!), but also because students' ability in home language supports their learning of SAE. Some time ago, Cummins (1976) proposed the Threshold Hypothesis. This basically says, you cannot be better in your second language than you are in your first. So if we want students to be successful in learning SAE, then we need them to have a strong home language. Including opportunities for them to explicitly make links between home and school language is one way to do this. Introducing the community *language* as the language for all students at the school to learn (instead of say French, Italian, Indonesian) is another way. Of course, that requires suitably qualified staff to do this – which is not always easy to achieve – however, it should certainly not be dismissed as a possibility and there are a number of schools around Australia where this is now happening. And where this is not possible, or even when it is, using resources such as books and magazines written in *language* in your classroom, putting up signs (e.g., welcome to school, school rules – as illustrated earlier in this chapter) and displaying local artefacts labelled bilingually are ways to show support for Aboriginal and Torres Strait Islander students' home language.

In turn these ideas provide opportunities to draw attention to the differences between home language and that which we use in schools. As we've indicated throughout, awareness is a crucial part of language and literacy learning (e.g., rather than simply suggesting Rhonda write something the 'proper way', actually highlighting the difference between how something is said and written down would have helped). Being aware of these differences is an important first step both for teachers and their learners. Without drawing attention to difference there is potential for confusion for AE, creole, and traditional language speakers, impacting on their success when interacting orally with SAE – especially in classrooms – but also on the development of their SAE written literacy. For instance, and as Rhonda experienced, sounding out words to spell them can be a fraught strategy if a non-standard variety is spoken. Similarly you may need to draw their attention to grammatical features that are influenced by the way things are said by students – such as tense e.g., *walks, kicks, sits* and plurals, e.g., *cats, kites, chicks*. The next step is providing input to students and drawing their attention to the form of the written language and how it might differ from how it sounds. Once again it is important to recognise that SAE words are not superior, but rather they are 'standard' and, therefore, are the appropriate ones to use in a written text. If problems arise for students, teachers should provide feedback to reinforce their students' explicit awareness. And, as we've indicated above, this should occur while embracing and supporting home dialect/language.

As teachers it is important that we model respect for everyone's language. We should use the correct local words, and do so respectfully and, where appropriate, with permission. By doing so we are better placed to discuss, quite explicitly, when it is appropriate to use some SAE words. One final comment about an issue that does arise for teachers when working with non-standard English speakers (be these Aboriginal or other cultural groups) is the use of swear words. In some cultures, particularly in groups who use a standard form of the dialect, swearing is often frowned upon. However, for others who may speak a non-standard dialect, including amongst some AE speakers, swearing doesn't carry the same connotations. They are just words, amongst other English words, albeit very expressive ones! Understanding this may help teachers respond in ways that do not escalate a verbal situation beyond what was intended by the speaker. This is not to say that students cannot have their attention drawn to the fact that it might not be appropriate – what is key is to deal with the language, rather than judging the person who might be using it.

Conclusion

In this chapter we have examined the language background of Aboriginal and Torres Strait Islander children. We have also reflected on the impact it can have for learning, but also for our teaching. We hope that by engaging with this chapter you will be sufficiently aware to think about ways for modifying your lessons in appropriate ways.

Reflective questions

1. We stated that the consequences of a mismatch in cultural understanding and communication, and the way assessment is done in school can be quite profound for Aboriginal and Torres Strait Islander students. What do you think some of these consequences might be and how might this be addressed in schools?
2. We mentioned linguistic discrimination – judging people because of the language or dialect they speak. Carefully consider your own biases. Have you ever felt you would like to 'correct' how someone speaks or are there particular accents, dialectal differences or language use related to linguistic background that you find you respond to in less than positive ways?
3. After reading this chapter, how will you respond to students who come to school with a language background that is not SAE?

References

Cummins, J. (1976). The influence of bilingualism on cognitive growth: A synthesis of research findings and explanatory hypotheses. *Working Papers on Bilingualism*, 9, 1–43.

McConvell, P. & Thieberger, N. (2001). *State of Indigenous languages in Australia – 2001*. Australia State of the Environment Second Technical Paper Series (Natural and Cultural Heritage). Canberra: Department of the Environment and Heritage.

Nguyen, B., Oliver, R., & Rochecouste, J. (2015). Embracing plurality through oral language. *Language and Education*, 29(2), 97–111. doi: 10.1080/09500782.2014.977294

Trudgill, P. (2012) *Dialects*. London: Routledge.

Wigglesworth, G., Simpson, J., & Loakes, D. (2011). NAPLAN language assessments for Indigenous children in remote communities: Issues and problems. *Australian Review of Applied Linguistics*, 34(3), 320–343.

Chapter 9

Teaching and learning

There is no one right way, but there are right things to do

Lillian Miller and Carly Steele

Who we are

Lillian Miller

Lillian Miller is a proud Dyribal, Mbarbarram, and Yidinji woman from the Atherton Tablelands area. Lillian has taught for 25 years within State and Independent schools in Queensland and New South Wales. Since 2007, Lillian has worked for Catholic Education Services, Cairns as an Education Officer for Indigenous Education. Her skills and expertise in curriculum development, particularly in Mathematics education, ensure that she is held in high regard locally and nationally. Part of this recognition includes her work on an Aboriginal and Torres Strait Islander Mathematics Project called 'Mandalany' and 'Yumplatok'. During 2014–2017, she sat on the ACARA Aboriginal and Torres Strait Islander Advisory Group. Lillian has recently completed her Masters in Indigenous Languages Education at the University of Sydney in 2018.

Carly Steele

Carly Steele is non-Indigenous and has taught for 12 years. During this time she shifted her teaching focus to Aboriginal and Torres Strait Islander education and has never looked back. She has since spent seven rewarding years working with Aboriginal and Torres Strait Islander students in northern Western Australia, Far North Queensland and the Northern Territory. She has recently completed her PhD at the University of Melbourne researching aspects of second dialect acquisition for Aboriginal and Torres Strait Islander EAL/D learners. Carly is currently a Lecturer of Aboriginal and Torres Strait Islander Education at James Cook University.

Introduction

This chapter is about effective ways for teaching and supporting the learning of Aboriginal and Torres Strait Islander students. These ways can be broadly categorised as 1) building relationships through valuing home language and culture, and connecting with students' families and home life; 2) practising culturally responsive teaching through adapting the curriculum and implementing Aboriginal and Torres Strait Islander pedagogies; and 3) empowering learners by holding high expectations and through developing Personalised Learning Plans (PLPs). Research presented throughout this chapter shows that these approaches have a positive impact on learning for Aboriginal and Torres Strait Islander students. However, how these approaches are implemented can vary greatly according to the environmental context, school, teachers, and students. Real-life examples are used to explore how these approaches can be implemented in different classrooms in effective ways.

Building relationships

Building relationships with your Aboriginal and Torres Strait Islander students and their families is imperative for successful teaching and learning in the classroom (Byrne & Munns, 2012; Harslett, Godfrey, Harrison, Partington & Richer, 1999; Hudsmith, 1992) and this should not be understated. We suggest that while building relationships is important for all students, it is crucial for the success of Aboriginal and Torres Strait Islander students. As indicated in Chapter 7, how teachers build relationships with each student will differ depending on a number of factors, including the personality of the students and their teacher. One key to building relationships with Aboriginal and Torres Strait Islander students is the valuing of students' home language and culture. This also involves making a strong connection with students' family and home life.

Valuing home language and culture

For teachers to value their student's home language and culture, they must first learn about their language and culture.

As described in Chapter 8 and the Our Land Our Languages Report (Australian Parliament, House of Representatives, 2012), language is important to every aspect of Aboriginal and Torres Strait Islander peoples' lives. Including Aboriginal language and cultural programs into our teaching has significant benefits both for individuals and their education: "early childhood Aboriginal language and cultural programs lead to increased self-esteem, improved academic performance, improved school attendance, reduced drop-out rates and better proficiency in reading skills in both the Indigenous language and English" (p. 99). (See also Gower & Byrne, 2012; Harrison, 2011; Sarra, 2011.) Furthermore, learning about languages is beneficial for both Aboriginal and Torres Strait Islander and non-Aboriginal and Torres Strait Islander peoples because it leads to better understanding between different people, their cultures and identities. It can also work to support and promote reconciliation. Finally, for us as teachers, an understanding of Aboriginal and Torres Strait Islander culture, language, and history is a vital component of the Australian Institute for Teaching and School Leadership (AITSL) Teaching Standards 1.4 and 2.4:

- **1.4 Strategies for teaching Aboriginal and Torres Strait Islander students:**
  Design and implement effective teaching strategies that are responsive to the local community and cultural setting, linguistic background and histories of Aboriginal and Torres Strait Islander students

- **2.4 Understand and respect Aboriginal and Torres Strait Islander people to promote reconciliation between Indigenous and non-Indigenous Australians:**
  Provide opportunities for students to develop understanding of and respect for Aboriginal and Torres Strait Islander histories, cultures, and languages.

The role of languages other than Standard Australian English (SAE) in the classroom can be contentious. However, it is important to recognise students' language and culture in the classroom and to provide a safe space for students to use their language/s. Students' language/s can be an important tool for learning and this should be actively encouraged in the classroom. Teachers can provide support for students learning SAE as an additional language or dialect (EAL/D) by helping them make connections between their language/s and SAE by using both languages, also known as a "translanguaging" approach (García & Wei, 2014). Often this can be aided by other students or by an Aboriginal or Torres Strait Islander educator within the school to build knowledge and understanding in the classroom. In the following account, Lillian explains how she used students' language and culture in the classroom to support students to build their mathematical knowledge.

A story from practice: Valuing home language and culture

Lillian was working with Aboriginal students in Far North Queensland. She noticed that students were not connecting with the mathematical resources that were available to them. She also noticed that the schooling environments were devoid of Aboriginal language and culture. She decided to develop a resource for a 'Closing the Gap' project that would develop mathematical concepts using Aboriginal language and culture.

The mathematical resource was called 'Building on Success', and it aimed to build on students' strengths as mathematicians. The language used in the resource was Kuku Yalanji which is the Aboriginal language of the Mossman Area. The main aims of this approach included:

1. To work with local Aboriginal Traditional Owners in a language-related project.
2. To promote Aboriginal culture in schooling environments, particularly in everyday classroom practice.
3. To ensure the preservation and continuation of Aboriginal languages.
4. To empower Aboriginal students through successful and engaging learning experiences and to promote a sense of belonging inside the classroom.
5. To develop community partnerships and involvement.

The key mathematical elements of 'Building on Success' were:

- Engaging before explaining – this stage employed a hands-on approach to learning, real-life examples, and making it enjoyable to provide students with opportunities to experience success (see Figure 9.1).

▲ Figure 9.1

Hands on approach

- Making mathematics experiential – this involved building language experiences and solving problems in collecting and organising of materials i.e. the "experience" as opposed to other methods of acquiring knowledge (see Figure 9.2).

▲ Figure 9.2

Building experiences

- Involving processes of investigation – this part provided opportunities for students to engage in the process and meaningfully connect with language (see Figure 9.3).

▲ Figure 9.4

Implementing strategies

▲ Figure 9.3

Engaging with the process

- Implementing strategies for working mathematically – this involved using students who are naturally competent thinkers to share their strategies for working mathematically (see Figure 9.4).

Building on Success enables teachers to provide engaging teaching and learning activities and to support the local language. It is beneficial for all students as they connect maths with learning language and culture. The response from teachers has been overwhelmingly positive and they are keen to embed language and culture in other learning areas.

Other teaching approaches and strategies that you can use in your classroom that support learning based on Indigenous language and culture include:

- Creating a language tree or similar classroom display with all the languages/cultural backgrounds of the students in your class (Berry & Hudson, 1997);
- Helping students create their personal family trees;
- Using 'Getting to know you' activities – e.g. draw the outline of a person and students colour the parts of their bodies that represent their different languages and cultures; student questionnaires – 'all about me'; using the iPad to create a personal video;
- Learning a few words in your students' languages and using them in the classroom;
- Adding words from your students' languages to your classroom displays and labels;
- Having students use their other language/s in the classroom to understand and explain their new learning to peers;
- Taking the time to learn about students' languages and cultures – often there are Aboriginal and Torres Strait Islander employees at the school who can help you or direct you to learning resources located in the school;
- Adopting a "translanguaging" approach (García & Wei, 2014) in your classroom (see Chapter 8);
- Listening to Aboriginal and Torres Strait Islander traditional music and stories in classroom;
- Explore the AITSL Illustrations of Practice, particularly: Teaching an Indigenous language; Implementing an Indigenous language program; Community perspectives on an Indigenous language program; Traditional language and Early career Indigenous language teaching.

Connecting with students' families, home life, and culture

Sadly, many Aboriginal and Torres Strait Islander people are often still impacted by the legacy of events or policies in their cultural history. Trauma caused by colonisation, including prohibiting the use of traditional languages and the practice of forced removal of children has had devastating consequences not only on the generations that experienced it, but also those that followed. This trauma, passed from generation to generation in families and communities, is known as 'intergenerational trauma'. Therefore, it is important to view the challenges faced by many Indigenous communities in the context of this history (including within the living memory of those who are still alive), as this still impacts on Aboriginal and Torres Strait Islander people today.

As educators we also need to be aware of the educational consequences of previous policies, such as Aboriginal people being barred from school and having to work from a very early age or, if enrolled in school, being unable to speak their language/s and practise their culture. Schooling environments can provoke past and intergenerational trauma, often resulting in Aboriginal and Torres Strait Islander people avoiding school. Therefore, it is important for schools and teachers to build connections with the Aboriginal and Torres Strait Islander families that attend their school, and with their broader community. This can be achieved by creating inclusive schooling environments that seek to engage Aboriginal and Torres Strait Islander students, their families, and communities in schooling (see Chapter 14).

There are many strategies to create inclusive schooling environments – ones that promote engagement for Aboriginal and Torres Strait Islander students, their families, and the wider community. When implemented together they will serve to support those dealing with intergenerational trauma. These include:

- Raising the Aboriginal and Torres Strait Islander flags alongside the Australian one;
- Celebrating significant dates for Aboriginal and Torres Strait Islander peoples, including but not limited to National Sorry Day, the 1967 Referendum, National Reconciliation Week, Mabo Day and NAIDOC Week. Put these dates in the school calendar, write about them in the school newsletter, put posters up around the school, organise student learning activities for these dates;
- Including an 'acknowledgement of country', or if possible and appropriate – 'a welcome to country' for school functions and events;
- Including the local language/s or the language/s spoken by students in school displays and signage around the school. For example, 'welcome' and 'hello' in the different languages in the school office and on classroom doors, a greeting or word of the week in the school newsletter and/or assembly each week, translating the school rules into other languages;
- Building a relationship with the local elders or traditional owners in your area and seeking their input or involvement in your school;
- Establishing a committee to promote inclusion within your school;
- Hosting community events at your school so it is not just a 'school' but a part of the community;

- Holding parent–teacher afternoons in alternative locations that will encourage family attendance;
- Developing a School–Community Partnership Agreement; these agreements have been shown to have positive outcomes for students and schools (What Works, 2013);
- Explore the AITSL Illustrations of Practice, particularly respecting local culture, history, and language.

For teachers, there are many ways to make your classroom inclusive and to build relationships with your students and their families. As described in Chapter 7, building relationships with your Aboriginal and Torres Strait Islander students is one of the best ways to engage your students, their families, and the broader community in school. It is crucial for achieving positive personal, social, and educational outcomes for your Aboriginal and Torres Strait Islander students.

A story from practice: Connecting with home

Carly worked at a school where many Aboriginal students were from a local Aboriginal Community, a 45-minute drive from the school. The students commuted by bus and it was difficult for parents, who either worked in the community or in town (in the opposite direction to the school), to become involved in school events or even attend parent–teacher afternoons. To overcome this and to promote community engagement, she created a video and played it for the community at an afterschool event held in the community. The video contained a vignette of each of the teachers greeting the parents and telling them about their classrooms, as well as images of their children in the classroom learning and playing in the playground. The event was very well attended with many children and their families including siblings, aunts, uncles, and grandparents coming along to the event. They greatly appreciated the opportunity to see 'in action' what school life was like for their children and the video was watched multiple times.

Here are some other strategies you can implement to achieve connections between your students and their families:

- Make your first contact with home a positive experience i.e., "I was proud of the way that ... did ... today. It shows me ..." Continue to share positive experiences;
- Aim for regular casual conversations in preference to formal school meetings;
- Contact with home might be difficult, so find non-traditional means to connect with families outside school, such as at sporting events or organise to meet them in a convenient, neutral environment. This can mean travelling to local communities or perhaps sending messages through a Community Liaison Officer or a person in a similar role;
- Ask parents and caregivers about their children, i.e., what do I need to know about your child to empower them as a learner? What are our goals and how can we achieve these goals together?
- Teach your students about significant dates for Aboriginal and Torres Strait Islander peoples with learning activities, and acknowledge and celebrate these dates in class;

- Include the local language/s or the language/s spoken by students in classroom displays;
- Become involved in local community life (where appropriate).

In an effort to build connections with home and promote engagement with schooling, Lillian formalised some of these ideas and developed a resource to achieve this (see the story describing this below). Whilst it might not be possible for an individual teacher to create such a resource, it is something that a group of teachers could work on together to implement.

A story from practice: Connecting with home

In her work Lillian often receives requests for activities that could serve to reinforce learning at home. In response, Antoinette Cole and the Cairns Catholic Education Learning and Teaching developed the T.A.L.King (Thinking, Acting, Learning, Knowing) Together Kit to promote parent and community involvement and home interaction; then it was Lillian's role to teach families how to use these kits and she worked together with them to achieve this. The T.A.L.King Together Kit looked at different ways that parents, families, and the community could engage with their children's schooling in a non-threatening way.

Each T.A.L.King Together Kit contained:

- Blackboard;
- Peoplescapes Number Names 1-10;
- Peoplescapes subitizing;
- Peoplescapes Numbers 1-10;
- Peoplescapes Ordinal Numbers 1-10;
- Threading Wombat Ordinal Numbers;
- Threading Koala Numbers 1-10;
- Circular Numbers 1-10;
- Foam Numbers 1-10;
- 10 Shells;
- 10 Counters;
- Number Ladder;
- Around the Home;
- At the Beach.

The T.A.L.King Together Kit was produced mostly to assist parents and caregivers of students in Pre-primary and Year 1. It builds on developing mathematical experiences that teachers are using in these classrooms. It includes activities to help students develop those mathematical concepts being learned at school. The T.A.L.King Together Kits aimed to:

- Investigate the role of oral language as a precursor to the development of literacy and numeracy understandings and skills;
- Monitor students in Prep/Year 1 as they engage in meaningful oral language experiences in literacy and numeracy;
- Identify key stages within transition from home to school;
- Adopt a socio-cultural pedagogical model for enhancing Prep/Year 1 students' oral language.

Families have responded well to the kit and commented on its effectiveness, describing how all the materials have provided successful learning experiences. Parents have also commented about how the increased engagement in the activities has provided opportunities for increased oral language and communication. They look forward to the next task cards each month, and parents have created their own learning activities as well.

Culturally responsive teaching

Knowing and valuing your students' home language/s and culture is not only imperative for building relationships with your students, it is also vital for your teaching, for successful implementation of the curriculum, and for undertaking appropriate assessment. Over the last few decades many terms have been employed to highlight the importance and the role that culture plays in learning. Terms such as 'culturally appropriate', 'culturally relevant' and 'culturally compatible' have been used. For us, the term 'culturally responsive teaching' is preferred, as it highlights the relational and interactive processes involved in strengths-based teaching that is being advocated here (Ladson-Billings, 1995, p. 467). The term 'culturally responsive teaching' was first coined by Cazden & Leggett (1981) and by Erickson & Mohatt (1982). More recently the idea has been expanded by Gay, who describes it this way:

> Culturally responsive teaching is defined as using the cultural char-
> acteristics, experiences, and perspectives of ethnically diverse stu-
> dents as conduits for teaching them more effectively. It is based on
> the assumption that when academic knowledge and skills are situ-
> ated within the lived experiences and frames of reference of students,
> they are more personally meaningful, have higher interest appeal,
> and are learned more easily and thoroughly.
>
> (Gay, 2002, p. 106)

As a result, the academic achievement of ethnically diverse students will improve when they are taught through their own cultural and experiential filters.

According to Gay (2002) there are five essential elements of culturally respon-sive teaching: developing a knowledge base about cultural diversity, ensuring the curriculum includes ethnic and culturally diverse content, demonstrating caring within positive learning communities, communicating with ethnically diverse stu-dents, and responding to ethnic diversity in the delivery of instruction.

To effectively practise culturally responsive teaching, as we have described above, teachers must build relationships with their students and develop a knowl-edge and understanding of their home language/s and culture. The benefit of doing this is that the two are mutually compatible and serve to reinforce each other. In an Australian-based study involving teachers and community, Owens (2015) found that partnerships with the community and teachers valuing students' family and cultural heritage resulted in increased warmth and communication between school and community, which in turn impacted on the curriculum and teaching approaches used, which enhanced learning opportunities of Aboriginal and Torres Strait Islander students.

Another aspect of culturally responsive teaching is responding to ethnic diversity in the way that instruction is delivered (Gay, 2002). To this end, teachers need to adapt the curriculum and employ Aboriginal and Torres Strait Islander pedagogies in their classrooms.

Adapting the curriculum

As a teacher your role is to support equitable access to the Australian Curriculum for all learners. It is important to note that when students do not see themselves reflected in the classroom curriculum, they can find it difficult to engage (Borden, 2013). Therefore, as teachers we need to adapt the curriculum for our local com-munities so we can meet the diverse needs of our students – noting that there is a vast range of learning contexts throughout Australia. How do you go about

Access, curriculum and assessment questions in relation to equity (Stobart, 2005, p. 279)

Access questions	Curricular questions	Assessment questions
Who gets taught and by whom?	Whose knowledge is taught?	What knowledge is assessed and equated with achievement?
Are there differences in the resources available for different groups?	Why is it taught in a particular way to this particular group?	Are the form, content and mode of assessment appropriate for different groups and individuals?
What is incorporated from the cultures of those attending?	How do we enable the histories and cultures of people of color, and of women, to be taught in responsible and responsive ways? *Apple, 1989*	Is this range of cultural knowledge reflected in definitions of achievement? How does cultural knowledge mediate individuals' responses to assessment in ways which alter the construct being assessed? *Gipps and Murphy, 1994*

this? One way we have found useful is to consider the equity questions about access, curriculum, and assessment as raised by Stobart (2005, p. 279) as shown in Table 9.1.

Teachers need to carefully consider each of these questions in the context of their current classroom environment. Based on their answers they may need to adapt their lessons, the curriculum, and how they design assessments to ensure equity for their students. For example, in Table 9.2 we give some suggestion as to how this could be achieved.

In the story below, Carly describes how she incorporates access, curricular and assessment responses (shown in Table 9.2) to write her HASS unit to ensure culturally responsive teaching.

Suggested responses to improve equity for Aboriginal and Torres Strait Islander students

Access response	Curricular response	Assessment response
Ensure students can use and access their additional language/s in the classroom to promote learning	Teach Aboriginal and Torres Strait Islander knowledge (cross-curricular priority)	Ensure that Aboriginal and Torres Strait Islander knowledge is assessed and equated with achievement.
Include Aboriginal and Torres Strait Islander persons in the school community and broader community	Teach knowledge in different ways, incorporating Aboriginal and Torres Strait Islander pedagogies, for example, the 8 ways of learning (Yunkaporta, 2009)	Consider non-traditional modes of assessment that still adequately demonstrate knowledge and understanding (for example, how can new technologies be incorporated to demonstrate knowledge and understanding?)
Invite Aboriginal and Torres Strait Islander guest speakers with specialist knowledge	Learn about Aboriginal and Torres Strait Islander languages, history, and culture to ensure responsive teaching	
Invite students to share their cultural knowledge		

A story from practice: Culturally responsive teaching

Carly was teaching the HASS curriculum to a multi-age class of Aboriginal students in remote Australia. She first needed to address the challenges of working with a multi-age class, including what content and skills to cover. After careful consideration she decided that the Year 1, 2, 3 HASS Curriculum presented themes that were sufficiently similar to allow for shared learning experiences, but at the same time allowed for adequate differentiation according to year level and ability level of the students. The thematic focus was past, present, and future in the local Aboriginal community.

There were four key shared learning experiences:

1. An Elder visited the class and spoke to them in language about her life in the past – the games they played, foods they ate, their shelter and the first time she encountered a 'white' person;

2. An Aboriginal Education Worker (AEW) that worked in the school visited the class and spoke to them about life for her generation (the next generation from the Elder in the last visit). She spoke of life on the mission – the games, the food and shelter, as well the experience of returning to Country;

3. An exploration of cultural artefacts and photos. The school housed a range of cultural artefacts and photos of the pasts that spanned each generation, showing how life had changed in terms of food sources and shelter;

4. A class excursion on Country to build shelter from the natural environment as was done in the past. Students were taught the relevant skills by community members.

These shared learning experiences provided students with the opportunity to build a rich understanding of key content in the HASS learning area. Assessment of learning was differentiated to enable students to successfully meet the achievement standards for their relevant year level in the HASS learning area.

There was a wide range of ongoing assessment tasks:

Year 1 – Picture sort into 'past' and 'present', explain how life has changed according to pictures, label map of community, describe community using map and directional/location terms, share stories of past and present using terminology to denote passing of time.

Year 2 – Choose one of the guest speakers and describe their significance in the local community, explain the significance of moving back to Country (i.e. why places are important to people), categorise and sort pictures according to food, shelter, entertainment, pose questions about the past based on photos and cultural artefacts, compare ways of doing things in the past and present (i.e. making food (flour), providing shelter, recreational activities), create a labelled map of the community, create a narrative about the past (present and future) using language to describe direction, location, and the passing of time.

Year 3 – Create a timeline (using pictures and cultural artefacts) of the recent past from first contact, missions, and return to Country, identify the individuals and events that played a significant role (label sources of information), create a table of continuity and change in the community, create maps of the community changing over time using basic cartographic conventions, describe aspects of the community that have changed and remained the same over time using timelines, maps, and tables as support.

The above provides an example of how the Australian curriculum can be contextualised to become relevant for the students in your classroom. In this example, local Aboriginal knowledge was taught to meet the demands of the Australian Curriculum and the HASS learning area achievement standards in multiple year levels. Different ways of learning and knowing were incorporated through interactions with community members and the local natural environment. Most importantly, students enjoyed the learning that took place. They delighted in poring over old photos and making family connections with who was who (a particular highlight for them was a photo of an Elder when they were much younger with dreadlocks wearing flared pants and playing guitar!). They learned cultural knowledge from community members and were not only very successful in building their shelters, they learnt a great deal about the past (see Figure 9.5).

▲ Figure 9.5

Students taking a 'nap' in the houses they built

In this way, Carly was able to teach all the requisite content descriptors in the Australian Curriculum and the students were able to meet the Achievement Standards appropriate to their year level and Aboriginal knowledge was equated with achievement.

Here are some other strategies you can use as a teacher to incorporate culturally responsive teaching in your classroom:

- Consider Stobart's (2005) equity questions about access, curriculum, and assessment;
- Adapt the curriculum and lesson delivery at assessment to meet local context;
- Ensure Aboriginal and Torres Strait Islander knowledge is taught, valued, and equated with achievement;
- Emphasise and promote the ways that Traditional Owners and community members can add value to the school and the classroom;
- Extend special invitations to Elders and community members to join in not only significant events but all school events, to have a positive presence in the school community;
- Use alternative or non-literacy-based forms of assessment in the classroom, e.g., the use of technology and other ways of representing learning.

Aboriginal and Torres Strait Islander pedagogies

As noted in previous chapters, Aboriginal and Torres Strait Islander students share a cultural worldview that often stands in stark contrast to that of the Western

Lillian Miller and Carly Steele

culture of schooling (Berry & Hudson, 1997; Malcolm & Grote, 2007). Teachers must include Aboriginal and Torres Strait Islander pedagogies in their teaching to ensure equity of access to learning for these students as discussed above. It is also important that Aboriginal and Torres Strait Islander pedagogies are implemented from a culturally responsive viewpoint. That is, not all Aboriginal and Torres Strait Islander peoples are the same and just using one pedagogy is not the answer. Teachers need to learn about the local context and the Aboriginal and Torres Strait Islander students in their class in order to respond to their needs. Aboriginal and Torres Strait Islander pedagogies provide options for doing this, but they need to be employed in a responsive way to avoid a reductionist view (Donald & Rattansi, 1992; McConaghy, 2000; Castagno & Brayboy, 2008). Due to the diversity of Aboriginal and Torres Strait Islander peoples' histories, languages, cultures, and experiences, it is important that all learning needs are contextualised within the local environment.

One example of a pedagogical approach for Aboriginal and Torres Strait Islander students is the 'two-way' or 'both ways' approach that was implemented through the Department of Education, Western Australian with their Tracks to Two-Way Learning program (2012). 'Two-way' cultural learning involves learning about both cultures, and valuing both equally. Because of the differing languages and cultural practices of Aboriginal and Torres Strait Islander students, teachers often find that cultural misunderstandings and miscommunications can be commonplace in the classroom (Eades, 1984). 'Two-way' cultural learning provides a bridge to explore these cultural and linguistic differences to aid mutual understanding and most importantly, learning in the classroom.

Teachers may also have access to the CSIRO's Inquiry for Indigenous Science Students (I2S2) in their school. This program also employs a 'two-way' learning approach that is designed to illustrate "how Aboriginal and Torres Strait Islander peoples used high-level science inquiry skills within cultural practices" and highlights "the links between Indigenous and Western science knowledge and ways of working" (CSIRO, 2019). The program is based on the premise that Aboriginal and Torres Strait Islander peoples are Australia's and the world's first scientists. This premise can be explored in many other subject areas as well, particularly English and Art (for example, Aboriginal and Torres Strait Islander peoples as the first story tellers or the first artists), to produce some very rich teaching and learning experiences. An example (Fire: a burning question) of this program in action is shown on the Australian Curriculum website in their Illustrations of practices for Aboriginal and Torres Strait Islander Histories and Cultures (ACARA).

The '8 ways of Aboriginal learning' (Yunkaporta, 2009) is designed to meet the learning needs of Aboriginal and Torres Strait Islander students. However, the strategies employed are beneficial for all students. As such, the framework presents an opportunity to include Aboriginal perspectives whilst simultaneously catering for a wide range of diverse learning needs in your classroom. Because it is a pedagogical approach, teachers can continue to teach learning area content while at the same time embedding Aboriginal perspectives in their lessons. The pedagogical framework is expressed as eight interconnected

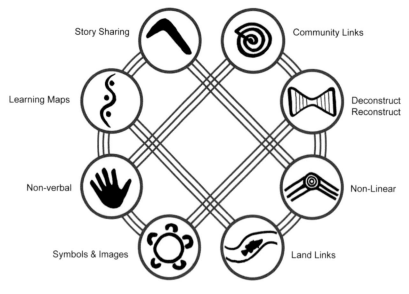

Story Sharing

Community Links

Learning Maps

Deconstruct
Reconstruct

Non-verbal

Non-Linear

Symbols & Images

Land Links

▲ Figure 9.6

8 ways of Aboriginal learning (Yunkaporta, 2009)

strategies for learning (shown in Figure 9.6). There are "8 ways to start the process… Tell a story. Make a plan. Think and do. Draw it. Take it outside. Try a new way. Watch first, then do. Share it with others" (NSW Department of Education, 2020).

Yunkaporta's (2009) techniques include:

- Learning through narrative;
- Planning and visualising explicit processes;
- Working non-verbally with self-reflective, hands-on methods;
- Learning through images, symbols, and metaphors;
- Learning through place-responsive, environmental practice;
- Using indirect, innovative, and interdisciplinary approaches;
- Modelling and scaffolding by working from wholes to parts;
- Connecting learning to local values, needs, and knowledge.

It is also important for teachers to consider the preferred interaction styles of some Aboriginal and Torres Strait Islander students. Teachers need to find ways of accommodating their preferred interaction styles in the classroom to cater for their students' learning needs. Frequently, the interaction styles of many Aboriginal and Torres Strait Islander students are not compatible with the expectations of classroom teachers, which again, can lead to breakdowns in communication (see Chapter 8). Prolonged or enforced eye contact and specific types of

Lillian Miller and Carly Steele

questioning can result in feelings of shame (Harkins, 1990) for some students. These situations are not necessary to teaching and there are other ways of doing things in the classroom that focus instead on building students' confidence in a safe and secure environment. Using indirect questioning or other means of determining student knowledge and understanding have been shown to be effective when teaching some Aboriginal and Torres Strait Islander students (Galloway, 2003). For example, instead of beginning the lesson with teacher-directed questioning, the lesson could begin with a small group interactive task that revises learning – and this could be written, oral, or completed through drawing or another type of visual representation, such as using iPads, or acted out, etc. Additionally, like all students, Aboriginal and Torres Strait Islander students respond well to positive reinforcement in the classroom (Galloway, 2003). This involves actively making the effort to avoid classroom situations which may initiate or invoke shame; instead teachers should work to ensure there are plenty of opportunities for success and positive reinforcement.

A story from practice: A maths lesson employing Aboriginal and Torres Strait Islander pedagogies

In her role, Lillian frequently demonstrates maths lessons that employ Aboriginal and Torres Strait Islander pedagogies. This is one example from a Prep classroom. The lesson focused on the following content descriptors from the Australian curriculum for mathematics:

- ACMNA 001 – Establish understanding of the language and processes of counting by naming numbers in sequences, initially to and from 20, moving from any starting point;
- ACMNA 289 – Compare and order and make correspondences between collections initially to 20, and explain meaning.

First, Lillian read the book Cassowary Coast – Count on Country by Pamela Galeano and talked with students about ways of counting in the local Jiddabul language. She then taught students the following key words in Jiddabul language that they would use throughout the lesson:

- Maui – food;
- Mandalay (pronounced man-da-lanj) – children's games;
- Yunggal – number for 1.

Next students engaged in mandalay (children's games) for learning about numbers. A blue mat was placed on the floor with maui (in the form of fish) spread across it as shown in Figure 9.7. The maui had number names, numerals and quantities shown on them. Students were asked to engage it different mandalay, such as:

- 'Find another maui like this one';
- 'Show me maui 8';
- 'What maui did I point to?';
- 'Find and catch all the maui for yunggal';
- 'Find all the maui for 10'.

These mandalay were extended to include sequencing, counting backwards and forwards to and from 20 – starting from any point. Because there were many different mandalay that could be played, it was very easy to differentiate learning according to the students' needs and specifically target the students' current ability level.

At the end of the lesson, students engaged in a 'yarn about' their reflections of their learning, sharing it with each other.

Therefore, in this lesson Lillian was able to teach students about Aboriginal language and culture while teaching key mathematical content. Her lesson also included many elements of Yunkaporta's (2009) 8 pedagogical ways for creating an engaging learning experience for all students.

▲ Figure 9.7

A student participating in Mandalany to learn key mathematical concepts

Aboriginal and Torres Strait Islander pedagogies are not just for Aboriginal and Torres Strait Islander students, which is a common misconception. They represent an opportunity for teachers to expand their teaching repertoire to cater for the diversity that is present within any Australian classroom. They also help to provide a balance of perspectives in learning, rather than privileging Western Eurocentric knowledge and cultural norms. Exploring the different knowledges and ways of learning that Aboriginal and Torres Strait Islander pedagogies embody will enrich the education of all, which is at the heart of the Australian Professional Teacher Standard 2.4.

Here are other ways you can incorporate Aboriginal and Torres Strait Islander knowledges and pedagogies into your teaching toolkit:

- Use dialogue or 'yarning circles' in your classroom (Mills, Sunderland & Davis, 2013);
- Employ 'two-way' learning in the classroom;
- Employ Yunkaporta's (2009) '8 Ways of Learning';
- Find out whether you can access CSIRO's Inquiry for Indigenous Science Students (I2S2);
- Explore the new science elaborations addressing Aboriginal and Torres Strait Islander Histories and Cultures cross-curriculum priority;
- Consider the preferred interaction styles of your students and ways to accommodate these styles in your teaching, such as the use of interactive tasks in preference to direct questioning;
- Use positive reinforcement;
- Provide opportunities for student success;

Lillian Miller and Carly Steele

- Always contextualise Aboriginal and Torres Strait Islander pedagogies and perspectives to the students in your classroom;
- Explore the AITSL Illustrations of practice, particularly 8 ways of Learning and Fire stick farming.

Empowering learners

This chapter is about teaching and learning. Effective teaching empowers learners. This can be achieved by holding high expectations and developing approaches in your classroom such as Personalised Learning Plans (PLPs) for your Aboriginal and Torres Strait Islander students.

High expectations

This book takes a strengths-based approach to the teaching of Aboriginal and Torres Strait Islander students. One way to achieve this is by holding high expectations for your students to overcome barriers to learning imposed by deficit perspectives (Ionn, 1995). Sarra, Spillman, Jackson, Davis, & Bray (2018) provide guidance for teachers to enact high-expectations relationships. Key to establishing high expectations is building an understanding of the student's personal circumstances and developing responsive strategies that will enable that student to achieve the high expectations set for them. This is what Sarra et al. (2018) label 'High-expectations relationship (enacting)' in Table 9.3. It is important to note that 'high expectations' is not treating all students the same, irrespective of personal circumstances. This is what Sarra et al. (2018) label 'High-expectations rhetoric (believing)'. Table 9.3 from Sarra et al. (2018, p. 7) clearly illustrates what high-expectation relationships look like in the context of schools. It is important to note in the examples that high-expectations does not just relate to teacher expectations of students, but rather is about how the teacher conducts themselves in all facets of their role as teacher and their responses to various situations that present.

High expectations are vital to improving school attendance and academic achievement for Aboriginal and Torres Strait Islander students (Bissett, 2012; Harrison, 2011; Milgate & Giles-Browne, 2013; Sarra, 2011; Sullivan, Jorgensen, Boaler & Lerman, 2013). Whilst many teachers may attest to holding high expectations for Aboriginal and Torres Strait Islander students, it is the communication of these high expectations that is significant to achievement. One way to formalise this and to promote accountability between all parties can be through the development of PLPs.

Personalised Learning Plans (PLPs)

PLPs are designed to recognise the strengths, needs and goals of individual students and map the pathway to achieving these goals (What Works, 2011) (also see Chapter 13 for a description of a Strengths Analysis approach). They are expected to be both a collaborative and an active process (DEEWR, 2011). PLPs have

▼ Table 9.3

Examples of the difference between high expectations rhetoric and a high-expectations relationship (Sarra, Spillman, Jackson, Davis and Bray, 2018, p. 7)

Situation	Low-expectations response	High-expectations rhetoric (believing)	High-expectations relationship (enacting)
A student arrives at school without a uniform.	Ignore the absence of the uniform, believing that confrontation is not worth the time, effort or potential conflict.	Send the student home for not following the school rules.	Talk with the student about why they are out of uniform Engage in a conversation with parents/carers about options, for example, the school providing uniforms if cost is an issue.
A student is not attending school regularly.	Refrain from talking to the student or contacting parents or carers—It is not the teacher's role to get students to school.	Suspend or punish the student for not adhering to school policy.	Work with the student to explore the reasons affecting attendance Talk with the family to work together to find solutions.
A student enters your classroom visibly upset because of relationship difficulties with another student.	Ignore the student, or state that the demonstrated behaviour is 'ridiculous' and unnecessary.	Insist that students keep their problems 'out of the classroom' because everyone is there to learn'.	Talk to the student to determine what support they need in order to engage in the class or if another option is appropriate Make a time to talk to the student further.
Two students are fighting in the playground.	Stop the fight and follow the school's procedures for unacceptable behaviour, thinking that it is typical of those students and they are on their way to a suspension.	Follow the school's procedures for unacceptable behaviour and divorce yourself of any further responsibility.	Stop the fight, follow the school's procedures for unacceptable behaviour and actively engage with both students individually and together to identify the cause of the fight and address those issues. Encourage students to reflect on their behaviour and accept responsibility for their part.
An Aboriginal or Torres Strait Islander parent or Elder complains about how elements of Indigenous history or cultural studies are being taught in your classroom.	Listen to the complaint and decide to refrain from teaching Indigenous studies again.	Listen to the complaint and respond that as the teacher you are responsible for what is taught and that parents/elders should not interfere.	Engage in an open conversation with the parent/elder to better understand their concerns. apologise for the distress. Consider options to address their concerns. for example, invite parent/elder to contribute to future lessons on Indigenous studies.
Students are heard using racist language when talking about a particular individual or group in the school (or in society).	Pretend not to hear the comments, as the situation is too complex, or it is harmless because it does not involve physical violence or casually tell the students to 'cut it out' without any follow-up.	Confront the students and implement school's procedures for unacceptable behaviour.	Intervene and explain that their language is inappropriate, implement school's procedures for unacceptable behaviour and organise a time to meet each student individually to discuss motivating factors and potential harm of their comments and attitudes.
A student refuses to participate in or complete a classroom. homework or assessment task that it is 'too hard'.	Accept the student's attitude, and make concessions for their inaction.	Demand that the student completes all set tasks and outline the consequences if student does not comply.	Discuss their concerns and explain the importance of the task, work with the student to understand what 'too hard' means to them and which parts of the task need additional scaffolding and if there are other forms of support that the student may require in order to complete the task.
Teacher shows a video in class.	Show a video loosely tied to the curriculum without an introduction to the purpose and context and without follow-up activities as a way of simply keeping the students quiet in the classroom.	Use the video to deliver the established curriculum inflexibly believing this will deliver on high expectations. with no consideration for student interests, capabilities or preferences.	Develop an understanding of students' interests and cultural backgrounds to deliver curriculum based on culturally responsive pedagogies

Lillian Miller and Carly Steele

evolved from an MCEETYA (Ministerial Council on Education, Employment, Training and Youth Affairs) recommendation to "ensure that schools, in partnership with parents/caregivers, deliver personalised learning to all Indigenous students that includes targets against key learning outcomes and incorporates family involvement strategies" (DEEWR, 2011, p. 8); all school systems and sectors in Australia agreed to this recommendation in 2008.

What Works (2011, p. 4) suggests key questions for developing PLPs:

1. Where is the student now?
2. Where should the student be?
3. How will they get to where they should be?
4. How will be know when they get there?

It is recommended that these questions be integrated into the teaching and learning cycle of assessment of student learning in order to establish goals for learning, and to plan for appropriate teaching and learning approaches (What Works, 2011, p.4). As with all we have described, how this will look in each school is dependent on the local context. School systems and sectors across Australia provide implementation advice and guidance for their schools. Beyond specific jurisdiction advice, there are two key general guides to assist schools in implementing a process for developing PLPs:

- DEEWR (2011). Guide to developing Personalised Learning Plans for Aboriginal and Torres Strait Islander students – A professional learning resource.
- What Works (2011). The Work Program: Core Issues 10. Using Personalised Learning Plans.

A story from practice: Developing PLPs

Carly developed PLPs for Aboriginal and Torres Strait Islander students at the schools where she worked and in doing so found some processes to be more effective than others she had tried.

At one school, the whole-school approach involved visually displaying goals. Within the classroom they built displays with a picture of each student; beside their picture the students had a bucket and in it they had a collection of juggling balls. Each ball had a different goal on it, and when they achieved this goal, it was placed in the air and it looked like the students were juggling the balls – that is, the goals they had achieved. Each student knew their goals and when they were working in class, Carly would put their relevant goal on their desk to remind them of what they were working towards. The students delighted in achieving their goals, their family members and the wider community enjoyed coming into the school and seeing the pictures of the students achieving their goals. This created a cycle of success, where success led to further success. Students were more willing to give it a go because they had experienced success in the past. In this approach, the paperwork for the teachers was not onerous, they simply discussed long-term goals with their students and their families. Then as teachers, they broke the long-term goals down into little achievable steps, which were the goals communicated and explained to the students. In the PLPs, teachers wrote key strategies for achieving student goals that were included in the teacher planning. Because, the PLPs were being communicated through the visual display and the strategies were in the teachers' planning, it wasn't a document that was completed, filed and forgotten; it was an active process that was at the forefront of what teachers and students did every day.

In contrast to this successful situation, at another school where Carly worked, the PLPs were an exhaustive document that took time to complete. Furthermore, it was not completed in the presence of the students or explained to them, rather it was sent home for the caregiver/s to sign and return to the school. The students were not aware of the goals being set and teachers were begrudgingly completing this paperwork as a school requirement. Clearly this was not an effective process.

Conclusion

Throughout this chapter we have endeavoured to highlight the importance of getting to know your students and their families, and the local community context in which you might be teaching. Without knowledge of your students, their families, and the community, you cannot implement culturally responsive teaching, Aboriginal and Torres Strait Islander pedagogies, hold high expectations nor develop useful PLPs. This knowledge should underpin everything that you do or don't do in the classroom. The title of this chapter – 'There is no one right way, but there are right things to do', speaks to this approach. How you teach should always be in response to the students in your classroom. Therefore, you need to get to know them first. Once you know your students, it is easy to do the right things in the right way for these students.

Reflective questions

1. What challenges might you anticipate (personal or otherwise) in getting to know your students, families, and communities? Suggest some ways you can overcome your identified challenges.
2. How can Aboriginal and Torres Strait Islander pedagogies be employed in responsive ways to avoid a reductionist view?
3. What does it mean to hold 'high expectations' for students and how can this sometimes come into conflict with 'empathy and understanding'? How do you think you can achieve a useful balancing act?

We will introduce ourselves to position ourselves within this chapter:

References

ACARA. (2019). Fire: a burning question. https://www.australiancurriculum.edu.au/resources/aboriginal-and-torres-strait-islander-histories-and-cultures/illustrations-of-practice/fire-a-burning-question/

Australian Parliament. House of Representatives. Standing Committee on Aboriginal and Torres Strait Islander Affairs & Neumann Shayne (2012). *Our land our languages: language learning in Indigenous communities*. Canberra: Parliament of the Commonwealth of Australia.

Berry, R., & Hudson, J. (1997). *Making the jump: A resource book for teachers of Aboriginal students*. Broome: Catholic Education Office, Kimberley Region.

Bissett, S. Z. (2012). Bala ga lili: Meeting Indigenous learners halfway. *Australian Journal of Environmental Education*, 28(2), 78–91.

Borden, L. L. (2013). What's the word for…? Is there a word for…? How understanding Mi'kmaw language can help support Mi'kmaw learners in mathematics. *Mathematics Education Research Journal*, 25(1), 5–22.

Byrne, M. & Munns, G. (2012). From the big picture to the individual student: The importance of the classroom relationship. In Q. Beresford, G. Partington, G. Gower (Eds.) *Reform and Resistance in Aboriginal Education* (revised edn). Crawley, WA: UWA Publishing, pp. 379–402).

Castagno, A., & Brayboy, B. M. (2008). Culturally responsive schooling for Indigenous youth: A review of the literature. *Review of Educational Research*, 78(4), 941–993. 10.3102/0034654308323036

Cazden, C., & Leggett, E. (1981). Culturally responsive education: Recommendations for achieving Lau remedies II. In H. Trueba, G. Guthrie, & K. Au (Eds.) *Culture and the bilingual classroom: Studies in classroom ethnography*. Rowley, MA: Newbury House, pp. 69–86.

CSIRO (2019). Inquiry for Indigenous Science Students (I2S2). https://www.csiro.au/en/Education/Programs/Indigenous-STEM/Programs/I2S2/About-I2S2

Department of Education, Employment and Workplace Relations (DEEWR) (2011). *Guide to developing Personalised Learning Plans for Aboriginal and Torres Strait Islander students – a professional learning resource*. Canberra: DEEWR.

Department of Education, Western Australia (2012). *Tracks to two-way learning*. Western Australia: WestOne Services.

Donald, A. & Rattansi, J. (1992). *Race, culture and difference*. New York: Sage Publications

Eades, D. (1984). Misunderstanding Aboriginal English: The role of socio-cultural context. In G. McKay and B. Sommer (Eds.) *Applications of linguistics to Australian Aboriginal contexts*. Melbourne: Applied Linguistics Association of Australia, pp. 24–33.

Erickson, F., & Mohatt, C. (1982). Cultural organization and participation structures in two classrooms of Indian students. In G. Spindler (Ed.) *Doing the ethnography of schooling*. New York: Holt, Rinehart & Winston, pp. 131–174.

Galloway, A. (2003). Questions: Help or hindrance? Teachers' use of questions with Indigenous children with conductive hearing loss. *Australian Journal of Teacher Education*, 27(2), 25–38.

García, O., & Wei, L. (2014). Translanguaging and education. In O. Garcia & L. Wei (Eds.) *Translanguaging: Language, bilingualism and education*. London: Palgrave Macmillan, pp. 63–77.

Gay, G. (2000). *Culturally responsive teaching: Theory, research, and practice*. New York: Teachers College Press.

Gay, G. (2002). Preparing for culturally responsive teaching. *Journal of Teacher Education*, 53(2), 106–116.

Gower, G., & Byrne, M. (2012) Becoming a culturally competent teacher: Beginning the journey. In Q. Beresford, G. Partington, & G. Gower (Eds.) *Reform and resistance in Aboriginal education* (revised edn). Crawley, WA: UWA Publishing, pp. 379–402.

Harkins, J. (1990). Shame and shyness in the Aboriginal classroom: A case for "practical semantics". *Australian Journal of Linguistics*, 10(2), 293–306.

Harrison, N. (2011). *Teaching and learning in Aboriginal education* (2nd edn). South Melbourne: Oxford University Press.

Harslett, M., Harrison, B., Godfrey, J., Partington, G., & Richer, K. (1999). Cultural authorisation of research in Aboriginal education: A case study. *Issues in Educational Research*, 9(1), 15–22. http://www.iier.org.au/iier9/harslett.html

Hudsmith, S. (1992). Culturally responsive pedagogy in urban classrooms. *Australian Journal of Indigenous Education*, 20(3), 3–12.

Ionn, M. A. (1995). Aborigines and Torres Strait Islanders and equitable educational outcomes: A focus on how school and society maintain misconceptions. *Australian Journal of Indigenous Education*, 23(4), 37–44.

Ladson-Billings, G. (1995). Toward a theory of culturally relevant pedagogy. *American Educational Research Journal*, 32(3), 465–491.

Malcolm, I. G., & Grote, E. (2007). Aboriginal English: Restructured variety for cultural maintenance. In G. Leitner & I. G. Malcolm (Eds.) *The habitat of Australia's Aboriginal languages: Past, present and future* (vol. 179). Berlin: Walter de Gruyter, pp. 153–180.

McConaghy, C. (2000). *Rethinking Indigenous education: Culturalism, colonialism and the politics of knowing*. Flaxton, Australia: Post Pressed.

Milgate, G. & Giles-Browne, B. (2013). Creating an effective school for Aboriginal and Torres Strait Islander students (Paper). http://research.acer.edu.au/indigenous_education/32

Mills, K., Sunderland, N., & Davis, J. (2013). Yarning circles in the literacy classroom. *The Reading Teacher*, 67(4), pp. 285–289.

NSW Department of Education. (2020). 8 Ways. https://www.8ways.online

Owens, K. (2015). Changing the teaching of mathematics for improved Indigenous education in a rural Australian city. *Journal of Mathematics Teacher Education*, 18(1), 53–78.

Partington, G., Richer, K., Godfrey, J., Harslett, M., & Harrison, B. (1999). *Barriers to effective teaching of Indigenous students*. Paper presented at the *Combined Conference of the Australian Association for Research in Education and New Zealand Association for Research in Education*, Melbourne.

Sarra, C. (2011). *Strong and smart – towards a pedagogy for emancipation*. London: Routledge.

Sarra, C., Spillman, D., Jackson, C., Davis, J., & Bray, J. (2018). High-expectations relationships: A foundation for enacting high expectations in all Australian schools. *Australian Journal of Indigenous Education*, 49(1), 32–45. doi:10.1017/jie.2018.10

Sullivan, P., Jorgensen, R., Boaler, J., & Lerman, S. (2013). Transposing reform pedagogy into new contexts: Complex instruction in remote Australia. *Mathematics Education Research Journal*, 25(1), 173–184.

Stobart, G. (2005) Fairness in multicultural assessment systems. *Assessment in Education*, 2 (3), 275–287.

What Works. Commonwealth of Australia (2011). *The work program: Core Issues 10. Using personalised learning plans*. Victoria: National Curriculum Services.

What Works. Commonwealth of Australia (2013). *The work program. Sustainable school and community partnerships – a research study* (1st edn). Victoria: National Curriculum Services.

Yunkaporta, T. (2009). Aboriginal pedagogies at the cultural interface (Doctoral dissertation, James Cook University).

Chapter 10

Critical selection of curriculum materials

Tools for educators

Beth Madsen, Ren Perkins and Marnee Shay

Who we are

Beth Madsen

I am a Murri woman from South East Queensland, who grew up in Meanjin (Brisbane) on Yuggera country. My first teaching experience was in Goondiwindi, on Bigambul country. I will be forever grateful to the students that I worked with during this phase of my career, who truly taught me more than I taught them. While teaching across a variety of schools, both rural and urban, I have been asked by many teachers to help them embed Aboriginal and Torres Strait Islander perspectives into their teaching. They often profess their best intentions, while simultaneously explaining their fears and hesitations about saying the wrong thing, offending people, and being unsure where to start looking for resources to use. These interactions with colleagues have fostered in me a deep passion for equipping teachers with the skills needed to appropriately embed Aboriginal and Torres Strait Islander knowledges across all curriculum areas. I acknowledge that this can be confronting and difficult for some teachers, especially for those who weren't taught any Indigenous perspectives in their own schooling. However, I hope that this chapter can inspire teachers to be brave and take the first step in embedding. Aboriginal and Torres Strait Islander history is Australian history, and vice-versa. By acknowledging our shared history, we can work towards true reconciliation as a nation.

Ren Perkins

I am a Quandamooka man with connections to Minjerribah or North Stradbroke Island. I also have connections with the Aboriginal community of Cherbourg, Queensland. Growing up Indigenous in an urban setting like Brisbane provided many challenges, barriers, and emotions for me, particularly regarding my Aboriginal identity. Growing up as an Indigenous young person in the 1970s and 1980s was difficult. In my experience, Australian society then was, by and large, white, Anglo-Saxon, and racist. There was little Indigenous culture present in any curriculum across Australia. This helped perpetuate the myth that Aboriginal people were 'dying out', that Australia was 'colonised' by the English, and that the unfolding 'white' history of Australia was to be celebrated and enshrined in our national identity. I had the privilege of teaching Aboriginal Studies at TAFE for many years in NSW. What I was witnessing was how little knowledge Australians had regarding Australia's First Nations peoples. I had the opportunity to move back to Brisbane to undertake my Master's Degree at the Australian Catholic University and part of this opportunity included a teaching load. This experience gave me an insight into the contribution I could make to our future educators. I have had diverse experience in embedding in the curriculum, including in a Deputy Principal position at a flexi school in Alice Springs that included classroom teaching. I was working directly with the Australian Curriculum and I could see the gaps that were evident in embedding Indigenous perspectives across the curriculum. The focus of this chapter, identifying appropriate resources for teachers to embed Indigenous perspectives into their teaching, has been a skill I have developed over a long period of time. I look forward to continuing to contribute in positive ways to the field of education in Australia, by helping to prepare the next generation of Australians for an ever-changing modern society.

Marnee Shay

I identify as a Murri educator and researcher. Although my family connections (through my mother) are to Wagiman country in the Northern Territory, I have spent most of my life living and working in South East Queensland, where I have many community connections and therefore use the term Murri when identifying myself. I took my first post as a high school teacher at a flexi school on the Sunshine Coast, or Gubbi Gubbi/Kabi Kabi country. Nothing could have prepared me for how rewarding, challenging, and exciting teaching could be. I was also a teacher in communities south and west of Brisbane, where I worked in schools with high numbers of Murri students. By virtue of my culture and who I am, I brought many aspects of Indigenous knowledges and perspectives into my teaching. But embedding Indigenous knowledges and perspectives across all curriculum areas and whole of school practices was a specific skill that I felt my teacher training didn't quite prepare me for. I had an undergraduate degree in Indigenous Studies so I was eager to use this knowledge as well in developing curriculum, but I was challenged by what at the time seemed like limited resources to draw from. Fortunately, there is now a growing body of quality resources, Indigenous-authored stories and films and more willingness for schools to work collaboratively with communities. I hope this chapter will help in supporting teachers to embed Indigenous knowledges and perspectives and enrich learning about this great country and its 65,000 years of history for all Australian children and young people.

Introduction

As a group of Indigenous educators, we have observed the positive impact embedding Indigenous knowledges and perspectives in classrooms and schools can have for all Australian students. We have had varying experiences across different education sectors in how well supported we have been as Indigenous educators in our endeavours to embed this knowledge. Similarly, we have also had varying experiences of observing and supporting our non-Indigenous colleagues in doing so. In this chapter, we will share our collective experiences of our practices as classroom teachers. We will focus specifically on the skills needed to locate

Indigenous curriculum resources and materials as this is a core skill that teachers need in order to ensure they are not re-producing colonial and racialised ideas that should have no place in contemporary Australia. We also provide a tool for teachers that is a practical framework for selecting resources to ensure the materials are authentic, appropriate, and fit for purpose.

Chapter overview

In this chapter, we endeavour to give future teachers the historical and cultural context in relation to Australian histories to consider the implications for how these have been represented through social, political, and cultural discourses. A discussion about the power of language, cultural protocols, and the influence of the media will deepen teachers' understanding of Indigenous knowledges and perspectives. We provide a framework for teachers in selecting curriculum materials that represent Indigenous knowledges and perspectives, which we have called the YARNS tool. Our hope is that by the end of this chapter, teachers will be better equipped to embed Indigenous knowledges and perspectives within their own classrooms, using quality resources and materials to accurately represent diverse Indigenous peoples, knowledges, cultures and perspectives

Creating a balanced representation of our shared histories

Aboriginal and Torres Strait Islander cultures are the longest continuing cultures in the world. There is scientific evidence of Indigenous people's occupation in Australia for over 65,000 years (Clarkson et al., 2017). For a culture to continue for that amount of time, there is a huge wealth of knowledge, spanning all aspects of histories, pre and post colonisation. In this chapter we discuss the importance of embedding Indigenous knowledges in the curriculum, but to do so we must first look to history to understand why this can be a complex task. It goes without saying that Australian history was by and large written by non-Indigenous peoples. As Sarra and Shay (2019, p. 1) outline, "[T]he history of the First Australians has often been represented through the lenses of non-indigenous perspectives with little to no historical perspective recounting the lived realities of Aboriginal and Torres Strait Islander people".

The silencing of Indigenous knowledges began with James Cook's arrival on Eora country (now known as Botany Bay). Under 18th-century International Law, Britain could not 'settle' a country if it was inhabited (NSW Department of Education, 2015). If a country was inhabited, Britain could either purchase the land off the First Nations peoples or invade and conquer. Rather than admitting to stealing land that belonged to the Eora nation and the many hundreds of Aboriginal Nations that existed, the British colonisers chose to declare the land *Terra Nullius*, a legal fiction that means 'empty land', which was later overturned by the high court of Australia in 1992 (Reynolds, 1996). Therefore, the First Nations peoples of Australia were essentially classified as non-human, and grouped into a homogeneous culture that was classified as inferior to the European colonisers (Reynolds, 1999). It was much easier to portray a narrative of Indigenous peoples as 'primitive natives' who were desperate for a superior race to provide enlightenment, than to acknowledge the British invasion.

Most Australians have heard of the concept of *Terra Nullius*, but many do not understand the ongoing implications that it has on social, political, and cultural constructs of Indigenous and non-Indigenous people. The denial of Indigenous humanity and the false idea of European superiority has been deeply ingrained in policy formation and national politics, ideology, and values. Through the protection-ist era, Indigenous people were separated from their country and forced into missions, allowing the British government complete control over Indigenous peoples' lives (McConnochie, 1982). On these missions, Indigenous people were not allowed to speak their languages, practise spiritual beliefs or follow their culture in any way. During the assimilation era, Indigenous children were removed from their families (commonly referred to as the Stolen Generations), with the intent to force them to forget their Indigeneity and assimilate into Anglo-Australia culture, thus obliterat-ing Indigenous culture altogether (Australian Human Rights Commission, 1997).

These histories are what is often referred to as 'hidden histories', as they have not been included, or only superficially touched upon in the mostly Eurocentric curriculum – one that has ensured Australian history has only been recounted and learned about through the coloniser's lens (Hart, Whatman, Mclaughlin, & Sharma-Brymer, 2012). Phillips (2012, p. 10) explains that while all Australian his-tory is our shared history, it is often "understood as separate". Phillips unpacks why this is problematic; on the one hand, when an Indigenous person recounts experiences this becomes known as 'black history', while at the same time a non-Indigenous experience becomes the "collective Australian story" (p. 10).

In 1967 a Referendum was held to allow Indigenous peoples the right to vote and be counted in the census. Over 90% of the Australian public voted to allow Indigenous peoples the same constitutional rights as every other Australian (Thomas, 2017) showing the beginning of a change in the perceptions of the pub-lic towards Indigenous peoples. Since that time, there have been repeated calls for constitutional recognition, treaties, as well as an increased understanding of the importance of recognition of Australia's Traditional Owners through signifi-cant policy changes, such as Indigenous histories and knowledges becoming a cross-curriculum priority in the national curriculum. Understanding the way that Australian histories have been positioned within the curriculum, policy, and also socially and ideologically, is critical to our understandings of how we view differ-ent materials and sources of information.

Judging a book by its cover – the power of language and imagery

Despite a clear legal precedent overturning the doctrine of *Terra Nullius* (see *Mabo vs Queensland*), many Australians do not accept the use of the word 'invasion' and instead use the terms 'colonisation' or 'settlement'. Amongst many Australians, there is a persistent level of ignorance and desire to look away from our his-tory of dispossession, violence, and abuse, and pretend that Australian history is free from bloodshed. Quite some time ago this phenomenon was described as the 'Great Australian Silence' (Stanner, 1969). We suggest that repeated denial of historical wrongs, along with the denial of 65,000 years of Indigenous knowledge, prevents Australians from moving forward towards a shared future. We need to recognise that Aboriginal and Torres Strait Islander history *is* Australian history and that it is only through acknowledging our shared history and being critical of the language describing this that we can develop a shared sense of what our full and embodied histories mean in this country.

We say this because language and power are interconnected (Mayr, 2008). More than one term may be used to describe events in any historical narrative. For instance, conscious use of terms such as 'settlement', 'occupation', 'colonisation' and 'invasion' will depend on the different worldviews and perspectives of the language users. The power of language to recognise, validate, or dismiss Australian histories is interconnected and will impact upon how we re-present particular ideas in our classrooms and in our work with children, young people, and their families. Language is particularly important as a means to educate us about the world we live in. For the First Peoples of Australia, this is vitally important. Language is not static, and our use of that language changes as well (Birner, 2020). It is, therefore, important that when selecting curriculum materials and resources that teachers understand the significance of language and its use for representing Indigenous peoples, non-Indigenous peoples, and Australian histories and cultures more broadly.

An example of how language use can shift over time is how the term 'Indigenous' has been used. The term 'Indigenous Australians' is an imposed term introduced by the Australian Government. It can be used to encompass both Aboriginal people and Torres Strait Islander people, though preferably not for one or the other when it is known which group is being spoken about. There are many language guides available, for example, Oxfam (2015) developed a language guide in consultation with many Aboriginal and Torres Strait Islander people. Although language guides are not definitive, the Oxfam guide explains simply how the terms Indigenous and Aboriginal and Torres Strait Islander have been used and their use now in contemporary Australia. They explain why using both terms need capitalising in writing and why the term Aboriginal and Torres Strait Islander should not be abbreviated.

It is also important for teachers to understand that although one person may prefer the term Indigenous, another may not like it. As Indigenous people are not a homogeneous group, it is to be expected that people have different preferences with relation to language and how it is used.

The actual definition of the word 'indigenous' is 'occurring naturally in a particular place' (Oxford Dictionary, 2020). The term is used to describe First Nations peoples worldwide, such as in the United Nations Declaration on the Rights of Indigenous Peoples. When used in an Australian context, it homogenises Aboriginal and Torres Strait Islander cultures into one group, denying the rich and varied knowledges and traditions. For this reason, some Aboriginal and Torres Strait Islander peoples reject the use of the term. However, 'Indigenous' can still be appropriately used, so long as the audience understand the meaning of the word, and are aware of the diversity of Aboriginal and Torres Strait Islander. For example, within this book, the term is used interchangeably with the phrases 'First Nations peoples' and 'Aboriginal and Torres Strait Islander peoples', as the authors are working off the assumption that you, the reader, have an understanding of the diversity of Aboriginal and Torres Strait Islander cultures. In a classroom context, the use of the term 'Indigenous', can be appropriate, so long as it is foregrounded by an explanation of the diversity of Aboriginal and Torres Strait Islander cultures.

For these reasons, when selecting teaching resources, it is crucial to be discerning about the language they contain, and also as the teacher to be conscious to contextualise it. For example, teachers may wish to use historical records or policy documents within their teaching. Many of these documents use what would be considered today inappropriate and offensive terminology when talking about Aboriginal and Torres Strait Islander peoples, terms such as 'half-caste' and 'Aborigines'. The Aborigines Act 1905 goes so far as to give definitions of the terms. In the era, 'half-caste', 'quadroon' and 'Aborigines' were terminologies that were commonly used to describe our people. In today's context they are extremely offensive and derogatory terms. That's not to say that the Aborigines Act 1905 would not be an appropriate resource to use within a classroom setting, as it may be an excellent resource to demonstrate the historical conditions experienced by Indigenous Australians and for students to understand how Indigenous peoples were treated. However, it's crucial that it is given appropriate framing before being introduced and that there is a suitable introduction around the content to support students to understand why these terms are now so offensive. That is, students need to be walked through contemporary and appropriate terminology as well as the historical and political contexts of the resource.

Teachers must also be aware of the dynamic within their classrooms, as well as the maturity levels of their students, when presenting resources that may have inappropriate terminology. For example, whilst it may be appropriate to embed such content (as described above) within a year 12 Legal Studies unit, embedding this within a year 8 history lesson, such as about the Stolen Generations, would need to be done with caution, as students may be unable to understand the complexity of changing terminology throughout history and it could lead to introducing inappropriate terminology to young students who do not understand the racist undertones. There is clearly much to be considered to ensure maximum educational outcomes for all students, as illustrated in the example below.

A story from practice: From the outback to the city

Ren: Whilst working at Alice Springs, I had the opportunity to take some local Aboriginal students to a Sydney private school as a shared experience. The visit was to a large academic focused school, with high expectations, and at that time, there were no Indigenous students enrolled. The week was spent with our students sitting in on different subjects throughout the school. One of the subjects was science. Our students thoroughly enjoyed the experience, but I remember having a conversation with the teacher after the lesson. They asked me how they could embed Indigenous perspectives into that subject. They were wary of showing disrespect or getting things wrong and were seeking some advice. I pointed her to ACARA's illustrations of practice and their science elaborations to provide ideas and support for embedding Indigenous perspectives.

Creating dialogue and trust are important in supporting teachers in embedding Indigenous perspectives across the curriculum. This experience demonstrated to me that there is still much work to do with all Australian teachers, to support their practice, to ensure that all students had the opportunity to engage with the world's oldest living culture, knowledge, and history.

Understanding cultural protocols

Aboriginal and Torres Strait Islander peoples place considerable importance on respect and observing cultural protocols. Using the correct language and observing protocols in the right place and context demonstrates respect to the local Aboriginal and Torres Strait Islander communities. Some words and phrases, both written and spoken, may offend Indigenous Australians. For example, advice should be sought before using regional terms such as Koori (New South Wales), Nunga (South Australia), Yolngu (Northern Territory), Noongar (Western Australian) and Murri (Queensland) and on the use of the word 'black' in various contexts. It is, therefore, important that teachers also demonstrate this respect in embedding Indigenous knowledges and perspectives in their classrooms.

As outlined earlier, authoritative reference resources, for example, federal and state government style guides, are clear on the use of capitalisation of Indigenous terms, for example, whether to use elder or Elder, to avoid the incorrect use of important terms. Curriculum writers generally try to abide by these guidelines and use the correct language when writing learning materials. Furthermore, government style guides are updated regularly to ensure language changes are kept up to date so they can they can evolve and reflect contemporary Indigenous language contexts (Note: Some of these are listed at the bottom of this section).

Teachers often make use of third-party resources, including works authored by Indigenous Australian people, for teaching purposes. It is important that teachers are aware of the guidelines (as indicated above) when they copy or re-write and that the language they use, and its meaning, is not removed or changed in inappropriate ways. A simple example of this could be the use of capital letters which are used to show respect and/or acknowledgement, for example, the use of the word 'Elders'. It is also important to acknowledge the contribution of the Aboriginal and Torres Strait Islander writer. When older works are used, it will be obvious that the language may not be contemporary and unacceptable at the time. There are appropriate resources to assist teachers in the protocols around the use of language in Aboriginal and Torres Strait Islander resources. Some of these include:

- AIATSIS - Guidelines for the ethical publishing of Aboriginal and Torres Strait Islander authors and research from those communities (https://aiatsis. gov.au/sites/default/files/2020-09/ethical-publishing-guidelines.pdf);
- Respect Relationships Reconciliation (https://rrr.edu.au/);
- ABC–IndigenousContent(https://edpols.abc.net.au/guidance/abc-indigenous-content/);
- Reconciliation Australia – Share Our Pride (http://www.shareourpride.org.au/).

Fake news? Understanding the role of the media

Through appropriate embedding of Indigenous perspectives, Australian teachers can challenge the negative representations and stereotypes of Indigenous peoples that are so prevalent in the media today. In this way all Australian children can learn to "understand and acknowledge the value of Indigenous cultures and possess the knowledge, skills and understanding to contribute to, and benefit from, reconciliation between Indigenous and non-Indigenous Australians" (Education Council, 2019, p. 8). However, to do so, it is crucial to understand the role media plays in shaping our perspectives.

Whilst the Australian media plays a role in providing information about the society in which we live, it is important to understand that it also actively constructs that picture of our society and does so by choosing what it reflects and the relationships it creates and in this way it is influential in shaping public opinion. Think about the last time you saw a story about Indigenous Australia on the news. Was there some kind of controversy involved? Were the Indigenous peoples portrayed in a positive or negative light? Was there a non-Indigenous person commenting on Indigenous affairs? Was the report unbiased, or did it intentionally try to sway people's perceptions?

Often, when Indigenous Australians are presented in the media, they are portrayed as a 'problem' or an 'issue' and it is not uncommon for the majority of mainstream media representations of Indigenous peoples to be mediated, if not reported, by non-Indigenous people. There is also often some sort of controversy (for example, changing the date of Australia Day) within such reports. So, while the media plays a primary role in informing people about the issues concerning Indigenous Australians, it also plays a central role in the way this information is constructed – even controlling the discourse about what and who is seen to be Indigenous (and for that matter, non-Indigenous as well). There has been a long history of racist, distorted, and even offensive representation of Aboriginal people in Australia (Langton, 1993), and the Australian media continues to pander to racist stereotypes (Bullimore, 1999).

One way teachers can counter this is to utilise Indigenous media outlets. Fortunately, there is now an increasing Indigenous media presence available for teachers to draw from. These provide students with media that encapsulate the voices and lived experiences of Indigenous peoples, providing Indigenous voices and perspectives on current issues that students may otherwise not be exposed to. Some examples of Indigenous media that teachers can use to build curricular resources include:

- NITV – National Indigenous Television. This is a channel dedicated to Indigenous news, documentaries, sport, arts, movies, series;
- Indigenous ABC – ABC hosts a range of Indigenous dramas, documentaries, news, and current affairs;
- Koori Mail – iconic fortnightly newspaper (also available online), 100% Aboriginal owned and operated;
- First Nations Telegraph – free online national First Nations e-newspaper, 100% Aboriginal owned and operated;
- 'Speaking Out' – politics, arts and cultures from a range of Indigenous perspectives on ABC local radio (also available on podcast) by Prof Larissa Behrendt;
- @IndigenousX – rotating Twitter account launched to provide platforms for diverse Indigenous voices including actors, activists, authors, academics, teachers, doctors, university students.

A story from practice: Media influence

Beth: I was teaching a year 9 unit about cultural influences on sport participation. Throughout the term the class had been extremely culturally aware and very appropriate when discussing cultures that were different from their own. Late in the term, I had a student put her hand up to say: "my Mum said that all Aboriginals get free health-care, and that her tax money shouldn't be spent so they can get stuff for free." This student did not mean offence and was just repeating what she had been told at home. I asked the class where people might find out this kind of information, and a few quickly mentioned various forms of media: the TV, radio, and social media. As a class, we discussed how everyone in Australia can access free healthcare, and how the media sometimes tells 'untruths'.

I was able to appropriately and calmly respond to this student, because I am knowledgeable on this topic. But it made me wonder how a colleague might respond, who is not Aboriginal themselves? How would they have the knowledge to skilfully unpack these racist ideologies that often present in classrooms? This highlighted to me the importance of teachers being aware of media manipulations, and where they can access media that comes from Indigenous authors.

When teaching any subject, it is important to be aware of the influence of the media in perpetrating and maintaining stereotypes about Aboriginal and Torres Strait Islander peoples and its role in promoting racism. One example of this was when a popular commercial morning television program featured a panel with no Aboriginal or Torres Strait Islander participants, to discuss a very sensitive and complex issue surrounding Aboriginal and Torres Strait Islander children. These non-Indigenous panel members gave their opinions about this topic, by making strong negative generalisations about Aboriginal and Torres Strait Islander peoples as a group.

As educators, we have a responsibility to be aware of the negative influence the media can have on our society and remain vigilant about how to counter this powerful force. Teachers should encourage their students to critically discern what they hear and see in the media, in all its forms. By providing appropriate, factual, and relevant resources within your classroom, you are enabling young people to be in a better position to deal with the negative attitudes that are espoused by sections of the media.

Indigenous knowledges and perspectives

As educators we are in the privileged, but also powerful position of working with large numbers of young people. However, with great power comes great responsibility. In this case, teachers can be responsible for changing the narrative around Indigenous Australians (as well as the taken-for-granted assumptions produced about non-Indigenous people), by having a firm understanding of the truths detailed above. The information above regarding history, media, language, and cultural protocols is only the tip of the iceberg, and our hope is that educators would use this chapter as a diving board to continue their own education. These topics are both relevant background information, and Indigenous knowledges and perspectives that can be embedded into classrooms. In addition to this, there is 65,000 years' worth of knowledges and perspectives that can be incorporated into every Australian classroom.

What do we mean by the terms 'Indigenous knowledges' and 'Indigenous perspectives'? It is important to understand that the terms 'Indigenous knowledges' and 'Indigenous perspectives' are often used interchangeably. The Department of Education and Training defines Indigenous perspectives thus:

> Perspectives are ways of seeing the world. Perspectives affect the way we interact with the environment and the perceptions we have about ourselves, our culture and the way we see others.
>
> (2011, p. 21)

Indigenous knowledges are defined by Walter (2011) as

> Aboriginal and Torres Strait Islander scholarship, pedagogy, the cultural and specific knowledges of the many Aboriginal and Torres Strait Islander nations as well as the shared epistemological tenets such as relationality that define and delineate Indigenous knowledges from the Western frame predominant within the sector.
>
> (p. 1)

So, whilst differences are described in these and many other definitions, the key point to remember is that these terms are interconnected and shouldn't be viewed as separate entities: you can't understand Indigenous knowledges without Indigenous perspectives, and you can't understand Indigenous perspectives without Indigenous knowledges.

Quality embedding of Indigenous knowledges and perspectives benefits all students. The Australian Curriculum acknowledges this importance, highlighting two major benefits, including:

- that Aboriginal and Torres Strait Islander students are able to see themselves, their identities and their cultures reflected in the curriculum of each of the learning areas, can fully participate in the curriculum and can build their self-esteem;
- that the Aboriginal and Torres Strait Islander Histories and Cultures cross-curriculum priority is designed for all students to engage in reconciliation, respect and recognition of the world's oldest continuous living cultures.

(Australian Curriculum, Assessment and Reporting Authority, 2020)

It is crucial that Indigenous knowledges and perspectives be included in our understanding of culture and Australian history, recognising the enormous contribution that Indigenous culture can make to all Australian students' understanding of their country.

Identifying quality curriculum materials for embedding

The ability to select quality teaching resources is a key skill that all educators across all subjects and topics need to develop. Via the internet, teachers have an unlimited access to resources and materials. However, the importance of being discerning about which resources to use for different learning activities is even more critical. Educators need to ensure that resources that they select are appropriate, meaningful, and that they represent the stories, knowledges, lived experiences, and perspectives of Aboriginal and Torres Strait Islander people rather than simply re-presenting historical misunderstandings and ideas that are underpinned by racialised ideas.

These curriculum resources provide teachers with cross-curriculum priorities in order to assist with embedding Aboriginal and Torres Strait Islander perspectives

Beth Madsen, Ren Perkins and Marnee Shay

across all subjects. The Australian Curriculum provides specific examples of resources that can be used to embed Indigenous knowledges and perspectives. While these resources are an excellent starting point for educators, ideally, teachers should be aiming to embed more localised knowledge and perspectives within their teaching.

It is important to note that Aboriginal and Torres Strait Islander knowledges and perspectives should be present throughout all teaching units. Often, educators fall into the trap of planning whole units surrounding Aboriginal and Torres Strait Islander perspectives, and while this is certainly important, Aboriginal and Torres Strait Islander knowledges should be embedded throughout other units. For example, within an English unit on Romeo and Juliet, students might compare and contrast the play with the story of Warri and Yatungka. This could be one activity amongst many in a lesson but gives students an insight into Aboriginal culture in Western Australia while focusing on curriculum-mandated materials.

A story from practice: Fear and avoidance

Beth: Across my various teaching positions, I have often been approached by colleagues to assist them with embedding Aboriginal and Torres Strait Islander perspectives. To their credit, many are already doing a fantastic job with the attempts that they are making. However, they are often wracked with concerns, telling me that they don't know if they're saying the right thing, or if they are being offensive, or exclaiming how hard they are finding this requirement of the profession. I once had a colleague ask me: "But I'm not Aboriginal so why should I teach about that culture?" To which I asked: "Can a non-Italian Home Economics teacher present a lesson about how to make pasta?" One teacher asked if it is 'appropriate' for her to be teaching a culture that is not her own. A term later, I saw this same teacher deliver a year 8 history unit about Polynesian expansion – a culture that is not her own.

In my experience there seems to be a deep fear amongst non-Indigenous teachers of saying the wrong thing and causing offence, and this fear has led to an accepted avoidance of embedding. Yet by not incorporating Indigenous perspectives, teachers are sending the message that Aboriginal and Torres Strait Islander perspectives are unimportant compared to Western knowledges. While avoidance is unacceptable, this 'fear' shows that teachers are, generally, aware that there are huge gaps in their own knowledge. Within my six years of classroom teaching, I have taught many times outside of my trained subject areas, and I know this is an experience shared by many teachers. When I was first assigned to Science, Business, History, and Geography classes, I was terrified – how could I, as a PE teacher, possible learn the technicalities of these subjects? But I researched and upskilled myself in order to teach my students to the best of my ability. Embedding Aboriginal and Torres Strait Islander Perspectives needs to be viewed in the same light. By starting small (such as using the YARNS selection tool outlined below to demystify the process), all teachers should be able to select appropriate resources to use within their teaching.

YARNS First Nations resource evaluation tool

Often, teachers from English and Humanities subject areas find embedding much easier, but with a little bit of innovative and lateral thinking, Indigenous knowledges and perspectives can be embedded across all subject areas in meaningful and appropriate ways. While the most obvious way to embed knowledges is to use resources to explicitly teach, there are also other ways that Indigenous knowledges can be embedded in teaching.

First, however, there are a few quality checks to ensure that what is selected and taught is appropriate. The YARNS tool is one way that teachers can make sure that the source they have found is appropriate. While many guides previously existed, the YARNS tool is an amalgamation of our own experiences as Aboriginal teachers, along with ideas from other frameworks including:

- *Selecting and Evaluating Resources Guide* (2007) by the Queensland Studies Authority;
- *Embedding Aboriginal and Torres Strait Islander Perspectives (EATSIPs)* (2010) by the Queensland Government;
- *The Aboriginal Education K-12 Resource Guide* (2003) by NSW Department of Education and Training.

This tool can be applied when embedding an Aboriginal and/or Torres Strait Islander resource into lesson planning and be used to analyse resources before their introduction into lessons (see Table 10.1).

As an example, the CSIRO Indigenous seasonal calendar (CSIRO, 2019) has been analysed using this tool. This resource shows traditional seasonal knowledge from seven Indigenous language groups and can be used across a variety of subjects. It must be remembered, however, these calendars demonstrate a

▼ Table 10.1

YARNS First Nations resource evaluation tool

YEAR	When was the resource written/made?
	Is it up to date?
	Does the year reflect contemporary Indigenous Australia?
	What contextual information would you need for students to understand the resource?
AUTHOR	Does the author identify themselves as Aboriginal and/or Torres Strait Islander?
	Were Aboriginal and/or Torres Strait Islander peoples consulted in the making of the resource and were they recognised for their contribution?
	Does the author identify the traditional owners of the country on which the resource was produced?
	Does the author (if non-Indigenous) clearly name their cultural standpoint and position they are writing from?
REPRESENTATIONS	Are Aboriginal and/or Torres Strait Islander people presented in a balanced way, showing both historical and contemporary cultural practices?
	Does the resource use racist terms (uncivilised, primitive) for Aboriginal and/or Torres Strait Islander peoples?
	Are there diverse representations of Aboriginal and/or Torres Strait Islander peoples through images?
NOUNS	Are accepted descriptions/names for Aboriginal and/or Torres Strait Islander peoples used in the resource?
	Are capitals used correctly in the resource?
	Is the language used contemporary and does it reflect contemporary language guides?
SENSITIVITY	Does the source name all Aboriginal and/or Torres Strait Islander peoples pictured or group them into a homogeneous group?
	Is there cultural information that may not be appropriate to re-present (for example men's business or women's business)?
	Does the resource have images of Aboriginal and or Torres Strait Islander peoples who have deceased and is there a warning about this?

Beth Madsen, Ren Perkins and Marnee Shay

YEAR	When was the resource written/made? Is it up to date? Does the year reflect contemporary Indigenous Australia? What contextual information would you need for students to understand the resource?	The resource was produced in 2019, making it quite recent. Students would need to understand the location of each language group for context and if not teaching in these contexts explain that there are knowledges like this in their areas.
AUTHOR	Does the author identify themselves as Aboriginal and/or Torres Strait Islander? Were Aboriginal and/or Torres Strait Islander peoples consulted in the making of the resource and were they recognised for their contribution? Does the author identify the traditional owners of the country on which the resource was produced? Does the author (if non-Indigenous) clearly name their cultural standpoint and position they are writing from?	The resource is produced by the CSIRO, a non-Indigenous group. However, it does state that Traditional Owners were consulted in the creation of the resource. This is clearly stated on the website. Overall, the authors go to great lengths to acknowledge the Traditional Owners of the information.
REPRES-ENTATIONS	Are Aboriginal and/or Torres Strait Islander people presented in a balanced way, showing both historical and contemporary cultural practices? Does the resource use racist terms (uncivilised, primitive) for Aboriginal and/or Torres Strait Islander peoples? Are there diverse representations of Aboriginal and/or Torres Strait Islander peoples through images?	The resource uses present-day language, explaining that Aboriginal people 'hold' knowledge, rather than held. This shows the user of the resource that Aboriginal people are still holders of much knowledge. No ethnocentric terms are used.
NOUNS	Are accepted descriptions/names for Aboriginal and/or Torres Strait Islander peoples used in the resource? Are capitals used correctly in the resource? Is the language used contemporary and does it reflect contemporary language guides?	The resource shows the diverse knowledge of country across language groups. No derogatory names are used.
SENSITIVITY	Does the source name all Aboriginal and/or Torres Strait Islander peoples pictured or group them into a homogenous group? Is there cultural information that may not be appropriate to re-present (for example men's business or women's business) Does the resource have images of Aboriginal and or Torres Strait Islander peoples who have deceased and is there a warning about this?	No Aboriginal or Torres Strait Islander peoples are pictured. All cultural knowledge shared is done so with permission from Traditional Owners.

small fraction of traditional knowledge around weather systems, land management, animal migration, and food availability. The YARNS tool is unique, in that teachers may also use it as a way of framing resources. In the example below of using YARNS to analyse the CSIRO calendar, when considering the author, many frameworks would not allow this resource as it is not authored by an Aboriginal and/or Torres Strait Islander person. The YARNS tool allows the teacher to see that the Traditional Owners have been consulted and properly recognised. When presenting the resource to the class, this understanding would allow the teacher to discuss the importance of Indigenous knowledges and knowledge holders (Table 10.2).

From this analysis, we can see that this resource is very appropriate for use in classrooms. Teachers may choose not to write out their analysis using the framework in this way, but it is a way to employ a critical framework for the selection of resources and materials.

Conclusion

Ideally, in the future, Indigenous knowledges and perspectives will be an integral part of the Australian Curriculum, rather than just an add-on as happens in many classrooms in present-day Australia. It is crucial that educators have a firm understanding of Australian history from diverse Indigenous perspectives, as well as the many Indigenous knowledges. Furthermore, an understanding of language, cultural protocols, and the influence of the media and how these are implicated in the ways in which Indigenous knowledges and perspectives are portrayed, is critical in providing all Australian students with quality information. These understandings, when paired with the YARNS tool, will hopefully lead to increased confidence for educations to embed Indigenous perspectives across their teachings.

Reflective questions

1. We discussed concerns raised to us by teachers who struggle to embed Aboriginal and Torres Strait Islander knowledges and perspectives. Do you have any concerns about your ability to do this as a future teacher? Who could you go to for help with embedding?
2. Think back to when you were a student at school. What were you taught about Aboriginal and Torres Strait Islander knowledges and perspectives? If so, how was this done?
3. After reading this chapter, how do you think could you embed Aboriginal and Torres Strait Islander knowledges and perspectives within your subject area?

References

Australian Curriculum, Assessment and Reporting Authority (2020). Aboriginal and Torres Strait Islander histories and cultures. https://www.australiancurriculum.edu.au/f-10-curriculum/cross-curriculum-priorities/aboriginal-and-torres-strait-islander-histories-and-cultures/

Australian Human Rights Commission (1997). Bringing them home report. https://www.humanrights.gov.au/our-work/bringing-them-home-report-1997

Birner, B. (2020). Is English changing? https://www.linguisticsociety.org/content/english-changing

Bullimore, K. (1999). Media dreaming: Representation of Aboriginality in modern Australian media. *Asia Pacific Media Educator* (6), 72–81.

Clarkson, C., Jacobs, Z., Marwick, B., Fullagar, R., Walis, L., Smith, M., … Pardoe, C. (2017). Human occupation of northern Australia by 65,000 years ago. *Nature*, 547, 306–310. Doi:10.1038/nature22968.

CSIRO (2019). Indigenous seasons calendars. https://www.csiro.au/en/Research/Environment/Land-management/Indigenous/Indigenous-calendars

Department of Education and Training (2011). Embedding Aboriginal and Torres Strait Islander perspectives in schools. https://earlychildhood.qld.gov.au/fundingAndSupport/Documents/eatsips_2011.pdf

Education Council. (2019). Review of the Melbourne Declaration, Alice Springs (Mparntwe) education declaration. https://uploadstorage.blob.core.windows.net/public-assets/education-au/melbdec/ED19-0230%20-%20SCH%20-%20Alice%20Springs%20(Mparntwe)%20Education%20Declaration_ACC.pdf

Hart, V., Whatman, S., Mclaughlin, J., & Sharma-Brymer, V. (2012). Pre-service teachers' pedagogical relationships and experiences of embedding Indigenous Australian knowledge in teaching practicum. *Compare: A Journal of Comparative and International Education*, 42(5), 703–723. 10.1080/03057925.2012.706480

Langton, M. (1993). *Well, I heard it on the radio, and I saw it on the television*. North Sydney: Australian Film Commission.

Mayr, A. (2008). *Language and power*. London: Continuum International Publishing Group.

McConnochie, K. R. (1982). Aborigines and Australian education: Historical perspectives. In Sherwood, J. *Aboriginal education: Issues and innovations*. North Perth, WA: Alpha Print Pty Ltd., pp. 17–32.

NSW Department of Education (2015). Terra Nullius. https://www.racismnoway.com.au/teaching-resources/factsheets/terra-nullius/

Oxfam. (2015). Aboriginal and Torres Strait Islander cultural protocols. https://www.oxfam.org.au/wp-content/uploads/2015/11/2015-74-ATSI-Cultural-Protocols-update_WEB.pdf

Oxford Dictionary. (2020). Indigenous. https://www.oed.com/

Phillips, J. (2012). Indigenous knowledge perspectives: making space in the Australian centre. In J. Phillips and J. Lampert (Eds.) *Introductory Indigenous studies in education*. Frenchs Forrest, NSW: Pearson, pp. 9–25.

Reynolds, H. (1996). *Aboriginal sovereignty: Three nations, one Australia*. St Leonard, NSW: Allen & Unwin.

Reynolds, H. (1999). *Why weren't we told?* Victoria: Penguin Books Australia.

Sarra, G. (2011). Indigenous studies in all schools. *International Journal of Inclusive Education*, 15(6), 611–625. 10.1080/13603110903265040

Sarra, G. & Shay, M. (2019). Indigenous education. Critical perspectives to enhance learning practices. In Michael A. Peters (Ed.) *Encyclopedia of teacher education*. Singapore: Springer, pp. 1–8. doi:10.1007/978-981-13-1179-6_195-1

Stanner, W. (1969). *The Boyer lectures 1968 – after the dreaming*. Sydney, NSW: Australian Broadcasting Commission.

Thomas, M. (2017). The 1967 referendum. https://www.aph.gov.au/About_Parliament/Parliamentary_Departments/Parliamentary_Library/FlagPost/2017/May/The_1967_Referendum

Walter, M. (2011). Embedding Aboriginal and Torres Strait Islander presence: Opening knowledge pathways. In report commissioned for the Behrendt review of indigenous higher education by the Department of Education, Employment and Workplace Relations, Canberra.

Chapter 11

Culturally responsive pedagogies and perspectives in mathematics

Grace Sarra and Bronwyn Ewing

Who we are

Grace Sarra

Associate Professor Grace Sarra is an Indigenous academic and researcher in the School of Early Childhood and Inclusive Education at the Queensland University of Technology (QUT).

I am of Aboriginal heritage from the Birrigubba nation and Torres Strait Islander heritage of Mauar, Stephen, and Murray Islands. I have had experience in teaching and leadership roles in schools and universities for almost 30 years and my research work utilises Indigenous knowledges and frameworks with theoretical frameworks to contest prevailing assumptions and stereotypes that contribute to the lack of success of Aboriginal and Torres Strait Islander young people in schools and juvenile detention centres. Furthermore, my work focuses in the area of Indigenous education on pedagogy and community engagement, school change and leadership, social justice and inclusive education.

Bronwyn Ewing

Associate Professor Bronwyn Ewing is an academic and researcher in the QUT School of Teacher Education and Leadership, course coordinator for the Masters of Teaching (Primary) program and member of the STEM Education Research Group operationalised through the Faculty of Education.

My research interests relate to problems of education failure for low socio-economic, Indigenous and special needs children and young people with a specific focus on pedagogy and mathematics. I use a transdisciplinary frame of study for my work and anchor most of it in theoretical approaches that emphasise pedagogical, contextual, and multi-sensory influences on individual learning.

Introduction

As the oldest living culture in the world with a history dating back over 65,000 years (Rose, 2015; Clarkson et al., 2017), Aboriginal and Torres Strait Islander peoples continue to maintain their connections to country and place. Cultural knowledge and practices are passed down to generations through oral traditions, cultural ceremonies and performances, traditional languages, and through cultural heritage to protect sacred sites and artefacts. These connections and some of the cultural knowledges and practices that can be shared should not only be of importance to Aboriginal and Torres Strait Islander people, but to all Australian people. Such connections can be acknowledged and transferred into the education system through culturally responsive pedagogies and respecting Indigenous peoples' cultural continuity and the relationships that have been sustained between Indigenous people and their environments for thousands of years.

Valuing these connections can be achieved by incorporating culturally responsive pedagogies that consider the social and cultural knowledge of the student (Gloria Ladson-Billings, 1995; Lewthwaite, Owen, Doiron, Renaud, & McMillan, 2014; Sarra, 2014). This process requires contextualising the students' knowledges and lived experiences, as it is through these that students' engagement in learning may be increased.

This chapter focuses, in particular, on student engagement in mathematics education. It focuses on integrating culturally responsive pedagogies and practices to actively engage and improve the mathematics achievement of Aboriginal and Torres Strait Islander students. We also suggest that these will be of benefit to many students. Culturally responsive pedagogies refer to the intersection of culture with teaching and the curriculum. It makes visible students' culture and draws on their cultural knowledge and experiences to inform and guide teachers' planning and instruction (Gloria Ladson-Billings, 1995; Lewthwaite et al., 2014; Sarra, 2014). Engagement refers to reflective involvement in deep understanding, valuing what is being done, and actively participating in learning (Munns & Woodward, 2006). Including these practices helps secure a sense of satisfaction and investment in learning for our students. In addition, we will explore how an inclusive learning environment is important for teachers in establishing high expectations for their students.

Background

In 2008, the Federal Government and the Council of Australian Governments (COAG, 2008), approved the National Indigenous Reform Agreement which set out 'Closing the Gap' targets, focusing on: closing the life expectancy gap; halving the gap in mortality rates for Indigenous children under five, ensuring access to early childhood education for Indigenous children four years of age in remote communities; halving the gap in reading, writing, and numeracy achievements for children; halving the gap for Indigenous students in Year 12 attainment rates by 2020; and, halving the gap in employment outcomes between Indigenous and non-Indigenous Australians. Of these targets, only 1 of the 6 areas has been successful: the 2018 National Assessment Program: Literacy and Numeracy (NAPLAN) data for numeracy showed improvement against the national benchmarks for Year 9 students (ACARA, 2018). Whilst this success is important, the mathematics performance of Indigenous students continues to be below that of non-Indigenous students overall, so our aim is to provide teachers with some tools to address this issue.

Indigenous students' participation

Improving Australian Indigenous students' participation in numeracy (and reading and writing) is critical to increasing their participation at school, at university, and in their future employment. Yet NAPLAN (ACARA, 2019) results show the mean scores for numeracy (and literacy) at Year 3 are lower for Indigenous students when compared to non-Indigenous students. At 15 years of age, the mean score for Indigenous students is significantly lower than the OECD (2019) average as identified by the Programme for International Student Assessment (PISA) (Thomson, De Bortoli, Underwood, & Schmid, 2019, pp. 20–21). Indigenous students continue to be outperformed by their non-Indigenous peers by the equivalent of two years. It is interesting to also note, while Indigenous student performance has not changed significantly over time, non-Indigenous students' performance has declined in all domains over the longer term. This is despite educators in Australia having done a great deal of work to enable all students to excel (as measured by international standards). There remains a particular sense of urgency for Indigenous students and their teachers to address this need. We suggest this can be achieved through culturally responsive pedagogies, which are described next.

Culturally responsive pedagogy: Terminology, theory, and practice

Culturally responsive pedagogies (CRP) have been described using various terms (Krakouer, 2015; Lopez, 2016; Morrison, Rigney, Hattam & Diplock, 2019). For instance, CRP has been described as culturally relevant pedagogy, culturally centred education, to name a couple, but all terms express individual nuances and histories (Morrison et al., 2019). So in this chapter, while we use the term CRP, we acknowledge that a range of alternative expressions are also used to refer to this.

CRP is orientated towards two different theories; constructivism (from Dewey, Bruner, Piaget) and socio-cultural learning (which draws on the work of Vygotsky) (cf. Boon & Lewthwaite, 2016; Morrison, Robbins, & Rose, 2008). From both these perspectives, learning is seen as socially mediated and interconnected with students' cultural experiences. Constructivism is based on the understanding that student opportunities for learning and for power come through problem-solving and communication with their teachers. Nonetheless, this theory has not been free of criticism or challenge. For example, the exclusive focus on the individual has increasingly come under question, particularly from those subscribing to a socio-cultural perspective. In contrast, the second theoretical perspective focuses not only on the individual, but on social interaction, such as between a child and adult, and the cultural context in which they live (Ernest, 1994; Lave & Wenger, 1991; Renshaw, 1992; Saxe, 1991; Voigt, 1994). Furthermore, a number of studies (e.g., Saxe, 1991; Lave & Wenger, 1991) have shown that knowledge and understanding are influenced by participation in cultural practices, including things as simple as shopping at a supermarket, going to the park, and playing with friends. It is on this basis that many researchers claim priority in the classroom should be given to social and cultural processes (Engestrom, 1996; Forman & McPhail, 1993; Levine, 1996; Minick, 1996; Voigt, 1994), such as by using CRP, and that such an approach is key to an individual's cognitive development. In the classroom context, this is achieved by scaffolding the learner (Bruner, 1985) and by taking account of the cultural knowledge and learning of the student (Diaz, Neal & Amaya-Williams, 1990).

Arising from the civil rights movement in the United States of America, which drew attention to the educational inequities experienced by students of colour, CRP drew attention to the need for teachers to respond to and address the diverse ways of knowing, thinking, and communicating (Howard & Rodriguez-Scheel, 2017; Pirbhai-Illich, Pete, & Martin, 2017). Thus, CRP is viewed as having an unapologetic political dimension that 'speaks to hegemonic educational discourses' (Howard & Rodriguez-Scheel, 2017) (i.e., questions the beliefs, understandings, accepted knowledges etc. that we incorporate within our teaching). And it is important to understand the impact of such 'hegemonic discourses' – the taken-for-granted things we do in education contexts. This is because all we do within education is based on ideological assumptions, such as about the nature and practice of education. In Australia, for instance, there is a taken-for-granted assumption that Western knowledges and ways of teaching are the norm and knowledges and other ways of teaching, such as Indigenous knowledges and pedagogies, are outside this norm. To address this CRP works to positively influence student achievement by including recognition of Indigenous knowledge systems in our teaching, while challenging inequities in schools. Indigenous knowledge systems include cultural knowledges, languages, storytelling, cultural heritage and spiritual connections to land, sea, waterways, and sky. In this way, Indigenous culture is not an obstacle, but rather serves to enhance education.

CRP also involves listening to and privileging Indigenous voices to ensure decision-making processes are more adaptive and reflective. This allows the creation of inclusive and culturally safe learning environments that cater for the needs of all students. By incorporating these aspects into teaching approaches, it allows Indigenous students to have a strong sense of pride and belonging, and promotes positive cultural identities (also see Chapters 4 and 5). However, CRP does require educators to be open-minded and to reflect on their own underlying cultural assumptions and beliefs about Indigenous students and the knowledge they bring to learning contexts.

CRP brings together three principles: (a) a focus on student learning; (b) developing students' cultural competence; and (c) supporting their critical consciousness (Ladson-Billings, 2017). Furthermore, these principles underpin the actions of a culturally responsive teacher, who is characterised as:

- Socially and academically empowering by setting high expectations for students with a commitment to every student's success;
- Multidimensional, because they engage [students'] cultural knowledge, experiences, contributions, and perspectives;
- Validating of every student's culture, bridging gaps between school and home through diversified instructional strategies and multicultural curricula;
- Socially, emotionally, and politically comprehensive as they seek to educate the whole child;
- Transformative of schools and societies by using students' existing strengths to drive instruction, assessment, and curriculum design; and,
- Emancipatory and liberating from oppressive educational practices.

(Aronson & Laughter, 2016, p. 165, based on Gay, 2010)

In this way a culturally responsive teacher acknowledges and respects "the cultural characteristics, experiences, and perspectives of ethnically diverse students as conduits for teaching them more effectively" (Gay, 2010, p. 106).

Within the mathematics curriculum teachers can make the learning experiences of their students connect to their cultural understandings and experiences, by attending to different ways of knowing and doing in their classrooms (Morrison et al., 2019). To achieve this, they need to draw on what students can contribute to their learning through their cultural knowledges, which then offers teachers further ways to engage with them.

Drawing on different aspects of student's worldviews is also important for bringing about change (Hardy, Palmer, & Phillips, 2000). A change process that acknowledges students' culture and ways of knowing and doing provides opportunities for educators to become culturally competent teachers who have high expectations for their students (Sarra, 2011). As Ladson-Billings in Greer et al. (2009) indicates:

> all students can be successful in mathematics when their understanding of it is linked to meaningful cultural referents, and when the instruction assumes that all students are capable of mastering the subject matter.
>
> (p. 190)

This is particularly important with respect to Aboriginal and Torres Strait Islander students who have experienced a long history of educational inequalities when compared to non-Indigenous people (Bodkin-Andrews & Carlson, 2016). This includes educational policies and guidelines, curriculum content, deficit perceptions, low expectations, racism, and negative stereotyping (see Chapters 2 and 7). The issues arising for Aboriginal and Torres Strait Islander students in our schools are often blamed on outside factors, yet educators can be blinded by their own negative mindsets and perceptions of Indigenous students as underachievers. We suggest that CRP is a critical tool for countering some of the existing issues that are connected to racism and deficit ways of thinking that have impacted the outcomes of Indigenous students.

Good teaching practices that incorporate culturally responsive pedagogies (CRP) provide their students with access to effective education that can make a difference to student learning. So, too, can teachers who approach the task with high expectations for their students, creating emancipatory environments that transform their classrooms. Hugh Lacey (2002) has described emancipatory activity as a collaborative activity, engaged in and by people who experience oppression and by those in solidarity with them to alleviate sufferings being experienced and to create conditions for effective change (p. 10). Setting high expectations for students means trusting that students are capable decision-makers and have the ability to achieve when in a learning environment that enables this. This also works to encourage the engagement of Aboriginal and Torres Strait Islander students.

A learning environment that is underpinned by shared beliefs and assumptions that are anchored in high expectation relationships, such as around mathematic understanding and achievement, acknowledges and embraces students' Aboriginal and Torres Strait Islander identity. Such a practice demonstrates to students that they are capable of achieving what has been asked them of them (Perso & Hayward, 2015). In this way, setting high expectations utilises

Grace Sarra and Bronwyn Ewing

strengths-based approaches for Aboriginal and Torres Strait Islander students, such as through a Stronger Smarter philosophy (Sarra, 2011) which honours a positive sense of Aboriginal and/or Torres Strait Islander cultural identity, and acknowledges and embraces Indigenous and educational processes that are anchored in positive relationships. In turn, strengths-based approaches and perspectives in schools can make a difference to the engagement and learning experiences of young people. When teachers consider their teaching practices based on the strengths and capacities of students' intellectual, physical, and interpersonal skills (McCashen, 2010) that are informed from the communities in which they live, this can have a positive ripple effect. Therefore, a strengths-based approach, including CRP, enables connections to be made between the students' individual culture (meanings, beliefs, norms, languages, and lived experiences) that they use to interpret the world (Bourdieu, 1973), creating opportunities for learning, such as the two-way learning approach (see Chapters 6 and 12).

Building on the knowledge, strengths, and lived experiences of Indigenous people in communities can enhance the teaching and learning experiences of students when embedding Indigenous perspectives in mathematics (Ewing et al., 2013). An example of this occurred when working with students from a community in the Torres Strait Islands in a mathematics lesson. The students were required to sort objects (shells) into groups, allowing them opportunities to identify, label, and name various attributes of the objects using Yumplatok (creole), English or their own home language (see Chapter 8). Relating their understandings to their daily life experiences helped scaffold the students' learning, for instance using their knowledge of the attributes of edible and non-edible shell creatures for sorting. They were able to do this with ease because this cultural knowledge is taught to children from a young age when they go fishing or exploring the waters with their families.

RAMR pedagogical framework: connecting culture to teaching

This pedagogical framework was first designed by Matthews (2008) through storytelling and connected culture, experience, and mathematics. It focused on four critical elements including: reality, abstraction, mathematics, and critical reflection (RAMR) (see Figure 11.1). In this way the framework contextualises mathematics learning to Indigenous culture (Sarra & Ewing, 2014). It builds on the creativity of mathematics and its cultural symbols, whilst addressing the cultural bias inherent in mathematics which can work to marginalise and exclude learners.

The reality phase involves making observations about the lived realities of students, including where they come from, observing their local, cultural, and environmental knowledges and then considering how these aspects can be incorporated into their learning experiences. By taking this approach it is possible to ensure that students' existing knowledge is connected to the mathematics idea. Continuing this further, creating representations in the abstraction phase is achieved through a sequence of activities, which includes examples that could be physical, virtual, and pictorial to form a symbolic language called mathematics (Sarra & Ewing, 2014). During this phase, the use of two-way connections can be used to investigate particular attributes and behaviours to explore the students' real-life situations. From the mathematics phase, critical reflection occurs to ensure that the mathematical

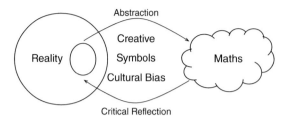

RAMR framework (Matthews, 2008)

representation that is created aligns with reality. (Note: This framework had been adapted and now informs the YuMi Deadly maths programs.)

YuMi Deadly maths (QUT, 2014) is a program that aims to improve performance and engagement in mathematics, especially for Indigenous students, and to improve the teaching practices and pedagogy for maths practitioners by providing support for them to deliver engaging lessons that embed Indigenous perspectives using a holistic framework (Sarra 2018). Following the RAMR framework (Figure 11.2) the lessons embed Indigenous perspectives through a series of Indigenous posters and interesting, culturally connected activities. Examples of mathematic lessons building on this are shown in Figure 11.2.

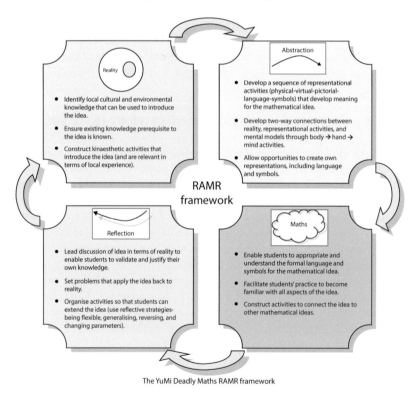

The YuMi Deadly Maths RAMR framework

YuMi Deadly maths RAMR framework (Figure 2, QUT, 2014, p. 32)

Examples of embedding Indigenous perspectives in mathematics (Tables 11.1 and 11.2, Figure 11.3)

Lesson one: measurement fish traps – full or empty

Learning goal	Students will:
	Explore the relationship between a container (what it could hold) and its contents (is there as much as or less in the container than it can hold).
	Experience and explore the attribute of capacity – full and empty.
	Use language full, empty, nearly full, nearly empty, half full, half empty.
Content description	Use direct and indirect comparisons to decide which is longer, heavier, or holds more, and explain reasoning in everyday language.
	Measure and compare the lengths and capacities of pairs of objects using uniform informal units.
Big idea	Change and relationship.
	Attribute – capacity.
	Unnumbered comparison.
Resources	Fish trap pictures, containers, water (if wet area available), sand, rice, uncooked popcorn, plastic spoons or scoops, boxes, small cubes to fit in boxes

Lesson plan

	REALITY
Activate Prior Knowledge	Discuss fishing, catching fish, ways to catch fish.
	YouTube: https://www.youtube.com/watch?v=qma1MC1_PAs (This clip is showing the actual fish traps at Oyster Bay, Albany, Western Australia.)
	Discuss what happens as the water comes into the trap. Students should be able to articulate that the trap starts with no water, and water gradually comes in and fish can come in until it is full. Use visual pictures (fig 1-6) to show examples of water empty and full in fish traps.
	Highlight language terms showing clips from video for full, empty, nearly full, nearly empty. Picture cards may also be used to discuss full and empty.
	Discuss other containers that can be full or empty e.g., cups, bowls, bins …
	ABSTRACTION
Body	Act out being the contents in a cup or jug that is being filled or emptied. Have students stand in own space with their arms above their heads and hands joined to show full. Students crouch down as low as they can with hands on the floor to show empty. Discuss, where might our hands be to show half full? What might nearly empty look like? Can you show me nearly full?
Hand Mind	Rotational activities: Sand play, water play, boxes with small cubes or items, digital game or activity that involves dragging pictures into a container on screen, provide picture cards of fish traps to sort and order from full to empty. Each workstation requires containers and scoops where students can explore full, empty, nearly full, nearly empty – promote language use and listen for student language and understanding that when something is full, there is no more space inside.
	Draw and label pictures of cups and containers that are empty, half full, nearly full, half empty, nearly empty and empty.
	Capture teachable moments at morning tea and lunch to talk about children's drink bottles and lunch boxes as full, nearly full, nearly empty and empty.
	Imagine that you are holding a cup of your favourite drink. Show me how happy you look when your favourite drink is full. Imagine drinking all of your drink. Show me how sad you look when your favourite drink is empty. Imagine filling your cup back up again – show me how you get happier and happier till your cup is full.

(Continued)

Lesson plan

MATHEMATICS

Language/Symbols Full, nearly full, half full/half empty, nearly empty, empty

Practice Provide children with opportunities to practice using activities discussed in

Connections Abstraction to reinforce concept and language.

This lesson is focusing on attribute of capacity but is also connected to measurement concepts of more than, less than, same as; measurement using direct comparison.

REFLECTION

Validation In reflection, ensure that children:

Application/ Know that a full container has no room for any more, and an empty container has

Problems no other substance inside it but has space to put things in.

Extension Are able to tell you which containers are full, empty when asked verbally.

Are able to show which containers are full, empty from a written instruction.

Can create and label full, empty containers when asked verbally and from a written instruction.

Discuss with students' other examples where we use the language full to mean complete or no more space e.g., fully grown, full marks, full schedule, full program, full stop.

Extend children to more than, less than, same as and informal measures of capacity.

A

B

C

D

E

▲ Figure 11.3

A-E Fish traps

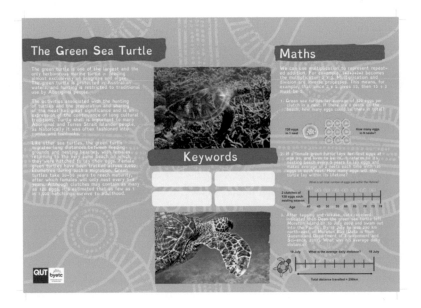

▲ Figure 11.4

The green sea turtle in maths, a poster (Ewing & Sarra, 2019)

Embedding Indigenous perspectives: marine life –the green sea turtle

The lesson identified in the poster in Figure 11.4 provides a different way of embedding Indigenous perspectives through a poster format design and aims to explore the mathematical concepts of multiplication and division. The written content about the green sea turtle is part of a school reading program and includes embedded Indigenous perspectives that provides young people with an opportunity to engage in conversations around the topic. This part of the lesson is teacher directed. Keywords and what they mean are then identified relating to the topic which is followed with the mathematics relating to the topic.

Mathematics educators working with Indigenous young people in a detention centre: key themes from teacher discussions.

The poster lesson above is part of a recent Australian Research Council Indigenous Discovery project (2016–2020) that aims to develop new knowledge concerning the mathematics learning potential of incarcerated Indigenous and low socio-economic status young people (10–17 years). It engages mathematics educators and students to design and develop a tailored mathematics intervention that is culturally responsive and embeds Indigenous perspectives into mathematics. The project draws on the conceptual framework of Sarra (2011) which acknowledges and embraces an Aboriginal identity and acknowledges and embraces a Torres

Strait Islander identity and aims to privilege Indigenous voices in the learning processes instilled in high-expectations relationships.

Over the duration of the project teachers from the detention centre engaged in interviews and teacher focus groups and a number of key themes were identified to inform their teaching pedagogies in their classrooms. These include:

1. Curriculum used;
2. Difficulties in learning;
3. Instructional strategies;
4. Perceptions of mathematics;
5. Making connections – real-life context;
6. Strategies to assess student understanding;
7. Differentiation strategies;
8. Indigenous perspectives;
9. Making connections – curriculum areas;
10. Making connections to mathematics;
11. Strategies for building knowledge;
12. Strengths of students in mathematics.

Some notable observations indicated that for improved teaching and learning to occur in the classrooms, differentiation strategies through individual learning plans and culturally responsive pedagogies that embed Indigenous perspectives are required to engage and improve outcomes for young Indigenous people.

Conclusion

Culturally responsive pedagogies can make a difference to learning in the class-room by providing students with opportunities to connect to their place and country by acknowledging and embracing their cultural identities. It shows as a teacher, there is a need to value who your students are and where they come from and this can assist in building high expectations for them. Embedding Indigenous perspectives into mathematics learning contributes to improving the mathematics outcomes of Indigenous young people in schools. It is important that as educators you consider what type of learning environment you create for all students, and particularly for Aboriginal and Torres Strait Islander young people.

Reflective questions

1. In what ways can you incorporate culturally responsive pedagogies and strength-based approaches in your teaching practice to engage your students in mathematics?
2. How might you embed Indigenous perspectives through contextualising and localising Indigenous knowledges into the mathematics learning in your classrooms?

3. An important factor in teaching is to connect and engage with your local Indigenous community. How might you engage your local Indigenous community when embedding Indigenous perspectives into the mathematics learning experiences in the classroom?

References

ACARA. (2018). National assessment program. Literacy and numeracy. Achievement in reading, writing, language conventions and numeracy. National report for 2017. http://www.nap.edu.au/docs/default-source/default-document-library/naplan-national-report-2017_final_04dec2017.pdf?sfvrsn=0

ACARA. (2019). National assessment program. Literacy and numeracy. Achievement in reading, writing, language conventions and numeracy. In *ACARA* (Series Ed.). https://nap.edu.au/docs/default-source/resources/2018-naplan-national-report.pdf?sfvrsn=2

Aronson, B. A., & Laughter, J. (2016). The theory and practice of culturally relevant education: A synthesis of research across content areas. *Review of Educational Research*, 86(1), 163–206.

Bodkin-Andrews, G. & Carlson, B. (2016) The legacy of racism and Indigenous Australian identity within education. *Race Ethnicity and Education*, 19(4), 784–807. Doi: 10.1080/13613324.2014.969224

Boon, H. J., & Lewthwaite, B.E. (2016). Signatures of quality teaching for Indigenous students. *Australian Educational Researcher*, 43(4), 18.

Bourdieu, P. (1973) Cultural reproduction and social reproduction. In R. Brown (Ed.) *Knowledge, education and social change: Papers in the sociology of education*. London: Tavistock, pp. 71–112.

Bruner, J. (1985). Vygotsky: A historical and conceptual perspective. In J. V. Wertsch (Ed.) *Culture, communication and cognition: Vygotskian perspectives*. Cambridge: Cambridge University Press, pp. 21–35.

Clarkson, C., Jacobs, Z., Marwick, B., Fullagar, R., Wallis, L., Smith, M., Roberts, R. G., Hayes, E., Lowe, K., & Carah, X. (2017). Human occupation of northern Australia by 65,000 years ago. *Nature*, 547(7663), 306–325.

Cobb, P., & Yackel, E. (1998). A constructivist perspective on the culture of the mathematics classroom. In F. Seeger, J. Voigt, & U. Waschescio (Eds.) *The culture of the mathematics classroom*. Cambridge: Cambridge University Press, pp. 158–190.

Council of Australian Governments (COAG) (2008). National Indigenous reform agreement (Closing the gap). http://www.federalfinancialrelations.gov.au/content/npa/health/_archive/indigenous-reform/national-agreement_sept_12.pdf

Diaz, R., Neal, C., & Amaya-Williams, M. (1990). The social origins of self-regulation. In L. C. Moll (Ed.) *Vygotsky and education: Instructional implications and applications of sociohistorical psychology*. Cambridge: Cambridge University Press, pp. 127–154.

Engestrom, Y. (1996). Work as a testbench of activity theory. In S. Chaiklin & J. Lave (Eds.) *Understanding practice: Perspectives on activity and context*. Cambridge: Cambridge University Press, pp. 64–103.

Ernest, P. (1994). The dialogical nature of mathematics. In P. Ernest (Ed.) *Mathematics, education and philosophy: An international perspective*. London: The Falmer Press, pp. 33–48.

Ewing, B. & Sarra, G. (2019) *Unlocking the learning potential of Indigenous and low SES young people in mathematics education*. Seminar presentation to *Queensland Department of Youth Justice*, Brisbane.

Ewing, B., Sarra, G., & Cooper, T. (2013) YuMi deadly maths program: Efficacy and collaboration. *Education Today*, 13(1), 28–30.

Forman, E. A., & McPhail, J. (1993). Vygotskian perspective on children's collaborative problem-solving activities. In N. M. E. A. Forman & C. Addison Stone (Eds.) *Contexts for learning: Sociocultural dynamics in children's development*. New York: Oxford University Press, pp. 213–229.

Gay, G. (2010). *Culturally responsive teaching: Theory, research, and practice*. New York: Teachers College Press.

Greer, B., Mukhopadhyay, S., Powell, A. & Nelson-Barber, S. (2009) *Culturally responsive mathematics education*. New York: Routledge.

Hall, S. (1982). The rediscovery of "ideology": Return of the repressed in media studies. In T. M. Gurevitch, J. Bennett, J. Curran, & J. Woollacott (Eds.) *Culture, society and the media*. London: Methuen, pp. 56–90.

Hardy, C., Palmer, I., & Phillips, N. (2000). Discourse as a strategic resource. *Human Relations*, 53(9), 1227–1248.

Howard, T. & Rodriguez-Scheel, A. (2017). Culturally relevant pedagogy 20 years later: Progress or pontificating? What have we learned, and where do we go? *Teachers College Record*, 119(1), 1–32.

Kenway, J. (1990). Education and the right's discursive politics: Private versus state schooling. In S. Ball (Ed.) *Foucault and education: Discipline and knowledge*. London: Routledge, pp. 197–206.

Krakouer, J. (2015). Literature review relating to the current context and discourse on Indigenous cultural awareness in the teaching space: Critical pedagogies and improving Indigenous learning outcomes through cultural responsiveness. https://research.acer.edu.au/indigenous_education/42

Lacey, H. (2002). *Explanatory critique and emancipatory movements*. Paper delivered to the *Critical Realist Conference*, Bradford University.

Ladson-Billings, G. (1995). Toward a theory of culturally relevant pedagogy. *American Educational Research Journal*, 32(3), 465–491. Doi:10.2307/1163320

Ladson-Billings, G. (2017). The (r)evolution will not be standardized: Teacher education, hip hop pedagogy, and culturally relevant pedagogy. In D. Paris & H. S. Alim (Eds.) *Culturally sustaining pedagogies: Teaching and learning for justice in a changing world*. New York: Teachers College Press, pp. 141–156.

Lave, J., & Wenger, E. (1991). *Situated learning. Legitimate peripheral participation*. Cambridge: Cambridge University Press.

Levine, H. (1996). Context and scaffolding in developmental studies of mother-child problem-solving dyads. In S. Chaiklin, & J. Lave (Eds.) *Understanding practice: Perspectives on activity and context*. Cambridge: Cambridge University Press, pp. 306–326.

Lewthwaite, B., Owen, T., Doiron, A., Renaud, R., & McMillan, B. (2014). Culturally responsive teaching in Yukon First Nation settings: What does it look like and what is its influence? *Canadian Journal of Educational Administration and Policy*, 155, 1–34.

Lopez, F. A. (2016). Culturally responsive pedagogies in Arizona and Latino students' achievement. *Teachers College Record*, 118(5).

Matthews, C. (2008). Stories and symbols: Maths as storytelling. https://thinking101canada.files.wordpress.com/2018/04/maths-as-storytelling1.pdf

Minick, N. (1996). Teachers' directives: The social construction of "literal meanings" and "real worlds" in classroom discourse. In S. Chaiklin & J. Lave (Eds.) *Understanding practice: Perspectives on activity and context*. Cambridge: Cambridge University Press, pp. 343–374.

Morrison, A., Rigney, L.-I., Hattam, R., & Diplock, A. (2019). *Toward an Australian culturally responsive pedagogy: A narrative review of the literature*. Adelaide: University of South Australia.

Morrison, K., Robbins, H., & Rose, D. (2008). Operationalizing culturally relevant pedagogy: A synthesis of classroom-based research. *Equity & Excellence in Education*, 41, 433–452. Doi:10.1080/10665680802400006

Perso, T. & Hayward, C. (2015) *Teaching Indigenous students: Cultural awareness and classroom strategies for improving learning outcomes*. Australia: Allen & Unwin.

Pirbhai-Illich, F., Pete, S., & Martin, F. (2017). Culturally responsive pedagogies: Decolonization, indigeneity and interculturalism. In F. Pirbhai-Illich, S. Pete, & F. Martin (Eds.) *Culturally responsive pedagogy: Working towards decolonization, indigeneity and interculturalism*. Cham, Switzerland: Palgrave Macmillan, pp. 3–25.

Queensland University of Technology (QUT) (2014). *YuMi deadly maths: Overview booklet: Philosophy, pedagogy, change and culture*. Brisbane: Australia.

Renshaw, P. (1992, August). *Synthesising the individual and the social: Social-cultural theory applied to the mathematics education of young children*. Paper presented at the *Presentation at the Seventh International Congress on Mathematics Education*, Quebec City.

Rose, M. (2015) The "silent apartheid" as the practitioner's blindspot. In Price, K. (Ed.) *Aboriginal and Torres Strait Islander education: An introduction for the teaching profession* (2nd edn). Melbourne: Cambridge University Press, pp. 66–82.

Sarra. C. (2011) *Strong and smart – Towards a pedagogy for emancipation for First Peoples*. Oxon: Routledge.

Sarra, C. (2014). *Strong and smart–Towards a pedagogy for emancipation: Education for First Peoples*. Oxon: Routledge.

Sarra, G. (2018) *YuMi deadly maths: Embedding Indigenous perspectives. Aboriginal and Torres Strait Islander Mathematics Alliance Conference, 10–13 July 2018*, Melbourne.

Sarra, G. & Ewing, B. (2014) Indigenous students transitioning to school: Responses to pre-foundational mathematics. *SpringerPlus*, 3(1), 685. doi:10.1186-2193-1801-3-685

Saxe, G. (1991). *Culture and cognitive development: Studies in mathematical understanding*. Hillsdale, NJ: Lawrence Erlbaum Associates.

Thomson, S., De Bortoli, L., Underwood, C., & Schmid, M. (2019). PISA 2018 In Brief I: Student performance. https://research.acer.edu.au/ozpisa/34/

Voigt, J. (1994). Negotiation of mathematical meaning and learning mathematics. In P. Cobb, & Yackel, E. (Eds.) *Learning mathematics: Constructivist and interactionist theories of mathematics development*. Dordrecht: Kluwer Academic Publishers, pp. 171–194.

Vygotsky, L. (1930). *Mind in society: The development of higher psychological processes* (trans. M. Cole). Cambridge, MA: Harvard University Press.

Chapter 12

Relational pedagogies and co-constructing curriculum

Danielle Armour and Jodie Miller

Who we are

Danielle Armour

I am a Kamilaroi woman from Northern New South Wales. My cultural links are through my paternal grandmother Isobel Armour nee Noel. Isobel's father was Noel Roberts, however, his name was changed to Robert Noel when he was a young. I am primary teacher trained and have taught in metropolitan, regional and very remote contexts. I now lecture and research in Aboriginal and Torres Strait Islander education in the Kulin nation. My perspectives are from an Aboriginal lens. Please be advised that there are names of Aboriginal and Torres Strait Islander people in this chapter that are now deceased. We use these names respectfully.

Jodie Miller

I am a first generation born Australian with no Indigenous heritage. My mother is Irish and my father is English. Both my parents arrived in Australia in the 1970s. As a non-Indigenous education researcher, I understand that although my own culture deeply influences the perceptions of the world around me, those views are not a defining assessment. In the context of my research I recognise that Aboriginal, Torres Strait Islander, and other Indigenous people (e.g., Maori and Pāsifika people) bring unique life experiences to the classroom. By addressing the diverse mindset of all involved in classroom interactions, we acknowledge and celebrate students as knowledge-makers who add to the collective understanding.

Introduction

Strength-based approaches in education stress the importance of co-constructed and culturally responsive teaching (Scerra, 2011) (see Chapter 11). Co-constructing learning requires the educator to enter the cultural life and lived experiences of the learner (Doige, 2003). All members of the learning community (teachers, students, teacher assistants, community members) are involved in co-constructing the learning experiences, which results in the empowerment of all members (Doige, 2003). Therefore, in the following chapter we describe how to develop co-constructed classroom pedagogies with both Aboriginal and Torres Strait Islander students, educators, and community members.

Effective teachers of Indigenous students demonstrate pedagogies that are based upon relationships rather than authority (St. Denis, 2010) (yet as Moreton-Robinson et al., 2012 indicate, we know teachers often struggle with building such relationships). Relationships are important to building two-way learning (Sarra, 2011), and for planning and decision making within the school and classroom contexts. In turn, two-way learning within the school contexts allows teachers to learn about local Aboriginal and Torres Strait Islander knowledge and community members learn about curriculum (Lewthwaite et al., 2015). By doing so culturally responsive pedagogies can be developed and implemented. This is important because culturally responsive pedagogy created in partnership with the community and students have the potential to impact deeply on the teaching and learning of all students, but in particular on Aboriginal and Torres Strait Islander students (Matthews, 2012).

To develop such co-constructed pedagogies, it is vital that respectful and meaningful relationships between all members of a school community are established (see Chapter 7). As the approach we describe in this chapter is based upon the importance of relationship building, we would like to open the chapter with a short introduction of ourselves, our experiences and perspectives about working with Aboriginal and Torres Strait Islander people. For the purpose of this chapter we use the term Aboriginal and Torres Strait Islander when describing the group of people who have identified as such. However, we also use the term Indigenous with reference to those people who identify as First Nations people in the broader literature, but we do so acknowledging that some Aboriginal and Torres Strait Islander people may be offended by this term.

Challenges faced by teachers implementing Aboriginal and Torres Strait Islander perspectives

Curriculum developers and decision makers in Australia's education systems have been slow to acknowledge the different worldviews Indigenous students bring to school (Nakata, 2002). In fact, the Australian educational curriculum developers have only acknowledged the value of Indigenous cultures and included them in curriculum documents over the past 20 years, despite the fact that Aboriginal and Torres Strait Islander education policies have been available in each state and territory for approximately 40 years (Harrison & Greenfield, 2011). It is important to be aware that these recent policies require teachers to embed Indigenous perspectives across all key learning areas (Lowe & Yunkaporta, 2013). Yet, Indigenous perspectives are still under-represented in Australian schools (Hickling-Hudson & Ahlquist, 2003). It has been suggested that one reason for this is that non-Indigenous teachers find it difficult to give an Aboriginal and Torres Strait Islander perspective as they do not possess Aboriginal knowledge (Pearson, 2009) and instead give their own perspective of Aboriginal people's knowledge (Martin, 2006). Hence, Indigenous perspectives implemented in schools are rarely a true reflection of Indigenous knowledge, as the majority of teaching staff is non-Indigenous.

Relational pedagogies: two-way learning

Research findings show that many Australian teachers have been unable, to date, to properly engage Indigenous students in learning. They have also been unable to use teaching processes that enable Indigenous students to show their strengths (Yunkaporta, 2009). Yet, for effective teaching to take place, students need to be supported to feel proud of their identity and their cultural heritage (Sarra, Matthews, Ewing, & Cooper, 2011). Two-way learning has been identified as one way to address these issues.

The two-way approach is where Aboriginal and Torres Strait Islander knowledges and Western knowledges find a space in which each is appreciated and respected, and by doing so meaningful exchanges can occur (Frawley, Fasoli, d'Arbon, & Ober, 2010; Marika, 1999) (see Chapters 6, 9, and 14 for examples). It is important to note that this does not necessarily mean an agreement about worldviews needs to be reached, rather it allows for an appreciation of all perspectives. Implementing a two-way approach, therefore, allows students to move between both worlds and knowledge systems (Indigenous and Western), allowing them to be two-way strong (Ober, 2009; Sarra, 2005; White, Ober, Frawley, & Bat, 2009). While there are many different interpretations of what two-way strong is, Aboriginal researchers suggest that it encapsulates being able to move and mix between Indigenous and Western knowledge in positive ways (Ober, 2009). Unfortunately, often in educational settings Aboriginal and Torres Strait Islander knowledges are rarely acknowledged and, instead, teaching and learning experiences are often dominated by Western perspectives, content, and pedagogies (Figure 12.1).

The advantage of the two-way learning approach is that it gives equal voice to Aboriginal and Torres Strait Islander perspectives. It also provides an opportunity for non-Indigenous teachers to start to think differently about the ways they teach in classrooms (Coff & Lampert, 2019). It also builds on the strengths and perspectives of the learners and provides a focus for their learning experience. For this to be successful, however, teachers do need to recognise their own standpoints, what

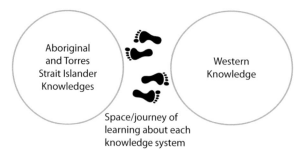

▲ Figure 12.1

Two-way learning – moving between two knowledge systems

Danielle Armour and Jodie Miller

their cultural lens and beliefs are, and how they see the world so that they can recognise the differences that exist (Coff & Lampert, 2019). They then need to access Aboriginal and Torres Strait Islander knowledges (with permission) in order to share these in their classrooms and begin implementing content and pedagogies that represent a different worldview. This can be challenging to do on their own and so they may need to build meaningful relationships with the local community so that Aboriginal and Torres Strait Islander knowledges can be shared. In the sections that follow we offer some practical suggestions about how this can all be achieved.

Building positive relationships

As indicated in our introduction, an important first step for teachers is to build positive and respectful relationships with Aboriginal and Torres Strait Islander students, educators, parents, and community members in order to create effective learning environments. For Aboriginal and Torres Strait Islander students, in particular, there needs to be trust between students and their teachers (Kearney et al., 2014). If trust and positive relationships can be fostered in the early years, these may be able to continue throughout the student's educational journey (Kearney et al., 2014). Once the relationships with Aboriginal and Torres Strait Islander students become strong, it is possible for the relationships between teachers, families, and the community to also evolve. To achieve this, however, effort needs to be given to building connections between home and school and to instilling a consistent sense of community and belonging (Kearney et al., 2014). To support this, teachers need to recognise their own behaviours to ensure Aboriginal and Torres Strait Islander people feel welcomed at school and in their child's classroom (again see Chapters 5 and 7).

One of the biggest hurdles faced by non-Indigenous teachers when trying to successfully implement culturally responsive pedagogies is understanding and learning about the backgrounds of their Aboriginal and Torres Strait Islander students (Sarra, 2011; Yunkaporta, 2009). However, by building strong relationships, not only with their students, but also with families and the local community, teachers will be able to achieve this. This is important because effective teaching builds upon understanding of the community and its history (Phillips & Lampert, 2012). Strong relationships begin by developing trust between teachers and their students and other community members who will begin to share stories about their family and their history (Lewthwaite et al., 2015). To be able to do this there is a need to engage successfully with Indigenous communities, which can be achieved in the following ways, by:

- Establishing trust by interacting respectfully and honestly;
- Showing appreciation of Indigenous histories, cultures and diversity in the local community;
- Valuing the skills and knowledges of the community and people;
- Demonstrating clarity of purpose and commitment in support of the community;
- Providing accessible and ongoing communication.

(Hunt, 2013)

By doing these different things teachers will be able to learn about the background of their students. With permission, they can also use this knowledge to create a positive, collaborative and two-way learning environment. It is important to note, that in line with Aboriginal protocols, non-Indigenous people need to gain permission to share Indigenous knowledges. In order to do this, you need to have close relationships with community members so they can inform you what is appropriate. You can not assume that this knowledge or permission is transferable between communities. Permission needs to be sought in each new place you teach.

Developing this depth of knowledge will take time, but the more teachers learn about the local Aboriginal and Torres Strait Islander community, the more culturally capable they will become, as it also provides them with opportunities to become more aware of their own cultural biases (Yunkaporta, 2009). It should be noted that becoming culturally capable is a journey. It does not just happen overnight and, at times, in can be a bumpy ride. Also, just because you may become culturally capable in one community, it does not necessarily mean that you will be culturally capable in another – this awareness is important for teachers to carry throughout their careers.

Along with students, their families and communities, another resource that can be central to success in classrooms where there are high enrolments of Aboriginal and Torres Strait Islander students are Indigenous teacher assistants (ITAs: Note, however, these have various titles in different education systems and sectors). These assistants have an important role in the classroom, including helping teachers to gain insights into the local community (Armour, Warren, & Miller, 2016). When relationships between assistants and teachers are strong, co-constructed expectations and learning based on local community knowledge can occur (Armour, 2016). They can also help to improve student engagement by providing authentic perspectives and the opportunity for this knowledge to be used (Blair, 2015). For this important collaboration between teachers and assistants to be successful we argue that there is a need to empower them in the classroom, which can be done by:

- Including ITAs in decision making in the classroom;
- Ensuring the ITAs are not only used for behavior management;
- Liaising with ITAs about student wellbeing;
- Involving ITAs in whole school professional learning;
- Including ITAs in all student support and learning activities.

(Armour, 2016)

Co-constructing learning experiences and classroom pedagogies

While Indigenous ways of knowing, being, and doing are becoming more common within education there are many ways that knowledge can be understood, and this can be challenging for educators if there is not input from local Aboriginal and Torres Strait Islander communities (Blair, 2015; Bennett, Redfern, & Zubrzycki, 2017; Martin, 2008). These challenges include misunderstanding of Indigenous ways of knowing and this knowledge being presented to students as 'other' because it is interpreted through a Western lens (Martin, 2008). To overcome this there is a need to embed Aboriginal and Torres Strait Islander knowledges within the curriculum through co-constructed teaching, planning, and learning.

Co-constructed learning takes place when students interact with teachers and with their peers, working together in partnership. Co-constructed learning allows personalisation, engagement and independent learning with student ownership. Co-constructed learning is an extension of pedagogical approaches that include student input, self and peer assessment, collaborative and explicit learning. Discussion becomes part of the classroom routine and students put forward ideas about the content to be covered and how they think that lessons should be delivered. This benefits students as it promotes students' confidence, encouraging them to communicate in and about their learning environment. Because traditional roles of teachers are broken down in this setting, with teaching and learning processes merging, co-constructed learning can create an environment that unleashes teachers' and students' creative energy. Giving such responsibility to learners in the learning process is not unique, but it has not been something that Aboriginal and Torres Strait Islander peoples have always had the privilege of doing.

To achieve a co-constructed approach, teachers of Aboriginal and Torres Strait Islander students need to implement a curriculum based on teaching practices that demonstrate links between school and the everyday realities of Indigenous peoples' lives, histories, and cultures (Lewthwaite et al., 2015; Sarra, 2011). They then need to facilitate learning experiences based on this knowledge. Achieving this might seem daunting, so in Table 12.1 we outline some questions that teachers can consider as they set up implementing such an approach. We also link these questions to the Australian Professional Standards for Teachers (APST).

As you can see, a co-constructed curriculum aligns closely to a strengths-based approach promoted throughout this text and provides a way forward for building upon the abilities and resilience of Aboriginal and Torres Strait Islander individuals. This is because it focuses on knowledge and capacities rather than on what people do not know or cannot do (as can be the case when a 'one size fits

▼ Table 12.1

Co-constructing learning with Aboriginal and Torres Strait Islander students and communities

Questions to think about	Strategies
Have I provided an opportunity for students to have input about what they are learning?	Ask students what they would like to learn. This can be done through discussion or pictures shown with the topics that align with curriculum. Do I know my students? (APST 1.4)
Have I built relationships with local Aboriginal Elders and community about local Aboriginal and Torres Strait Islander knowledges, history, and learning?	Make time to go to Aboriginal and Torres Strait Islander events so that a reciprocal relationship can be developed (i.e., it is important to not just take knowledge from communities). Are Aboriginal and Torres Strait knowledges and histories in the local area being shared with all students? (APST 2.4)
Have I asked the students would they like to learn?	Provide opportunities in your class to ask such a question and provide students the opportunity for discussion about this. Go into community and discuss the needs and interests of your students (also see Chapter 7).

all' curriculum is imposed). It recognises that the community is a rich source of resources; assumes that people are able to learn, grow, and change; encourages positive expectations of children as learners; and, perhaps most importantly, it is characterised by collaborative relationships (Scerra, 2011).

A story from practice: Building and establishing new relationships – co-constructing a science lesson using Aboriginal knowledge

Out of respect, and to maintain the confidentiality of the town and people who supported Elizabeth (non-Indigenous teacher) to implement co-constructed pedagogies, pseudonyms are used in the following vignette.

After five years of teaching Elizabeth moved and started teaching a composite class of year 4 and 5 in a school that had a high number of Aboriginal and Torres Strait Islander students. After being shown around the school and taken to her classroom, she asked her Principal if there was a community Elder who was involved with the school. He explained there were a couple of Elders and gave her the Elders' details and so she got in contact with Aunty Lisa and Uncle Paul. After exchanging text messages, she set up a meeting where they discussed local significant and sacred sites and some other information about the area and what sports the students played and what families in the area did on the weekends. They did not plan another time to meet up, but Elizabeth asked Aunty Lisa and Uncle Paul if she saw them around town if it was okay to stop and have a chat as she knew they were busy.

Next Elizabeth attended the local sporting events and social events Aunty Lisa and Uncle Paul had talked about. She saw a few familiar faces of school parents that had brought their children to school on the first day. Because that day can be quite hectic she did not get to talk to all of them, so at these events she made sure to say hello, reintroduced herself and asked them how their child was enjoying school. The parents seemed to appreciate her interest in their child. She also offered to open her classroom up so they could come and have a chat anytime. One parent took up this offer and came and sat in the classes for a couple of days. This was a great time for Elizabeth to get to know her and have a yarn at recess and lunch times. She also bumped in to Aunty Lisa quite a few times as well and always had a yarn with her. Her contact with Uncle Paul was not as frequent, but they always stopped and talked when they did see each other. The more she saw the parents and Elders, the longer they talked. This was a great way to start good relationships with well-respected community members.

Half way through first term Sheree, who was the Indigenous Teaching Assistant, suggested that a parent's morning tea in our classroom should be held. Aunty

Lisa and Uncle Paul were invited along with the parents. Sheree and Elizabeth also thought it would be a good time to yarn about what would be good learning and teaching in the classroom. Both Elders attended and brought other community members with them. There was quite a good turnout and there was lots of good discussion about what the students, parents, and community would like to see happening in the classroom.

What the parents and community members indicated was that they wanted more inclusion of Aboriginal and Torres Strait Islander knowledge. The students, on the other hand, indicated that they wanted to do fun things, but when this was unpacked it came down to a more hands-on approach so that they could make, collect, play with and build things. After the morning tea Elizabeth sat down with the students and asked them what they would like to learn about. The students came up with the idea of looking at bush medicine because some of the students in the class had mosquito bites. Elizabeth was pleased because bush medicine provides a good link with the Science, History and English curriculum and the cross-curriculum priorities of Aboriginal and Torres Strait Islander histories, cultures and sustainability.

Next the lessons were co-constructed with Elizabeth asking the students what they thought was the best way to start the unit of work. They suggested that she talk to their parents and Aunty Lisa about what were the best bush medicines to use and when that was determined, the class should walk down to the bush and find it. This was done with input from Sheree (ITA), Aunty Lisa and also two parents who went on the walk to find the bush medicine.

The students were excited about their co-constructed lesson and as they walked in the bush with everyone, they taught Elizabeth the names of plants in their language and showed her places that they often visit. Once it was cooked and cooled the medicine was applied to the mosquito bites. As a final step the group discussed what they did and why they did it this way. This information was used to write up a procedure (Australian National Curriculum English - Year 4 ACELY1688; ACELY1690; Year 5 ACELY1704, ACELY1705) of how to collect and make bush medicine (Australian National Curriculum Science - Year 4 ACSSU074).

Danielle Armour and Jodie Miller

Co-constructive culturally responsive teaching experiences

An effective learning environment for Indigenous students has many dimensions. For example, as we saw above, it includes creating situations where students can connect to and understand the importance of learning. It also involves the teachers providing hands-on experiences which convey the social meaning of the idea (Matthews, Howard, & Perry, 2003; St. Denis, 2010). These things can be achieved by building on the knowledge and experience that ITAs have about their community. Together these aspects entail working in your classroom to establish a meaningful, effective, and culturally safe learning environment (St. Denis, 2010).

While this might seem easier to achieve in some subject areas than others, with careful consideration such a co-constructed curriculum can be achieved across all of the curriculum. For instance, the following provides an example of how this can be achieved in a mathematics lesson.

A mathematical framework for co-constructing pedagogies: Goompi model (Chris Matthews)

It is important to acknowledge that mathematics is not free of culture and, therefore, is influenced by cultural bias (Matthews, 2009) (also see Chapter 11). This is reflected in many pedagogies for teaching mathematics which draw on Western perspectives. A model that diverges from this is the Goompi model (this is also named as RAMR model and cloud model) developed by Dr Chris Matthews (2009) (see Figure 12.2). This model forefronts students' culture and lived reality, and provides a framework to co-construct learning through examining creativity, symbols, and cultural biases to arrive at mathematical concepts. For many students, they only experience mathematics in the image depicted by the cloud (abstract), having limited opportunity to connect mathematics to their lives. This requires teachers to not only shift from a traditionalist approach to teaching mathematics, but also consider the lived reality and local context of their learners. As such, teachers may need to adapt learning materials that reflect the lived experiences for their students.

The Goompi model provides an opportunity to create a learning environment where students develop mathematical understanding by co-constructing the context and influencing the pedagogical approaches of the lesson. Hence, this model

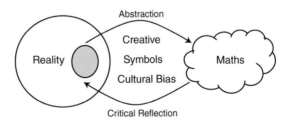

▲ Figure 12.2

Goompi model (Matthews, 2009)

can be used to create new pedagogies in mathematics forefront culture and cultural expression (Matthews, 2012). The key features of the model are:

- Students choose a particular reality or lived experience to situate the mathematics;
- Students create an abstract representation of the reality/real-life situation, using a combination of creative and symbolic language and representations;
- Students then use the mathematics in the abstract form to explore particular attributes and behaviours of the real-life situation and then communicate these ideas with others;
- Students then critically reflect on their mathematical representations to determine if it fits with the observed reality;
- This cycle between abstraction and critical reflection continues so that mathematical knowledge is created, developed and refined.

(Matthews, 2009, p. 47–48)

Examples of pedagogical approaches developed from the Goompi model are *mathematics as story-telling* and *mathematics as dance* (see Matthews, 2012, for examples of this; also visit the ATSIMA website: https://atsimanational.ning. com/). It can be used in both primary and secondary settings to teach mathematics.

A story from practice: Co-constructing a mathematics lesson drawing on students' lived experience

Sally was a new graduate teacher working in a Year 2 classroom. She had been working in a remote community for 8 months.

As a primary school teacher, she was aware that she needed to contextualise learning for her students. However, sometimes she found it challenging to teach mathematics for two reasons: first, she was not confident to link culture to mathematics, and second, she found the language of mathematics and mapping to students' home languages challenging, yet she knew to draw on her students' home language and contexts is important because it demonstrates that she values students' culture (see Chapter 6) and it also provides an opportunity for the students to connect mathematics with their everyday lives.

Despite these concerns, she was able to successfully implement the following measurement lesson with her students in a way that provided a more meaningful context for them.

Specifically, the lesson focused on comparing and ordering lengths (Australian National Curriculum Mathematics – Year 2 ACMMG037). The day prior to the lesson the class had compared and ordered lengths of objects in our classroom using non-standard units (ribbon). At the end of the lesson, there was a discussion about where measurement and comparison are used and how to order measurements in our everyday lives. Many students spoke about fishing with their families on the weekend and comparing the fish to know which they could take home and the fish they needed to return to the sea. For example, one of the students said: "My dad and I measure when we go fishing".

Following this, Sally worked with her co-teacher (an Indigenous Teacher Assistant) to determine which fish were located in the local area. We also invited a local fisherman into the classroom to discuss fishing with the students. Once we had a list of fish the students decided that they would like to make their own measuring tools to determine and compare the lengths of fish. The class worked together to make a class chart which the students wanted to take home to share with their families. With the Indigenous Teacher Assistant the students ensured that all the fish (where possible) were identified using local language names. The also created a mathematics vocabulary chart focusing on the language of comparing – moving between local language and English terms.

In this way it was possible to make this maths lesson a richer experience both for the students and for the teacher because they could all see the relevance of mathematics in their everyday lives.

Danielle Armour and Jodie Miller

Conclusion

Effective teachers of Aboriginal and Torres Strait Islander students understand their cultures, histories and place in contemporary life (Sarra, 2011). They work to develop good relationships with their students, their families, community members and Elders and are flexible in adjusting to the needs of the students. By doing so, they foster an environment where learning expectations, including empowerment and wellbeing are addressed. This also means students can feel safe in their environment and have a voice in what they learn. The pedagogy is based upon a co-constructed model of learning which allows teachers to focus on the knowledge and capacities of their students, promoting a strengths-based approach. Using a strengths-based approach celebrates the identity and culture of the students and is achieved through two-way learning and a culturally responsive curriculum. However, this is a process that takes time to develop and although it may be a long journey, it is an important one to take.

Reflective questions

1. How can you co-construct learning?
2. Why is localised learning important? How could you implement localised learning in your curriculum?
3. How can the Goompi model created by Matthews be used in your teaching?

References

Armour, D. (2016). *Aboriginal education officers working at the cultural interface: Nguli yoo boy ngoo Yulling Ngunya* (Unpublished doctoral thesis). Australian Catholic University, Brisbane, Australia.

Armour, D., Warren, E., & Miller, J. (2016). Working together: Strategies that support cross-cultural engagement of Indigenous teacher assistants working in Indigenous contexts. *Asia-Pacific Journal of Teacher Education*, 44(5), 421–435.

Bennett, B., Redfern, H., & Zubrzycki, J. (2017). Cultural responsiveness in action: Co-constructing social work curriculum resources with Aboriginal Communities. *British Journal of Social Work*, 48(3), 808–825.

Blair, N. (2015). *Privileging Australian Indigenous knowledge: Sweet potatoes, spiders, water-lilys, and brick walls*. Chicago, IL: Common Ground.

Coff, K., & Lampert, L. (2019). Mentoring as two-way learning: An Australian First Nations/non-Indigenous collaboration. *Frontiers in Education*, 4(4), 24. doi: 10.3389/feduc.2019.00024

Doige, L. A. C. (2003). A missing link: Between traditional Aboriginal education and the Western system of education. *Canadian Journal of Native Education*, 27(2), 144.

Frawley, J., Fasoli, L., d'Arbon, T., & Ober, R. (2010). The Linking Worlds research project: Identifying intercultural educational leadership capabilities. *Leading and Managing*, 16(1), 1–15.

Harrison, N., & Greenfield, M. (2011). Relationship to place: Positioning Aboriginal knowledge and perspectives in classroom pedagogies. *Critical Studies in Education*, 52(1), 65–76.

Hunt, J. (2013) *Engagement with Indigenous communities in key sectors*, Issue paper no. 5. Canberra: Closing the Gap Clearinghouse. http://www.aihw.gov.au/uploadedFiles/ClosingTheGap/Content/Publications/2013/ctgc-rs23.pdf

Hickling-Hudson, A., & Ahlquist, R. (2003). Contesting the curriculum in the schooling of Indigenous children in Australia and the United States: From Eurocentrism to culturally powerful pedagogies. *Comparative Education Review*, 47(1), 64–89. doi:10.1086/345837

Kearney, E., McIntosh, L., Perry, B., Dockett, S., & Clayton, K. (2014). Building positive relationships with Indigenous children, families and communities: Learning at the cultural interface. *Critical Studies in Education*, 55(3), 338–352.

Lewthwaite, B. E., Osborne, B., Lloyd, N., Boon, H., Llewellyn, L., Webber, T., Laffin, G., Harrison, M., Day, C., Kemp, C., & Wills, J. (2015). Seeking a pedagogy of difference: What Aboriginal students and their parents in North Queensland say about teaching and their learning. *Australian Journal of Teacher Education*, 40(5). 10.14221/ajte.2015v40n5.8

Lowe, K., & Yunkaporta, T. (2013). The inclusion of Aboriginal and Torres Strait Islander content in the Australian National Curriculum: A cultural, cognitive and socio-political evaluation. *Curriculum Perspectives*, 33(1), 1–14.

Marika, R. (1999). Milthun latju wanga womgu Yolŋu: Valuing Yolŋu knowledge in the education system. *Ngoonjook: A Journal of Australian Indigenous Issues*, 16, 107–120.

Matthews, C. (2009). Stories and symbols: Maths as storytelling. *Professional Voice*, 6(3), 45–50.

Matthews, C. (2012). Maths as storytelling: Maths is beautiful. In K. Price (Ed.) *Aboriginal and Torres Strait Islander education: An introduction for the teaching profession*. Melbourne, VIC: Cambridge University Press, pp. 94–112.

Matthews, S., Howard, P., & Perry, B. (2003). Working together to enhance Australian Aboriginal students' mathematics learning. In L. Bragg, C. Campbell, G. Herbert, & J. Mousley (Eds.) *Mathematics education research: Innovation, networking opportunity*. Geelong, VIC: Mathematics Education Research Group of Australasia, pp. 9–28.

Martin, K. (2006). *Please knock before you enter: An investigation of how rainforest Aboriginal people regulate outsiders and the implications for Western research and researchers* (Doctoral thesis, James Cook University, Townsville, Australia). http://eprints.jcu.edu.au/4745

Martin, K. (2008). Aboriginal worldview, knowledge and relatedness: Re-conceptualising Aboriginal schooling as a teaching-learning and research interface. *Journal of Australian Indigenous Issues*, 12, 66–78.

Moreton-Robinson, A., Singh, D., Kolopenuk, J., Robinson, A., & Walter, M. (2012). *Learning the lessons? Pre-service teacher preparation for teaching Aboriginal and Torres Strait Islander students*. Melbourne: Australian Institute for Teaching and School Leadership. (Prepared in partnership with the Queensland University of Technology Indigenous Studies Research Network.)

Nakata, M. (2002). Indigenous knowledge and the cultural interface. In A. Hickling-Hudson, J. Matthews, & A. Woods (Eds.) *Disrupting preconceptions: Postcolonialism and education*. Flaxton, QLD: Post Pressed, pp. 19–38.

Ober, R. (2009). Both-ways: Learning from yesterday, celebrating today, strengthening tomorrow. *Australian Journal of Indigenous Education*, 38S, 34–39.

Pearson, N. (2009). Radical hope: Education and equality in Australia. *Quarterly Essay*, 35, 1–105.

Phillips, J., & Lampert, J. (2012). *Introductory Indigenous studies in education: Reflection and the importance of knowing*. Frenchs Forest: Pearson Education.

Sarra, C. (2005). *Strong and smart: Reinforcing Aboriginal perceptions of being Aboriginal at Cherbourg State School* (Doctoral thesis, Murdoch University, Perth, Western Australia). http://researchrepository.murdoch.edu.au/id/eprint/1687

Sarra, C. (2011). *Strong and Smart – Towards a pedagogy for emancipation: Education for First Peoples*. Abingdon, UK: Routledge.

Sarra, G., Matthews, C., Ewing, B., & Cooper, T. (2011). Indigenous mathematics: Creating an equitable learning environment. In N. Purdie, G. Milgate, & H. R. Bell (Eds.) *Two way teaching and learning: Toward culturally reflective and relevant education*. Camberwell, VIC: Australian Council for Educational Research Press, pp. 173–185.

Scerra, N. (2011) *Strengths-based practice: The evidence*. Parramatta, NSW: Uniting Care Social Justice Unit.

St. Denis, V. (2010). *A study of Aboriginal teachers' professional knowledge and experience in Canadian schools*. Canadian Teachers' Federation and Canadian Council on Learning. https://www.oise.utoronto.ca/otso/UserFiles/File/ABORIGINAL_Report2010_EN_Web.pdf

White, N., Ober, R., Frawley, J., & Bat, M. (2009). Intercultural leadership: Strengthening leadership capabilities for Indigenous education. In N. Cranston (Ed.), *Australian leadership today*. Bowen Hills, QLD: Australian Academic Press, pp. 85–103.

Yunkaporta, T. (2009). *Aboriginal pedagogies at the cultural interface*. (Doctoral thesis, James Cook University, Townsville, Australia)

Chapter 13

Aboriginal and Torres Strait Islander students at school

Strengths analysis

Ellen Grote and Tomzarni Dann

Who we are

Ellen Grote

Ellen grew up in the north-eastern part of the United States and has German and Irish heritage. She taught English as an Additional Language in the USA, West Africa, and the United Kingdom before emigrating to Australia with her own family 20 years ago. When she arrived in Perth, her academic interests and activities shifted to research, focusing on teaching and learning English as an Additional Dialect. She worked on a number of Aboriginal English research projects, including for her own doctoral and post-doctoral studies. She spent time visiting remote communities in Western Australia's Kimberley region, working in partnership with Aboriginal colleagues to engage with community Elders to gain an understanding of their perspectives on various government services. Her more recent projects and publications have focused on different aspects of Aboriginal Education, including developing a Needs Analysis framework that teachers can adapt to build on the strengths and interests of Indigenous (and other) learners.

Tomzarni Dann

Tomzarni is from Broome, Western Australia with family connections to Nyul Nyul, Bardi and Nyinkina country in the Kimberley region of Western Australia. He has an Associate Degree in Indigenous Community Development and Management. He has been working with Aboriginal youth in leadership, mentoring, and career development for the past seven years. He is very passionate about seeing the youth of today become leaders of tomorrow.

Introduction

Teachers can help students to succeed in the classroom by adapting their teaching program in ways that build on learners' existing knowledge and skills to address their learning needs (Armstrong et al., 2012). Undertaking a systematic strengths analysis (SA) might sound quite technical, but it is simply the name of a strategy that provides a structure for guiding teachers as they collect information about the students by drawing on a range of sources and using a variety of methods. Teachers can then organise and analyse this body of information and use it to determine the best way to support Indigenous and other learners. It can help teachers identify such matters as their areas of interests, what motivates them, what they are good at, how they learn best and what they want to learn. This strategy enables teachers to find out practical information that can be used as the basis for developing a curriculum that capitalises on learners' strengths to scaffold their learning. The learning objectives, lesson plans, materials as well as teaching and learning strategies that result from this kind of SA is then credible and justifiable. This is because it is based on evidence that teachers gather together rather than on their own assumptions or intuition (Long, 2005).

Strengths analysis

Conducting an SA is particularly important for educators of Indigenous students (and of course all students) who are linguistically and culturally diverse, particularly as the teaching workforce remains predominantly non-Aboriginal. Indigenous students may speak a form of English that sounds like Standard Australian English (SAE), but many Indigenous children and young people speak Aboriginal English (AbE) as a first or additional language (Eades, 2013). Indigenous languages are spoken at home by approximately 1.9% of First Nations Australian people in urban areas and about 14.3% in rural and remote communities (ABS, 2017). Undertaking an SA offers teachers an opportunity to gain an understanding of their students as whole individuals so that they can adapt the curriculum in ways that value the linguistic and cultural backgrounds of Indigenous learners while addressing their learning needs (see Chapter 8 for a more detailed discussion of Indigenous students' home languages and communication practices).

Another advantage of conducting an SA is that it can provide opportunities for teachers to engage effectively to work in partnership with Indigenous learners and their families. The information collection process can help teachers to develop positive relationships with students and their families and communities. By understanding the students' backgrounds and home life experiences, teachers and students develop mutual respect, the basis of good relationships, which has been shown to be fundamental to students' learning (Byrne & Munns, 2012) (see Chapter 7).

Undertaking an SA provides additional benefits for the future learning of the students in your classroom. During transition time when information about students is 'handed over' to next year's teacher, the SA records kept regarding learners' interests, what motivates them and how they learn best can be passed on as well. This provides increased continuity for student learning and helps the next teacher in curriculum planning.

In this chapter we define what an SA is in relation to strength-based education and identify and describe the various aspects of learners' lives to consider in the SA process to ensure that it views learners as whole individuals and first and foremost works identifying from the young person's interests, strengths, skills, knowledges and support systems. We then offer practical guidelines for planning an SA. We discuss how information can be collected using different sources and methods as well as how to organise and analyse that body of information in a systematic way so that it can be analysed. We explain how teachers can plan to better support students based on the evidence that they have collected and make adjustments in the curriculum.

It is important to note that although the procedures for undertaking an SA are set out in a step-by-step way, the process is an iterative one. As such, it usually requires going back and repeating some steps, such as collecting more information from another source to verify what has already been collected. This will ensure that teachers can have confidence in what they find out from the process.

It is also important to acknowledge that on the surface an SA process is very much focused on students' strengths. However, it is essential that this process involves teachers looking critically at their own practices (and perhaps even their own needs) whilst also understanding the needs of students. The practice of critical self-reflection (see Chapter 3) is an excellent process that should be a part of the SA process. Moreover, conducting an SA should be seen as one part of an overall suite of educational approaches that teachers undertake to ensure that the educational outcomes of all Indigenous (and non-Indigenous) students are met.

The SA procedures outlined here constitute one model. As such, they might need to be altered in order to recognise the realities of the teaching situation and the time available. It is a model that is flexible so that it can be adapted as required to urban, regional, and remote school locations. What is important, however, is that multiple sources and methods are used, that the different dimensions of learners' lives are taken into account and that the SA is conducted in a systematic way.

What is an SA?

An SA is the process of systematically gathering and analysing information about students' strengths and learning requirements with the aim of developing or adapting an appropriate curriculum. It draws and builds on the research literature from the area of *needs analysis* which is usually applied to developing curricula for learning an additional language or dialect (Brown, 2015; Long, 2005; Oliver, Grote, Rochecouste, & Exell, 2013). As such, the SA model described in this chapter advocates for an evidence gathering process that emphasises a focus on the strengths that Indigenous (and other) learners already have.

The SA framework is also based on the understanding that learners, their families, and their communities are important sources of knowledge. They are the ones who are most familiar with what interests learners, what they are good at, what drives them to want to learn and how to engage them so they are more likely to learn. The SA model we discuss here also extends the needs analysis model to consider the various domains that can impact upon learning (Haig, 2018). These include the learner's physical health; social, emotional, spiritual,

Ellen Grote and Tomzarni Dann

Domains to be considered in an SA

Domain	Examples
Physical health	General health, hearing, vision, nutrition, sleep quality, substance abuse and other physical health issues that can affect learning ability
Social, emotional, spiritual, and cultural wellbeing	Stability of relationships and home environment, bereavement and other sources of stress that affect school attendance and participation; connection to culture; bullying and racism
Linguistic	Aboriginal English, Standard Australian English as an additional language or dialect, country
Educational	Subject area knowledge and skills (e.g., maths, science, history, Standard Australian English language and writing conventions and communication practices)
Other	Level of support at home, quiet space, books, academic role models, access to computers

and cultural wellbeing; linguistic background, as well as the educational realm. These are shown with examples in Table 13.1.

Although the categories in Table 13.1 are described as separate entities, they are not necessarily discrete. An issue identified in one domain often overlaps and affects aspects of those in one or more others. An example of this is conductive hearing loss which is associated with the physical health domain. Indigenous children are particularly vulnerable to chronic hearing loss with approximately 8% of Indigenous children aged 0 to 14 affected and those living in remote communities at greater risk (11%) (Australian Health Ministers' Advisory Council, 2017). Also known as otitis media, the disease can lead to temporary or even permanent hearing loss if left untreated (Australian Institute of Health and Welfare, 2018). For young Indigenous children who acquire Standard Australian English as an additional language or dialect (linguistic and cultural domain) at school, this ear disease can limit their capacity to hear the sounds of the language and makes it difficult for them to distinguish the subtle differences between similar consonant sounds such as *b, p* and *v* or *sh* and *ch* (Aithal, Yonovitz, & Aithal, 2008). Children's learning is further disadvantaged by the disease when developing reading and writing skills, which initially depend on understanding the relationships between sounds and letters (knowledge and skills domain). Children who are unable to hear properly are also less likely to engage fully in whole class activities. This, in turn, can negatively affect their relationships with other students (social, emotional, spiritual, and cultural wellbeing domain). Strategies that can be used for learners with conductive hearing loss are discussed in greater detail in Burrow, Galloway, & Weissofner (2009). Also see Thomson, Burns, & McLoughlin (2012) for an overview of other issues relating to physical health as well as social, emotional, spiritual, and cultural wellbeing.

It is important to note that the Aboriginal concept of spirituality is seen to be closely interconnected with social, emotional, and cultural wellbeing as well as physical health, each one having an impact on the others. (Note: in Table 13.1 we have placed physical health in a separate domain for the practical purposes of a Strengths Analysis). Unlike Western understandings, the notion of the spiritual is inseparable from that of the physical realm. From an Aboriginal perspective, spirituality is viewed as:

> a dynamic, evolving, contemporary expression of Indigineity. Spirituality connects past, present and future. Spirituality emphasises people's relationships with each other, the living (other entities — animals) and non-living (mating season, tides, wind and mythology) life forces premised by an understanding or experience of their place of origination.
>
> (Poroch et al., 2009, p. 2)

How to undertake an SA

The optimum time to embark on an SA is at the beginning of the school year after the teacher has had a chance to develop a good rapport with the learners. As discussed above, conducting an SA provides additional opportunities to develop positive relationships with students, their families, and members of their community by getting to know them better and developing mutual trust and respect. In this way the SA process can become part of relationship building which is pivotal to learning (again, see Chapter 7).

When planning an SA, it is advantageous to use a variety of sources and methods to collect information (or data) that teachers will later analyse, use to draw conclusions and then to adjust the curriculum. To gain a whole perspective of the student, important information can be gathered from individuals that the teacher has developed good relationships with such as caregivers, Elders, aunties, uncles, school support staff. Teacher observations as well as school records and other relevant documents can provide valuable information to develop the SA. Methods of collecting information that are useful can involve talking or yarning with people outlined above and observing learners in the classroom. Both require taking handwritten notes or making audio or video recordings (and then viewing and taking notes on the recordings later).

With regard to recording devices, it is important to be very cautious when introducing the idea of using such equipment. While some people may be fine with having their voices recorded, others might feel uncomfortable. Shay (2019) discusses how quickly the dynamic can change when introducing recording (audio and video) devices with some Indigenous peoples, particularly as these have been used to exploit and surveil Indigenous peoples in the past (and some might argue today). Moreover, the presence of recording instruments can signify to some people a formality and authority that will change the entire dynamic of an interaction or conversation. Removing the possibility of a recording device's potential negative impact may ensure the accuracy of the person's input. Therefore, whilst using these are effective for developing a clear picture and ensuring information is correct, there are alternatives. When writing information with the person observing, they can see what you are writing so it becomes a shared and transparent process.

Using different sources and methods is highly recommended because it increases the amount of evidence you can obtain. It also enhances the quality of the body of information. Another benefit is that it provides opportunities to compare and cross-check the information collected from the different sources and methods. This process, known as *triangulation*, ensures the trustworthiness of the information on which the teacher develops the curriculum (Long, 2005).

Sources

The sources used for collecting information for the SA will depend on the teaching situation and the age of the students. Typical sources of information about a learner's strengths and needs include the stakeholders in the learner's education, documents, questionnaires and a reflective journal (which may be part of normal teacher assessment records or may simply be notes jotted down in the margins of a daily work pad). An overview of sources with examples is displayed in Table 13.2.

Assuming a strengths-based approach to an SA, the students themselves become the starting point as they provide valuable insight and information. Talking or *yarning* with students at this point provides an opportunity to get to know them better and vice versa. (The practice of yarning is discussed in more detail below.) Explaining the purpose (the *why*) of the undertaking, the procedures (the *how*), the participants (the *who*) what you hope to learn (the *outcome*) and how this knowledge will be used are important components to include in such a conversation. Furthermore, students should be encouraged to ask questions so that the process is as transparent as possible and so that they are encouraged see themselves as valued contributors to the endeavour.

Other stakeholders who can be helpful in contributing to this might include the student's caregivers, family and community members and other staff members who might be familiar with the student such as their previous teacher, the librarian, chaplain, school principal or school-based Aboriginal and Torres Strait Islander Education Officers (note that these role titles vary across states). Including stakeholders who are familiar with the learners in the school setting, as well as those who know them at home and in their community, can give a more meaningful picture of the learner's strengths and needs. Moreover, if resistance is encountered from a student or family member, the Aboriginal or Torres Strait Islander Education Officer or another stakeholder who knows the student or family member well might be able to suggest an alternative strategy to assist in explaining the aims of SA and help the teacher to gain their trust and confidence

▼ Table 13.2
Potential sources of information

Sources	Examples
Stakeholders	Students, caregivers, Elders, aunties, uncles, cousins, sisters, brothers, teachers (the student's previous teachers or those that students have in other subjects), relief teachers, teaching aides, Aboriginal Education Officers, other relevant school staff
Documents	School records, test results, student's work
Questionnaires	Filled out by students, caregivers, relevant school staff
Reflective journal	Teacher's formal and informal observation notes

to facilitate the process. One of the features of the SA approach is the use of multiple sources and methods, so that various options are available to the teacher.

Documents

Some of the more obvious documents to consider as sources when gathering information for an SA include: any past and current official records held by the school or previous teachers, NAPLAN test scores, as well as student assignments and assessments. These documents can be helpful, but of course it is important to bear in mind that there is a power imbalance between those who record the documents (school administration and teachers) and those who they are about (the students). It is advisable that in ensuring an SA is accurate that teachers cross-check these documents with the perspectives and stories of students alongside them.

Perhaps less obvious, but still useful, are the unofficial types of writing that students produce in their free time. These can contribute useful insights into the learner's strengths and interests inside and outside the classroom. Inviting students to offer some of their personal writing such as their poetry, music lyrics or stories can shed light on their skills or suggest social, emotional, and spiritual wellbeing concerns. Teachers can ask the student's permission to photocopy them so that they have time to read or view them and include them in the analysis. Showing interest in a student's personal writing can also help the teacher get to know the learner better, develop a positive relationship and provide a more in-depth view of skills that might be transferable to the classroom setting (Grote, 2006).

Questionnaires

To obtain other kinds of information, you can develop questionnaires designed for the different stakeholders. Questionnaires should be carefully tailored so that they get the kind of information that learners, family and community members are likely to be able to share. The questions should also be worded carefully so that they can be easily understood by the respondent. Using plain language and avoiding teaching jargon will help to make sure that the questions are 'reader-friendly', cannot be misinterpreted or cause frustration. This is particularly important for caregivers and others who may not speak Standard Australian English as a first language or dialect. It is important to note that Indigenous students as well as family and community members may not feel comfortable filling out or responding to information requested in questionnaires. An alternative approach is to organise home visits and use the questionnaire topics as a guide when talking or yarning with them as a way of learning more about the learner. See below regarding talking or yarning (interviewing) techniques to gather information when making home visits to ensure that the interaction is undertaken in a culturally sensitive and appropriate manner.

To access the kind of information you are seeking and to make it easy for respondents to provide answers, different types of question or statement formats should be considered. Questionnaires can include both *closed-* and *open-ended* questions. Closed-ended questions, which usually require short answers, are useful

Ellen Grote and Tomzarni Dann

to obtain basic information such as siblings' ages, the number of hours spent on homework and *yes* or *no* answers. Open-ended questions provide opportunities for respondents to describe, explain, give examples, elaborate on an issue or raise a concern that has not been specifically mentioned. Because multiple methods will be used to gather information, the teacher can explore these open-ended question topics further when talking or yarning during a home visit. (This method is discussed in more detail below in relation to talking or yarning in interviews.)

Another type of survey can be used that asks the person (e.g., caregiver, teacher, other staff member or student) to rate the student's level of skills, knowledge, interest or other measurable qualities by offering general descriptive terms such as *excellent, good, fair, poor, very poor*. Another possibility is to make a statement and ask people to indicate the extent to which they agree or disagree with it by ticking a box or circling the answer. To make sure that the respondents understand how to respond, you can provide examples of questions with illustrations on how they should be answered. A summary of some of the basic forms of questions or statements that can be used to elicit information in a questionnaire is shown in Table 13.3.

Before distributing a questionnaire it is always a good idea to get feedback on the readability, clarity, and effectiveness of the questions. It is particularly important that the feedback be provided by an Aboriginal and / or Torres Strait Islander person. A practical way of doing this is to ask a friend, family member, or colleague to read through the questions and answer them. For a questionnaire intended for students, try it out on a child or young person near the age of the target students. It is also important to ensure that cultural protocols have been considered and that the language used in the questionnaire is appropriate to the local context. For example, asking specific personal questions may be considered rude in some cultural contexts.

▼ Table 13.3

Types of questions or statements that elicit information on a questionnaire

Question format	Example
Open-ended	Which school subjects does your child like the most? Why do you think that is?
Closed	Who usually helps your child with homework?
Closed (yes-no)	Does your child have access to a mobile phone to access the internet at home?
Rating	How interested is your child in science? (Please circle one.)
	No interest - some interest - a lot of interest
	On a scale of 1 to 10, how happy do you think your child is at school? (Please circle a number.)
	1 2 3 4 5 6 7 8 9 10
	unhappy *very happy*
Questions of degree, level or frequency	When doing homework, how often does your child ask for help? (Please circle one.)
	Never – Rarely – Sometimes – Often – Always
Level of agreement/ disagreement	Tick the box that seems right to you.
	My child looks forward to going to school in the morning.
	☐ *I agree strongly.*
	☐ *I agree.*
	☐ *I disagree.*
	☐ *I disagree strongly.*

Finally, consider the best strategy to distribute the questionnaires so that you will get them filled out and returned to you. For the caregivers of younger students, questionnaires could be posted or hand delivered when caregivers pick their children up. In other cases, you might need to contact the stakeholder directly, and ask them the best way to get them the questionnaire and get it returned to you. In some cases, it might also be useful to offer to make an appointment to take the questionnaire to individuals and assist them in filling it out. This can be a good way to meet and get to know families in your school community (see Chapter 12 for an example of how this can be done).

Reflective journal

Another valuable source of information is a reflective journal where you can record your observations about students' knowledge, skills, and other relevant information (see Chapter 15 for an example of this). This can be done by making brief notes in a journal (or as indicated in teacher records or in the margins of your daily work pad) throughout the day when possible, or soon afterwards when more time is available. By recording reflections, you can keep track of and look for issues that might require further exploration. Ideas that emerge from these might also be included in subsequent questionnaires or interviews. (Other ways a journal like this can be used for an SA are discussed below.)

It is critical to note, however, that prior to recording such observations, teachers should talk with students about what they are doing and why they are doing it. Being transparent about the process with students and even offering to share those observations with them are essential strategies to ensure that students know why a teacher is taking notes. Teachers must make it clear to students the purpose of the notes, how they are written, and how they will be used to contribute to the overall outcome of the process. As highlighted in other chapters, relationships are central and ensuring that these are not jeopardised is critical.

Methods

There are a number of ways to collect information about students' strengths and needs that a teacher can consider when doing an SA. The most common ones include talking and yarning with people close to the student, observing students while teaching and observing them while someone else is in charge. These are shown in Table 13.4. Deciding which methods to select again depends on the classroom situation and the time available. Nonetheless, all methods require some planning and preparation.

Talking or yarning

Yarning or having a yarn with someone is "telling and sharing stories and information" (Bessarab & Ng'andu, 2010, p. 38). As an oral tradition, it can be a

Ellen Grote and Tomzarni Dann

Methods of collecting information

Methods		Examples
Talking and or yarning		The teacher asks the person (student, caregivers or community member, etc.) to talk about an issue in relation to the student. The teacher records the responses by taking handwritten notes or, with permission, audio records the talk and takes notes later. (See above regarding concerns about using recording devices.)
Observing	…while teaching	The teacher observes and later records in a journal observations about the student(s).
	…while not teaching	1. The teacher observes students in a lesson lead by another staff member, or in another setting, and records handwritten notes in real time.
		2. The teacher video records the class or group during a lesson or activity, views the recording and takes notes.

formal exchange of knowledge, but most commonly it is an informal conversation. Nonetheless, it is a familiar and important means of establishing, developing, and maintaining relationships within and across communities. Yarning is also now recognised as an effective research method that is used by and with Indigenous and non-Indigenous researchers and research participants (Bessarab & Ng'andu, 2010; Kovach, 2019).

When planning to meet with caregivers or staff members, design the set of questions or topics so that they are culturally and linguistically appropriate. Using plain language without jargon is always best regardless of the age group or language background. If at all possible, when permission is given, it can useful to audio-record the interview because taking notes while conducting an interview can be challenging. However, the teacher must keep in mind the cautions outlined earlier, and only use these where there is an established relationship of trust and it will not compromise the process. If the person does not want the interview recorded, taking brief notes during the interview is possible, alongside the person so it is a co-written and recorded process (Shay, 2019). It is optimal to co-write these, because in doing so it clarifies the accuracy of the information in the moment (because the person is seeing what is written and can correct what is recorded at any time).

When contacting interviewees to arrange a meeting, you can offer to share with them a list of topics or questions in advance. Knowing in advance what will be discussed will help to put people at ease and gives them time to think about their response. It can also be a good idea to suggest that the person invite another family member or friend to sit with them during the meeting. Alternatively (or in addition), you could say that you will bring along an Indigenous colleague that knows the family, such as an Aboriginal Education Officer, so that they are not the only Aboriginal person in the room.

At the beginning of the interview it is important to develop a rapport before you start posing questions. You can 'break the ice' by using some simple strategies, including: smiling when you greet them, using their name(s), talking about the child (in a positive way), mentioning or enquiring about possible mutual connections you might have with other family or community members, or raising a neutral topic such as a recent sporting event. Above all, be genuine in your interest. It is also a good idea to review why you are doing the interview and that you hope they can help you learn more about the student by sharing what they know.

It is important to note that some Indigenous people can feel uncomfortable when asked direct questions. You might get more informative responses by using an indirect approach, particularly with topics of a sensitive nature. This can be done by reformatting questions as statements and encouraging the person to elaborate on them. For example: "I've noticed that Marlee seems to really like stories about animals and is very good at drawing them. Maybe you can tell me more about other things she likes or is good at," or "Perhaps you could talk a bit more about Kirra's love for basketball." Be aware that you might not get all the answers you are looking for, but if you keep the interview flexible and encourage them to elaborate, the interviewee is more likely to feel comfortable about sharing stories.

During an interview it is important to apply good active listening skills involving non-verbal and verbal signals, such as nodding in agreement or using verbal cues, such as "mmm", "uh huh" or "I see". Another strategy is to briefly summarise what they have said to let them know you have been listening and to clarify understanding. Some Aboriginal people, particularly those in the Kimberley region of Western Australia, might show that they are listening by interjecting "I hear you", "True" or "True God" to communicate agreement; sometimes they will make a clicking sound between the teeth and the inside of the cheek. Disbelief at what they are hearing might be expressed by "oh what!"

It is important to refrain from interrupting the other speaker or talking unnecessarily. Allowing for silences is critical. Some Indigenous people can be more comfortable with long silences than non-Indigenous people. Silences give the person time to think and respond when and how they want to. One should also be aware that making direct eye contact may cause discomfort. In some Indigenous communities, making direct eye contact can be impolite or disrespectful, particularly when speaking to Elders. Awareness of cultural protocols is important. A general rule is to be observant of the interviewee's non-verbal behaviour and follow their lead. (Cultural Capability Team, Queensland Health, 2015; Grote & Rochecouste, 2012)

Observing and taking notes

Your own observations of learners as they engage in whole class, group, or individual activities can provide a good source of information. This can be done while in the role of teacher or while someone else assumes that responsibility. Both methods, however, require a systematic approach. Again it is important to note that whichever approach you take, when observing students and taking notes about them, make sure that students are aware of what you are doing, why you are doing it, and of course how the notes that you are taking will be used.

Observing while teaching and taking abbreviated notes opportunistically is usually done over a period of days or weeks to ensure that information is recorded about every student. At the end of the lesson (or when time permits), teachers can expand on their notes, filling in details later. Observing students while not teaching requires more planning because it requires the assistance of another staff member. In this case, notes can be taken in real time in more detail.

In advance of both types of observations, it can be useful to develop an observation spreadsheet. This is a practical way to ensure that information is recorded about every student, including those who quietly get on with their work without attracting attention. One way of setting up an observation spreadsheet is to list student names on the left side and the domain areas (Table 13.1) across the top. The domains can be subdivided if appropriate for convenience or as particular issues of concern emerge. For example, the language domain might be subdivided into communication skills displayed by individuals while in whole class, group work, or pair work activities.

Analysis of the information collected

Organising and analysing the data you are collecting begins early on so that you can identify and explore areas requiring further attention. Once you have gathered some information and recorded these in your observation notes, questionnaires, or in your journal, it is useful to reread through it so that you become familiar with all the information. This will help you to begin noticing themes or patterns of behaviour. Consider how you might organise the themes or patterns so that you can bring the information (evidence) relating to each theme together in one place. This enables you to examine all aspects of them more closely and identify patterns.

One way of doing this is to set out the different types of information on a spreadsheet (Brown, 2015). This can be sketched out on paper or in an electronic format. Once again, the different domains might be a useful way to organise the information initially. These can be set out across the top row, one for each. As more information is collected, the columns can be subdivided as necessary. The student names can be arranged in a column on the left. As information accumulates, abbreviated notes on students' strengths and needs can be entered into the squares as appropriate for each learner.

Table 13.5 shows a sample of notes made by a teacher of Year 7 students who attend middle school in the Kimberley region of Western Australia. The table should be seen as a work in progress. The information is based on the profiles of actual learners though their names and some details have been changed to obscure their identities.

Colour-coding each domain heading can provide visual assistance in the analysing process. As you read through a questionnaire, interview or journal notes, you can use a highlighter pen to illuminate sections of text that relate to a particular domain. For example, if you notice that a student does not seem to be able to follow verbal instructions, this text section could be highlighted in blue for physical health because it might be a potential hearing problem. Doing it this way makes the information easy to locate later on. Alternatively, you may have observed that a particular student has a real artistic flair and engages best when classroom activities involve drawing as part of the task. Again this is information you can highlight and refer to later.

Sample spreadsheet for analysis

	Physical Health	Social & Emotional Wellbeing	Linguistic and Cultural	Educational	Other
Sarah	Generally active and healthy despite her frequent colds.	Appears to fully engage in the social aspects of school life; doesn't like to miss school. Often finishes tasks quickly, then helps others; downplays her skills; well-liked by peers. Recently, there have been times when Sarah appears to withdraw, daydream or just 'zone out'. This is possibly due to the grieving process she is undergoing following the loss of her mother 3 months ago and missing family in Meekatharra. Sarah has not engaged with a counsellor yet. Note: Useful to talk to her older siblings and auntie.	Family from Meekatharra, WA; AbE is the main home language; Yamatji & some words from a desert dialect are used by father and understood by children. Sarah has excellent oral language skills and is good at storytelling/ yarning She switches easily from AbE (when talking to friends) to SAE (when talking to me). She sometimes explains my instructions to another student using AbE.	Strengths: Reading, writing speaking, listening, maths, science, art. Displays creativity & imagination in oral/ written storytelling & artwork. Enjoys: Reading, writing, solving problems in science and maths. Interests: Animals, music, basketball, outdoors, fishing. In the short term, must provide more challenging tasks; in the long term, must talk to learning support teacher to discuss Sarah's enrolment in an enrichment program.	Sarah attends school fairly regularly, except when missing the bus; her absences are for a short time. Father is the main caregiver and is devoted to looking after his children. This is despite offers from other family members to step in. As an older parent (age 60) receiving a pension, he is able to stay home to look after the children. Sarah has 4 sisters (Years 2,4,9, 10) as well as 2 little ones at home (sister & brother). The Year 2 sister has serious health issues. Sarah's auntie (her 'mother sister', a local nurse) is aware of Sarah's potential and takes an interest in her education.
Warrin	Generally healthy, but prone to getting middle ear infections.	Appears to enjoy coming to school and being with other children. Note: Warrin's auntie, the AIEO, has been helpful in providing updates on Warrin's home situation.	A creole and Bardi are spoken at home. Speaks AbE and some SAE in classroom, but is self-conscious. His SAE improves as his reading & writing skills develop.	Literacy: Becoming more confident with reading & writing tasks, following ongoing one-to-one help from aide. Does well in science when topic is about nature, especially animals. Prefers maths tasks that relate to practical and other real world problem solving, such as weights, size and other measurements. Topic areas that engage Warrin: Nature, especially wildlife; sports. Outside interests: Basketball, fishing, hunting, BMXing. Continues to struggle with listening skills. Need to consult with family about checking on his ear health & hearing.	Attends school regularly, averaging 3 times a week; often late for school. One of Warrin's aunties is an AIEO at school, who is very helpful. Warrin & his younger sister live with another auntie* (his 'mother sister'), uncle and 4 younger cousins (2 male, 2 female). All children attend school.
Rianne					
Kirra					

Ellen Grote and Tomzarni Dann

The findings

When the information collected has been organised and analysed so that patterns or themes become evident, you can compile a list of *findings*. Some findings might be applied when adjusting what you teach or what approaches you use; others might require some form of action, such as contacting a caregiver to find out if the child's hearing needs to be checked. Some findings are more obvious than others and can be identified early on, while others might require going to an additional source or method to verify it. As mentioned above, the SA process is an iterative one, and using multiple sources and methods makes it possible, for example, to go back and collect more information through observations or interviews so that the finding can be confirmed. This cross-checking of information enables the teacher to be confident in the findings regarding issues that need to be addressed. The teacher can then draw up a plan to modify the curriculum as appropriate or take other forms of action where required.

For example, if one of the findings is that most of the Indigenous students in the class speak Aboriginal English or an Indigenous language at home, then English as an Additional Language strategies must be applied throughout the teaching program. If the teacher discovers that several students have a history of conductive hearing loss, strategies need to be put into place to address the needs of those students. Such strategies include managing the classroom environment to minimise noise and enhance listening; raising student awareness of issues that affect hearing; teaching language and literacy skills on linking sounds and letters; using whole class, group, or individual teaching arrangements; and implementing sound-field amplification technology involving a microphone (worn by the teacher), receiver, and loudspeaker (Massie & Dillon, 2006; Partington & Galloway, 2005). Teachers of adolescent students who discover that some students are prolific poetry writers or keep journals, as Grote found in her own research (2004), can use this knowledge by helping students build on these informal literacy skills and extend them to other more formal academic texts.

Conclusion

In this chapter we have described how to undertake an SA, using an evidence-based and strengths-based approach that enables teachers to identify students' existing knowledge and skills as well as areas requiring attention. Gathering information from a variety of sources and methods provides an abundance of real evidence which can be compared, cross-checked and analysed for patterns or themes in order to draw conclusions about learners' strengths and needs. Teachers can then use these understandings to adapt their teaching as required or take another form of action to enable student success. They can do this with confidence because they have based these modifications on verifiable evidence rather than on their intuitions or that of others (Long, 2005).

Importantly, because the caregivers and students themselves are central, the process of gathering information from them provides teachers a chance to get to know them better. This, in turn, can provide opportunities for teachers to develop positive relationships with students and their families, which is key to enabling Indigenous students to succeed at school.

We have also shown that collecting information about students with respect to their physical health, social, emotional, spiritual and cultural wellbeing, linguistic background as well as their knowledge and skills provides the teacher with a more holistic perspective of learners' strengths and needs. This multifaceted view acknowledges learners as complex individuals whose past and current life experiences outside of school impact on their learning on a day-to-day basis in the classroom. By having this knowledge, teachers can use students' strengths as the basis to address their needs as the learners navigate through this stage of their educational development.

Reflective questions

1. Which sources do you think would be most useful for the age group of students you are likely to teach? Why? Can you think of other sources that are not listed in Table 13.2?
2. What are some actively listening strategies (other than those mentioned above) that you believe can encourage the interviewee to talk?
3. Which methods shown in Table 13.4 do you think would provide the most useful information? Why? What other methods could you add to the list?

References

ABS. (2017). ABS celebrates Indigenous languages during NAIDOC. https://www.abs.gov.au/AUSSTATS/abs@.nsf/mediareleasesbyReleaseDate/1DBCFBCE6CACB75FCA25815400049DBA?OpenDocument

Aithal, S., Yonovitz, A., & Aithal, V. (2008). Perceptual consequences of conductive hearing loss: Speech perception in Indigenous students learning English as a 'school' language. *The Australian and New Zealand Journal of Audiology*, 30(1), 1–18.

Armstrong, S., Buckley, S., Lonsdale, M., Milgate, G., Kneebone, L. B., Cook, L., & Skelton, F. (2012). Starting school: A strengths-based approach toward Aboriginal and Torres Strait Islander children. https://research.acer.edu.au/indigenous_education/27

Australian Health Minister's Advisory Council (2017). Aboriginal and Torres Strait Islander Health Performance Framework 2017 report. https://www.aihw.gov.au/reports/indigenous-australians/health-performance-framework/contents/tier-2-determinants-of-health/2-21-health-behaviours-during-pregnancy

Australian Institute of Health and Welfare (2018). Australia's health 2018. Australia's health series no. 16. https://www.aihw.gov.au/getmedia/12c11184-0c0a-43ad-8386-975c42c38105/aihw-aus-221-chapter-6-4.pdf.aspx

Bessarab, D., & Ng'andu, B. (2010). Yarning about yarning as a legitimate method of Indigenous Research. *International Journal of Critical Indigenous Studies*, 3(1), 37–50.

Brown, J. D. (2015). *Introducing needs analysis and English for specific purposes*. Florence: Taylor and Francis.

Burrow, S., Galloway, A., & Weissofner, N. (2009). Review of educational and other approaches to hearing loss among Indigenous people. *Australian Indigenous Health Bulletin*, 9(2), 1–37. http://healthbulletin.org.au/wp-content/uploads/2009/04/ear_education_review.pdf

Byrne, M., & Munns, G. (2012). From the big picture to the individual student: The importance of the classroom relationship. In Q. Beresford & G. Partington (Eds.) *Reform and resistance in Aboriginal education*. Crawley, WA: UWA Press, pp. 304–334.

Cultural Capability Team, Queensland Health. (2015). Aboriginal and Torres Strait Islander cultural capability. https://www.health.qld.gov.au/__data/assets/pdf_file/0021/151923/communicating.pdf

Eades, D. (2013). *Aboriginal ways of using English*. Canberra: Aboriginal Studies Press.

Grote, E. (2004). An ethnography of writing: The writing practices of female Australian Indigenous adolescents at school. Unpublished doctoral thesis, Edith Cowan University, Mount Lawley, Western Australia.

Grote, E. (2006). Challenging the boundaries between vernacular and school-sponsored writing: Urban Indigenous teenage girls writing in an 'at risk' program. *Language and Education*, 20(6), 478–492.

Grote, E., & Rochecouste, J. (2012). Language and the classroom setting. In Q. Beresford & G. Partington (Eds.) *Reform and resistance in Aboriginal education*. Crawley, WA: UWA Press.

Haig, Y. (2018). English as an additional language learning: A specialist approach with young learners. In R. Oliver & B. Nguyen (Eds.) *Teaching young second language learners: Practices in different contexts*. London: Routledge, pp. XX–XX.

Kovach, M. (2019). Conversational method in Indigenous research. *First Peoples Child & Family Review*, 14(1), 123–136.

Long, M. H. (Ed.) (2005). *Second language needs analysis*. Cambridge: CUP.

Massie, R., & Dillon, H. (2006). The impact of sound-field amplification in mainstream cross-cultural classrooms: Part 1 educational outcomes. *Australian Journal of Education*, 50(1), 62–77.

Oliver, R., Grote, E., Rochecouste, J., & Exell, M. (2013). Needs analysis for task-based teaching: A case study of Indigenous vocational education and training students who speak EAL/EAD. *TESOL in Context*, 22(2), 36–50.

Partington, G., & Galloway, A. (2005). Effective practices in teaching Indigenous students with conductive hearing loss. *Childhood Education*, 82, 101–106.

Poroch, N., Arabena, K., Tongs, J., Larkin, S., Fisher, J., & Henderson, G. (2009). Spirituality and Aboriginal people's social and emotional wellbeing: A review. Discussion Paper No. 11. https://www.lowitja.org.au/content/Document/Lowitja-Publishing/DP_11_spirituality_review.pdf

Shay, M. (2019). Extending the yarning yarn: Collaborative yarning methodology for ethical Indigenist education research. *Australian Journal of Indigenous Education*, 1–9.

Thomson, N., Burns, J., & McLoughlin, N. (2012). The impact of health on the education of Indigenous children. In Q. Beresford, G. Partington, & G. Gower (Eds.) *Reform and resistance in Aboriginal education*. Crawley, WA: UWA Publishing, pp. 202–234.

Chapter 14

Learning on and from Country

Teaching by incorporating Indigenous Relational worldviews

Kathryn Coff

Who I am

Kathryn Coff

My name is Kathryn Coff and I am a proud Yorta Yorta woman living on Dja Dja Wurrung Country; I live at the foothills of Leaganook. I come from a family where our relationship with Country is strong and ongoing. You could say we were raised by Country. "You look after country … Country he look after you" Neidjie, 2015, p. 222. I feel her beneath my feet, hearing the voices of the wind, and the healing of the warmth of the sun and the cleansing of rain in my soul.

As a Yorta Yorta woman I would like to acknowledge Country and the pain that she holds. I acknowledge her resilience and her knowledge. How she whispers gently to me through the wind in the leaves and kisses me on the cheek to remind me, I'm home. I feel most at home in the depths of fresh water and when water is lapping at my feet. I acknowledge Leaganook mountain in whose foothills I live. She reveals something new to me through the day and wraps her arms around me at night. I acknowledge my Ancestors and all First Nations people, they remind me every day who I am and what I need to do. I would like to acknowledge the Elders that did not give up, it is because of them that First Nations people are still here today. I acknowledge the Elders who are still holding strong to what is important. I also acknowledge those emerging Elders, who are coming out strong, proud, so comfortable in their own skin. They are the leaders of tomorrow.

From the Western worldview I would introduce myself in this way: I have been working with children and adults that struggle to engage with the dominant non-Indigenous culture for nearly 30 years. I am a registered teacher and continue to teach within schools as well as being Indigenous Practitioner in Residence at La Trobe University. I also manage the First Nations Education programs in our local area.

Introduction

I began this chapter by introducing myself and I did so choosing my words carefully because the way we introduce our work and ourselves is important and clearly expresses our worldviews. I also acknowledged Country because this is important to who I am as a Yorta Yorta woman. You will also see by the way I have written this chapter and the language I use, certain other things are important to me. For instance, you will notice that I capitalise certain words – Community, Country,

Learning on Country

and Ancestors. This is because as a First Nations person with my belief system, they are proper nouns (Figure 14.1).

In this chapter I share other aspects of my worldview as a Yorta Yorta woman. I begin by describing what I have learned while working with Indigenous and non-Indigenous young people on Country as well as outlining how many teachers (including non-Indigenous teachers) can do this in their classrooms, too. I then describe the impact of the worldviews on our understanding and the impact this can have on our students. Next, I provide a case study of what can be done to address the needs of students in terms of their learning. I conclude with some considerations for all teachers.

Learning on and from Country

Over the years, I have learned many things on and from Country. Martin and Mirraboopa (2003, p. 3) describe Country as including "the land, skies, waterways, animals, plants, and all the elements such as wind or fire." It is important to point out that learning on Country is not just about taking your lessons outside or even using nature within the classroom, although these are certainly some ways that you can incorporate Country in your teaching. Rather, by taking Australia's First Peoples' view on Country, you can develop a deeper awareness and use this to transform your teaching practices.

Learning on and from Country is about changing the way you can see the world, merging our Indigenous Relational worldview with Western approaches to pedagogy in order for Country to be included in every part of how we teach and what is taught. Teachers can include content about Country, but more importantly, if they challenge their pre-existing beliefs and ideas about pedagogical approaches to teaching, Country can be included throughout the curriculum.

Incorporating Country is particularly pertinent in today's society where many people have become detached from their environment in which they live. For example, in my role as a university Indigenous Practitioner I go into classrooms to educate students, teachers, professionals, and lecturers, and when I state, "There are not four seasons in Australia as we don't live in Europe," the look of bewilderment is astounding. And when I tell them our trees are not deciduous – for many this is the first time they have heard this.

In contrast, for First Nations people everything – our whole being – is about our local Community and our local Country and many of us know it well. From a Western perspective a lot of this is taught within the classroom, but it is not embedded at an everyday level. In contrast,

> Learning, as Aboriginal people have come to know it, is holistic, lifelong, purposeful, experiential, communal, spiritual, and learned within a language and a culture. What guides their learning (beyond family, community, and Elders) is spirit, their own learning spirits who travel with them and guide them along their earth walk.
>
> (Battiste, 2010, p. 2)

A key part of this is learning about Country, as it represents

> our survival, our humanity, our worldview and language, our imagination and spirit, our very place in the world depends on our capacity to act for ourselves, to speak for ourselves, to engage in the world and the actions of our colonizers, to face them head on.
>
> (Smith, 1999, p. 198)

However, it is not just critical for us, but given the precarious state of our environment it is important for all. So please bring Country into your lessons.

When planning your lessons, take into consideration how you might teach from and about Country. Think about what your students can learn from Country. For instance, consider such questions as: What is the history of the Country where you live? What is the history of the land, both before and after colonisation? This is especially important in contemporary Australia where many people know more about the history of other countries than they do their own. Take your students outside so they get to know their landscape and come to understand different peoples' relationships with Country. Also have them consider their Country now and their Ancestors' Country before. As teachers you can model this, talking about your Community and where you come from. Talk from your 'heart' about your Country and your family, and get your students to do the same. This opens opportunities for sharing and understanding different worldviews.

As I will describe next, incorporating Country into a teaching program is relatively easy to do and also quite possible within our current national curriculum. Ways of including Country in your teaching could include:

- Taking students outside to teach. This can be done in any subject. I find this interesting as I hear many teachers think that they won't get as much work completed outside, and yet I hear many students say they do. They love the change of scenery, the fresh air clears their head, and changing up how you teach can refresh a session;
- Teaching how to care for Country by understanding Country. Create opportunities for students to feel and measure the wind and the rain, changes in temperature and observe changes in cloud formation. In this way you can teach through Indigenous pedagogy;
- Using raw materials from Country as resources for teaching. This could include materials brought into the classroom or using landforms and flora and fauna outside as key parts of your teaching. Interestingly this practice of using natural materials often occurs in early childhood settings with younger age level students, but sadly it seems to cease with older students. Yet there is much they can get out of such experiences;
- Raising awareness of the 'real' Australian seasons by bringing them into the classroom. Here use First Nations people's understanding of the seasons. This involves looking at where the stars are in the sky (and to do this they will need to learn the directions of North, South, East and West and, in turn, this is important to know where you are positioned in Country), the length of day and night, changes in the temperature, what birds and animals can be heard and even the sounds they are making, which birds are nesting, what plants can be seen, what is flowering and what is ready for harvest. (Note: many botanical gardens around Australia have this information on display for visitors);
- Making Country your classroom. This might include investigating an ecosystem and then establishing or supporting one nearby. For example, this might involve adding fish to a school pond or local dam and getting students to research which plants are needed to sustain life. Students can then monitor any changes that occur over time. Another option is to go on excursions to get students to physically explore and know the Country they live on. This is especially important in today's society where so many children have a lot of screen time, but do not know or engage in their local landscape;
- Using vegetable gardens for learning. Again this seems to be something that happens with younger age groups, especially around their science and mathematics programs, but less so in the older years – yet it can be equally valuable. In addition to growing conventional fruit and vegetables for consumption, it is also useful to incorporate local indigenous plants in your school gardens. This can also be used to show how the food web can be different for First Nations

people. By doing this you can also build on the previous suggestion of bringing Country into your teaching – by first observing such plants in nature and then planting and being responsible for growing something is a way to develop responsibility for Country;

- Having a school fire pit. Despite the potential concerns over safety, it can provide classes and the whole school community with a focus for 'coming together'. I give opportunities for conversations around a fire, and from a First Nations perspective, cleansing occurs through the smoke of fire;
- Bringing in local First Nations people to talk about Country. Whilst this may seem obvious and even simple to achieve, many difficulties can prevent this from happening. A first step is to build relationships with your local First Nations Community. If it proves too difficult, take students out to events. Going to events that are already happening in your region is a great way to engage and learn on so many levels.

These ideas for learning on and from Country are important in their own right and they also demonstrate a coming together by clear differences in the worldviews of Indigenous and non-Indigenous people. I will explain this in more detail next.

Worldviews

Most of you will know that the protocol of acknowledging the traditional custodians of the Country on which you meet has become a common practice in schools and other public domains. It is not just a sign of respect, but an important way of recognising Indigenous worldviews. (If you are uncertain, all State Departments of Education include information about how this can be done). Key to this are the following parts: Acknowledgement, Country, Community, and Ancestors. An Ackowledgement is like a big thank you for allowing you to be on the Country of First Nations people. I have already described how important Country is to Indigenous people and by providing an Acknowledgement, you signify your recognition of this. Equally, acknowledging Community and Ancestors, especially when you speak from 'the heart', gives due recognition to the history – past and present – of Indigenous people.

This last part of Acknowledging is particularly important for Aboriginal and Torres Strait Islander children in our Community who may not feel as safe at school as perhaps they should. Sometimes they may feel that they are not truly seen or understood for who they are and what they bring to school. One might even go so far as to say that schools might even feel threatening or dangerous for young people unless their, and other diverse worldviews, are understood. Sadly there is a shared belief amongst First Nations Community that to 'get through' school successfully Indigenous young people must assimilate into non-Indigenous ways of being, knowing, and doing. Too often this means letting go of who they are and suppressing their belief system and identity or leaving their language and culture at the door (Martin, 2016) (also see Chapter 8).

The reasons for the disconnect, as described above, is that Indigenous and non-Indigenous ways of understanding the world can be very different. That is not to say that ideas about the world don't also come together. While we would not want to risk implying that Indigenous people 'see the world differently' (this could be a terrible stereotype), Indigenous worldviews are fundamentally different from non-Indigenous worldviews. For example, within an Indigenous worldview ways of being, knowing, and doing are relational: "Humans are not central nor alone in knowledge construction. Instead knowledge construction is through the cyclical and equal relationship between Community, Country and the Ancestral Core" (Martin, 2008, p. 87). That is, boundaries between humans and nature are blurred. Things are not animate and inanimate, rather everything is more or less animate. Consequently, Aboriginal languages allow for talking to trees and rocks, an allowance not accorded in English. This is because in Indigenous culture "If everything is animate, then everything has spirit and knowledge. If everything has spirit and knowledge, then all are like me. If all are like me, then all are my relations" (Little Bear, 2000, p. 3).

As a First Nations person I gain knowledge about who I am and who I want to be from Country, Ancestors, and Community. As I have described, I gain knowledge from Country – it speaks to me and communicates with me every day. I also believe my Ancestors speak to me everyday. In non-Indigenous way this might be called your 'gut' feeling, but to me there is ancestorial memory that we hold in our cells. Community is people or family and together we operate like a giant organism. A beautiful anology I have heard is that Community is like a flock of birds. We move like a flock of birds, at times someone is at the front, but when that person gets tired, he or she moves to the back and someone else moves to take their place seamlessly.

Such a worldview is in contrast to the Western worldview. For example, how we gain knowledge from this perspective is about human-led experiences and knowledge production. Western worldviews are often built upon incremental knowledge and the study of things, rather than the experience with or in them (as is the case with Country for First Nations people).

Interestingly, however, by highlighting the differences in the worldviews it is possible to increase "the mutual understanding that is created between people" (McMahon, 2017, p. 89).

Figure 14.2 illustrates some of these fundamental differences between Indigenous and non-Indigenous worldviews. It is important to note that these represent generalisations as there is no one Indigenous nor non-Indigenous worldview. In fact, many individuals may hold aspects of both worldviews. For instance, Indigenous people can be both scientific and at the same time value what they know from their Ancestral knowledge. Therefore, it is important to try and avoid oppositional and binary thinking and to remember that there are many ways of being. Even so, it is useful to recognise that differences in worldviews may exist as this can help us understand and support Indigenous students.

It should also be noted that over the years, some non-Indigenous Australians have found it difficult to have their worldviews challenged, or even to understand the fact that people live with different views or belief systems. This is particularly difficult given the way that the dominant culture, one that constructs their

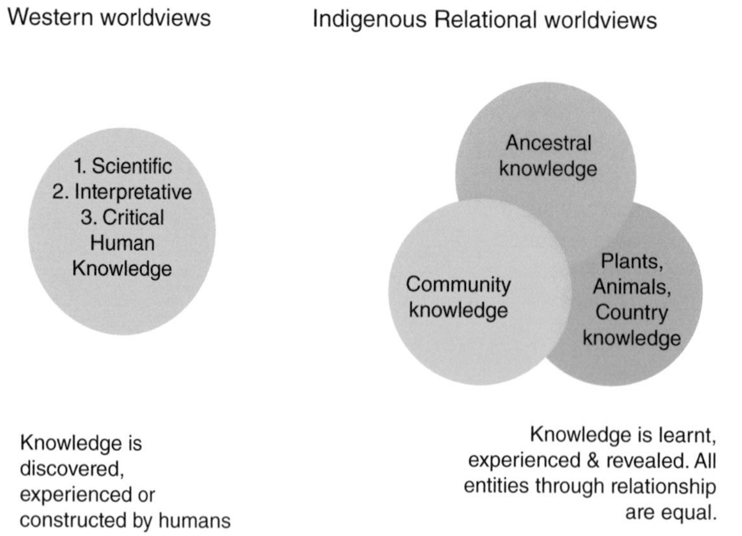

Western worldviews	Indigenous Relational worldviews

1. Scientific
2. Interpretative
3. Critical
Human
Knowledge

Ancestral knowledge

Community knowledge

Plants, Animals, Country knowledge

Knowledge is discovered, experienced or constructed by humans

Knowledge is learnt, experienced & revealed. All entities through relationship are equal.

▲ Figure 14.2

Western and Indigenous worldviews (McMahon, 2017)

privilege, is described and attributed to different groups in society, as many non-Indigenous people do not see themselves in that way. If you wish to explore this further, theories about White Privilege help explain how the dominant culture comes to be normalised as the only way of doing things (see Moreton-Robinson, 2004).

Many have spent their whole life not even thinking that there is any other way than the way they have lived and the beliefs that they hold. Mishel McMahon and Leroy Little Bear illustrate this by describing how we see a tree. Through the Western model, a tree only has meaning when we see it and say 'Oh, that's a beautiful tree'. Yet science is closer to First Nations peoples' way of seeing the world and would state that the tree holds all the memory of being a tree within it. From the Indigenous Relational worldview, because all is animate, knowledge is held in Country and everything that is alive holds all the information about everything else in it. Furthermore, it is revealed when needed. So I hold the same knowledge as a grain of sand, or as a tree. However, when Indigenous students come to school they are often walking into the Western way of seeing the world – a way that is new and different from the belief system they have grown up understanding. Be aware, too, that this occurs regardless of an Indigenous student's skin colour, as cultural understanding, beliefs, and 'ways of being' are not determined by how we look. Fortunately, learning with and on Country (as described above) can provide a way for all students to learn, to 'be seen' and to feel welcomed with our schools. So do consider how you can incorporate different worldviews and Country into your classroom.

To illustrate how teaching can be designed to extend students' worldviews, this section provides an example of an established education program, The Meeting Place, in the Loddon Mallee region of Victoria.

Kathryn Coff

Case study of a local Indigenous education program

Five First Nations teachers – two Elders and three Indigenous teachers – developed the Meeting Place program. At this point I would like to acknowledge the two Elders, Uncle Rick Nelson and Aunty Julie McHale. The group that worked on the program also involved other Community members, with Indigenous and non-Indigenous people working together. The purpose of the program was to address our concerns about Indigenous kids who were not doing well in school. Two very clear things were happening. First our kids in the community were not engaged in school: many were not at school or if they were going to school, they were struggling to stay in the classroom. Second, many teachers did not know how to reach our kids. We decided that as adults in our community we had to do something about this. So we wrote a list of what we felt would help our kids. We suggested it would be beneficial to:

- Create a setting and a program where our children could come to learn our way, at least part time. We proposed to set up a space where they could learn through Culture and Country;
- Have our Community's adults involved in their children's education. We believed this would impact student academic outcomes;
- Support non-Indigenous classroom teachers and principals by meeting with them to discuss curriculum, going into their classrooms to show them how you can teach it, mentoring them through the process, providing lesson plans, and writing units of work;
- Support First Nations teachers currently working in schools, as well as pre-service teachers;

- Provide support, as necessary, so we could all come together to support each other to write curriculum, provide practicum opportunities and employment;
- Commit to providing sustainable long-term support – being there all the way through our students' schooling and into their first training and or employment situation;
- Provide support to schools to increase attendance;
- Provide support to schools with literacy, numeracy, and homework, for all students;
- Create a homework centre at the schools and in other settings as appropriate;
- Encourage Indigenous students who were academically strong to move to the next step.

We supported these aims and by implementing associated approaches and structures, these initiatives were were able to make marked and sustainable changes. Two key aspects of this program was that 1) it was First Nations people who ran and led it, and 2) it was always strengths based. As Sarra (2014) notes, too many educational programs for Indigenous kids start from a deficit position. A recent independent evaluation completed on the Meeting Place and all of Nalderuns programs found that, "Through Nalderun the local Aboriginal community has increased pride, confidence, identity, visibility and access to leadership opportunities. 'Increased pride' was the most commonly expressed significant outcome by both Aboriginal and non-Aboriginal respondents. Aboriginal community members also have an increased sense of safety, connection, community and belonging" (Moxham, 2018, p. 7).

Most importantly because we involved everyone: teachers, other members of community and other organisations we created a web affect not just with the First Nations Community, but within the whole community. As Little Bear discusses in the article on Jagged Worldviews Colliding, "The 'spider web' of relations ensures that the welfare of the group is the most important thing in Aboriginal societies. The value of wholeness tells the members that, if all do their parts, then social order will be the result" (Little Bear, 2000, p. 8).

Ways for teaching

The framework for the program described above and one that I advocated here is based on "YOE, respect Yourself, Others and the Environment", as created by Aunty Julie McHale. It also reflects the Indigenous Relational model outlined previously. These approaches can create in students a feeling that they are a part of something bigger, that they have responsibilities to look after their Country and Community. Most importantly, these things support their feeling of having a place in this world.

Also important is a two-way or both-ways learning approach (Purdie, Milgate, & Bell, 2011): that is creating "a partnership relationship between First Peoples and Settler cultures in Australia ... a negotiated space ... 'third space', to imply that, like the cultural literal zone where land and sea meet ... it is dynamic and fluid, like that of a coast line". Two-way learning incorporates both worldviews into our teaching practice. Such a pedagogy should not divide us, but rather include everyone. Both ways are equally important and provide a way of creating a new space within the classroom. For example, to achieve this in our Meeting Place program we included both worldviews in how we taught our students. We did this by working out how we could work together without losing our ways of being, knowing, and doing (Martin & Mirraboopa, 2003). The Meeting Place started out initially as an after-school activity, but we realised how engaged our kids were and just how much they were learning when they were in the right environment. Reflecting Indigenous Community, learning happened in a multi-age setting, where our kids completed activities in skin groups, each with its own animal, plant, and place in Country. We advocated that because this program was educational it should be taught during school hours. So we went into schools to support teaching and learning, by building connections between both worldviews. When we did this we would sing, create songs, dance, go out on Country, but we would also write, design, articulate, delve into the why and the how of the world, our shared history, and how we can move forward in positive ways into the future.

Most First Nations people from around the world have similar components to teachings.

1. They teach us about how we should be in the world as people.
2. They teach us how something in nature is formed or why things are the way are.

Because our kids have heard and learned so many 'teachings' from across the world, we had no idea the impact this would have had until one memorable day. Two of our youngest children, both around seven years old, came up to us and said they wanted to perform a play. Normally, when children of such an age announce such a thing, especially when they are ad-libbing, you think you are going to get something a little silly. However, they created their own 'teaching' on the spot and it was about friendship, and that, yes, at times we might hurt each other, but through true forgiveness and love we can work through this – no matter the differences. Within the play they even moved from one character to another. After they had finished we spoke to everyone about what they had learnt. One student responded by asking the question, "Why are teachings from a long time ago, when the dreaming is always?" We knew then that what we were doing was keeping our culture alive.

The Meeting Place, and Nalderun (the overarching name for all our programs, a Dja Dja Wurrung word meaning 'altogether') has now been running for seven years. We believe because of this program our kids know and are proud of who they are. They gain strength from it and from each other. Our young people are writing and sharing their ideas about the world. For instance one of our kids wrote a book and she was interviewed by ABC Education. The book, *My Culture, the Beach and Me*, is written by Grace Coff who is a proud Yorta Yorta girl living on Jaara Country. She writes about her beliefs in Culture, Country, her respect for her Elders and the difficulties at times she faces about being an Aboriginal person with pale skin and how "being Aboriginal is in her heart" (Coff, 2017).

Our students are also building relationships in new ways. They have strong relationships with each other, and are mentoring each other within the group. Older students are supporting younger ones. Our students are also supporting their non-Indigenous teachers in new ways when they are in their mainstream classrooms. They know they are part of making change – they know they have a voice and they use it to make a difference. Engagement and attendance rates have improved and teachers and principals are supportive and engage with Indigenous content.

The Meeting Place has made a difference to our young peoples' aspirations and career pathways. Many have now completed school, apprenticeships, traineeships, and have enrolled in University. We support the organisations and our kids through this. Many of these kids were ones on whom the system had given up. As stated by one of the young participants involved in the Meeting Place, "If we didn't have it [Nalderun] I'd be sad. I'd do nothing. … It's important because you get to hang out with your own culture and history … It's good to be together as a community" (Moxham, 2018, p. 7).

As Nakata writes, unless we can build relationships at the cultural interface we cannot address the "contested space between Indigenous people, non-Indigenous people, and that body of knowledge of Australia's Indigenous people that establishes the order of things to the ways we can and cannot understand each other" (Nakata, 2011, p. 2). Unless we model a way to be every day, things will not change. In the Meeting Place, it just took a small group of people who had the same belief in wanting change, to change the whole belief of a community.

Final suggestions

It is important to note that non-Indigenous people can teach using Indigenous pedagogies. They can also teach Indigenous content, but it is vital that when doing this, Aborginal protocols are followed. This means acknowledging where the knowledge comes from. As a teacher, if you introduce any content or new ideas based on Indigenous knowledge, try and follow these simple rules:

1. Acknowledge the person or people who created the content. Published material is best as it then stays the property of the people that created it and is okay for it to be used;
2. Acknowledge the mob(s) or language group(s) that live on Country near to your school. This can occur by using local maps from your local Indigenous

Corporations, pictures of Country or even have Google Earth running on the smart board in their classroom;

3. Introduce Country appropriately – describe where is it in relation to your classroom. Consider your teaching in relation to the area, taking into account the flora, fauna, the climate and other environmental factors.

Recognising the Indigenous worldview can no longer be an 'add-on' to our curriculum. It is something that can and should be shared with all our students. As teachers we can combine it as a new pedagogical approach that brings both worldviews together, much as a conglomerate rock brings together different particles as a whole. By doing so we can teach in ways relevant for all our students.

Conclusion

Teachers need to be aware that this is a learning journey for us all. There are no simple answers, but what is important is to make a start. I have seen many times teachers wanting to learn and trying to get it right for Indigenous students, and this makes a huge difference. Providing opportunities to learn through Country supports our kids to feel respected. That is, incorporating Country into the curriculum for all students is a critical step for Indigenous education. Learning on and through Country, understanding and changing your worldviews involves opening your heart and mind to another way of seeing the world, and together this enables a 'shift' to a strengths-based approach, but we need to continue to move forward together.

Reflective questions

1. How would you identify your own worldview?
2. How do you think you could include Country in your teaching?
3. What could students learn about Country?
4. How do you think as a teacher you could become an agent of change?

Acknowledgement is given to Aunty Julie McHale's development of the framework 'YOE: respecting, Yourself, Others and the Environment'. This chapter is written in her honour. I would also like to thank Jo Lampert for her ongoing support.

References

Battiste, M. (2010). Nourishing the learning spirit: Living our way to new thinking. *Education Canada*, 50(1), 14–18.
Coff, G. (2017). *My culture, the beach and me*. Castlemaine: Nalderun.

Little Bear, L. (2000). Jagged worldviews colliding. In Marie Battiste (Ed.) *Reclaiming Indigenous Voice and Vision*. Vancouver: University of British Columbia Press, pp. 77–85. Walking together; First Nations, Metis and Inuit Perpectives in Curriculum, http://www.learnalberta.ca/content/aswt/worldviews/documents/jagged_worldviews_colliding.pdf

Martin, K. (2008). *Please knock before you enter: Aboriginal regulation of outsiders and the implications for researchers*. Teneriffe, Qld.: Post Pressed.

Martin, K. (2016). *Voices and visions: Aboriginal early childhood education in Australia*. Baulkham Hills BC: Pademelon Press Pty, Limited.

Martin, K., & Mirraboopa, B. (2003). Ways of knowing, being and doing: A theoretical framework and methods for indigenous and indigenist re-search. *Journal of Australian Studies*, 27(76), 203–214. doi:10.1080/14443050309387838

McMahon, M. (2017). Lotjpa-nhanuk: Indigenous Australian child-rearing discourses. PhD Thesis, College of Health Science & Engineering; School of Allied Health. Bundoora: La Trobe University.

Moreton-Robinson, A. (2004). *Whitening race: Essays in social and cultural criticism*. Canberra: Aboriginal Studies Press.

Moxham, N. (2018). Nalderun Aboriginal Services, Evaluation Snapshot. https://nalderun.net.au/wp-content/uploads/2018/05/Nalderun-Evaluation-Snapshot-16April2018-Leanganook-Yarn.pdf

Nakata, M. (2011). Pathways for indigenous education in the Australian curriculum framework. *Australian Journal of Indigenous Education*, 40, 1–8.

Neidjie, B. (2015). *Old man's story: The last thoughts of Kakadu Elder Bill Neidjie*. Canberra, ACT Aboriginal Studies Press.

Purdie, N., Milgate, G., & Bell, H. R. (2011). *Two way teaching and learning: Toward culturally reflective and relevant education*. Camberwell, Vic.: ACER Press.

Sarra, C. (2014). *Strong and smart – Towards a pedagogy for emancipation: Education for First Peoples*. Hoboken: Taylor and Francis.

Smith, L. T. (1999). *Decolonizing methodologies: Research and indigenous peoples*. Dunedin, New Zealand: University of Otago Press.

Chapter 15

Red ochre women[1]

Sisters in the struggle for educational reform

Jacqueline Amagula and Helen CD McCarthy

Who we are

Jacqueline Amagula

My name is Jacqueline Amagula. I am a Warnindilyakwa woman and my language is Anindilyakwa. I come from Groote Eylandt in the Gulf of Carpentaria in the Northern Territory. My diyabarrka (sister) Helen McCarthy and I feel privileged to share our story with you.

Firstly, I will write about my journey; my pathway to teaching as a young student teacher who wanted to achieve literacy and numeracy in my community. Growing up I was humble and a shy student teacher, but I really wanted to make a difference in my community especially through education. In those days life was tough, as we had the church missionary running the community, although that did mean every child would be at school. We had a strong village Council and they would round kids up and take them to school every day and on time. We would talk to Elders, parents and community in big community meetings about how they wanted their children to learn. The people would say that they wanted their kids to learn Two-Way, both Western and Indigenous learning.

As I became a little stronger I attended staff meetings, conferences, workshops and in-services, but I wasn't a strong leader, not strong enough to stand and fight for the rights of my people. My life continued with the journey of the struggle when I met a young teacher Helen McCarthy; we had worked together since the 1980s and Helen kept on talking to me to go on to do further teacher training. As the years passed I became stronger in dealing with conflict and issues in education. Not long after I met Jean Illingworth who was a lecturer and teacher. Jean came to my Community Education Centre and was a lecturer for 10 Indigenous students who were becoming teachers in their community. A lot of these students graduated with their degree – an Associate Diploma in Teaching in Aboriginal Schools from Batchelor College.

Jean then became a teacher for senior secondary girls, where me and another Indigenous lady were her Education Assistants. Having a big number of students was very tough and without her love, care and dignity these girls wouldn't have got out with a Certificate nor graduated from Year 12. A lot of these students Jean taught were from the local Angurugu community and parents and community members were very proud. These girls continued to seek proper jobs in the community and with the mining company on Groote Eylandt and still today continue to have good jobs.

Jean Illingworth, like Helen, in a traditional way is my sister. My father, Numaljawarma, gave her the name Dangmalgayukwa – the raindrops that come with the Eastern Mamarika winds. She is a special woman from the Amagula Clan and her name also means a message – for example, it could be a forewarning of a death or a new-born baby coming out to the world. Jean, like Helen, has been painted up attending the mortuary ceremonies and has kinship family connections right across from East to South Arnhem Land. She has taught Two-Ways culture with respect and always believed these kids could get to the level like every other child in Australia. I will now write about what happened with Ngakwurralangwa College and then Helen will write more about other things that happened within Indigenous education.

Back in 2005 we thought we could change things to help make things work better in our community on Groote Eylandt. We began with the establishment of the Ngakwurralangwa College making the story right for us to control it – have ownership. Ngakwurralangwa means 'Our Way': we own it and we lead it; we have our say and we have the voice. The story for us (about Ngakwurralangwa) concerns the journey for traditional women and going hunting for wild yams. When we find the vines of the yam, we follow the stem to the ground and dig a hole going down as long as it is long. If we break it half way, that means it is not good, the message will break, but if we keep on digging until we get to the end, that means a strong powerful message is going to happen.

I had an opportunity to step in and have the power to help lead that college; we changed how things happened, and we had control of the four schools on Groote Eylandt and reached out and built innovative partnerships with all the service providers across the Eylandt. As an Indigenous Director I made sure all new staff coming to our schools would understand or do Cultural Awareness before entering our schools. For instance, the local Aboriginal people ran the Cultural Competency induction training. The College Director would step back and say this is not my community, nor is it my culture, you lead and I will follow behind you and observe and we will walk and talk together. Ngakwurralangwa College performed very well in the Smart Schools Awards because of these partnerships and innovations. We were recognised for running our own College through community leadership and we had our own structures developed. We even ran workshops for Indigenous teachers and their tutors and mentors. Then the government said no more funding for the Director's position, although the College is still there.

We need to educate these kids by having community control and we continue fighting to make an improvement in the lives of my people because education leads to better lifestyles and is the key to a pathway towards a career. This is what my family wanted and it's been a struggle. Helen will now write about how we tried to build a better world together to break down the barriers.

***

Jacqueline's story around breaking down barriers to prevent Aboriginal learners disengaging from their education was first co-presented as a conference paper at the

Australian Institute of Aboriginal and Torres Strait Islander Studies (AIATSIS) 50ᵗʰ year Conference Breaking Barriers in Indigenous Research and Thinking in Canberra in 2014. She was frustrated and worried that after all this time nothing appeared to be improving in the lives of young black people. Refusing to accede, we co-presented our concerns at the 40 Year Celebration of Batchelor Institute in the Northern Territory again that year. Breaking down barriers to build a better world together was Jacqueline's life's work. Her commitment was to ensure that Aboriginal children learned in ways that recognised their complex social interactions, differences in aspirations, value systems, languages and life experiences. To acknowledge her important contribution to Aboriginal Education, Batchelor Press provided special permission to reprint part of our story in this chapter.

Helen CD McCarthy

I grew up on the great Southern Ocean sheltered by the hundred islands of the Recherche Archipelago. The youngest of 11 children, I knew the freedom to surf the beaches and roam the open coastal spaces where my Celtic ancestors had walked before me. It seemed fitting that when I graduated from university, I would go to another Archipelago at the opposite end of Australia and fall in love with an island called Groote, in the Gulf of Carpentaria.

My story is woven into Jacqueline's, based primarily from and around a collection of my pedagogical journals and diary entries drawing on artefacts and experiences lived and written. This type of reflexive documentation according to Chang is, "a rigorous attempt to achieve in-depth cultural understanding of self and others" (Chang, 2008, p. 57), celebrating the diversity and validity of each other's cultural systems together as allies. I derived this ultimately from living, working and playing basketball with Jacqueline Amagula. I spent 12 years in her community and school, being a part of her daily life and she of mine which included being trusted with the sacred rites of ceremony. I witnessed her mature from a young girl into an experienced educator and leader.

Introduction

Mindful that many of you are just beginning to embark upon your teaching journey we want to share with you our yarn, the story of our collaboration and the challenges that we faced. To begin this chapter, we have outlined our personal and professional backgrounds to explain our life and experiences as teachers and as learners on Groote Eylandt in the Gulf of Carpentaria. For over 40 years we worked together and observed many parents/carers and teachers express dissatisfaction with the way mainstream education has been delivered in community schools. This disparity never sat well with us. We have been critical about these warnikakakirumaka (non-Aboriginal) teaching practices. Working closely with Elders, teachers, and parents/carers, collectively we challenged this one-way worldview that was imposed upon our learners, irrespective of them having their own Indigenous knowledge systems. These ways of knowing are complex (see Chapters 4, 5, 6 and 14) as well as accomplished, yet seldom are they incorporated as part of the negotiated school curriculum.

> A negotiated curriculum improves the relevance and meaningfulness
> of learners' curriculum experiences. It exemplifies a strength-based
> approach to teaching and learning, where educators capitalise on the
> strengths and expertise of learners, rather than view learners in
> terms of their weaknesses – what they do not know and cannot do.
>
> (Gobby, 2017, p. 21)

We knew that living in the community, knowing the backgrounds and real-life experiences children brought with them to the learning environments, meant as teachers we could build on this richness and upon the students' passions, interests and ways they like to learn and then nurture, in a holistic way, all the attributes of the children. Kickett-Tucker describes these preferred ways of learning as "working in groups, cooperation, sharing common group goals and learning by observation, an understanding of the real-life significance of school based learning, and jovial social interactions in the learning environment" (as cited in Gray & Partington, 2003, p. 147).

We hope you are cognisant of these ways of working when you graduate and commence your teaching career. You may get to work in schools that are the heartbeat of the community. We have found from our experiences that they are the one place everyone wants to be part of and involved in. People from different communities are keen, for example, to work in the literacy centre, the canteen, on the sports programs, or as liaison officers. This can happen when schools are staffed with local Aboriginal educators who work side by side with non-Aboriginal teachers who, in turn, live in the communities in which they teach, sharing ideas and sharing language. These are schools who open their doors at seven o'clock to students with hair still wet from the shower and the soft scent of campfire smoke, who arrive keen to start the day. Once the daytime classes finish, the afternoon and night classes start. Working with community and school leadership, with Aboriginal teachers in team-teaching partnerships, you can work to construct an all-embracing emergent curriculum that evolves over time – a curriculum that interests and engages learners. You will know this because of the way the students appear to 'own' the burgeoning curriculum frameworks and how they propel it by their contagious vigour and by seldom missing a day of school. Living and learning are interchangeable terms, equally proper in outside spaces, in the bush, on the sea, near the ground. These environments which are "considered the third educator" (Gandini, 2012, p. 339) are valued places that create appropriate exploratory engagement. In true Indigenous teaching and learning ways, nature is nurtured.

Although university taught us much, the one thing that was never mentioned was that schools can be places of conflict and issues, too. Yunkaporta (2019) writes,

> Schools are sites of political struggle in this civilisation because they
> are the main vehicles for establishing the grand narratives needed to
> make progress possible. There is a reason ideological battles and culture
> wars filled with rhetoric about patriotism and nation-building
> are fought around schools and schooling.
>
> (p. 133)

Education is a revered attribute, yet it is often linked to economic outcomes and is shaped by powerful institutionalised forces that hardly consider cultural relativism as a shared responsibility. Connell (2013), affirms that

> Neoliberalism has a definite view of education, understanding it as human capital formation. It is the business of forming the skills and attitudes needed by a productive workforce—productive in the precise sense of producing an ever-growing mass of profits for market economy.
>
> (p. 104)

However, this view of education is not one that Jacqueline and I shared. In the following case studies, we describe some of the challenges we experienced because of this view being imposed on learners. These stories also reflect the deep concern amongst families about the low expectations and aspirations of educators and the disregard for bicultural and bilingual knowledge schooling afforded to their children. We describe how Aboriginal and some non-Aboriginal teachers and staff shared in the belief that they needed to craft proper ways of imparting knowledge and culture that were different to those often reflected in the mainstream curriculum. These case studies also show what occurred when school managements were uncompromising and did not listen to the call for reform, but instead insisted on schooling systems that ran counter to culturally sensitive and strengths-based approaches. We end the story with an affirmation showing how with cooperation and shared aspirations eventual success was achieved – how Jacqueline's work, along with that of many others, finally led to the right for Aboriginal communities to take back the power to make the decision for their schools to be bilingual and bicultural.

As you read in her story at the beginning of this chapter, Jacqueline helped established Ngakwurralangwa College, so you can imagine how very angry she was when she told me that funding had been cut to the school. She asked why is it whenever good results are being achieved the government shuts down the programs or withdraws funding? Throughout our contemporary Australian educational history there are many examples where grass roots, community initiated and led programs, ones that have been operating successfully, suffer from government intervention at some level and the place or program was shut down . Over the years we continued to listen to the parents/carers and to the community Elders. We listened to their concerns about how the mainstream ways of schooling prejudiced their ways of knowing, unfairly eroding their cultural uniqueness by undermining their identity.

In our early time working together we fretted as many students became disengaged, leaving school at 14 or 15 years of age with underdeveloped literacy, numeracy, and life skills. We witnessed young adults reject what school was offering at that time which inevitably

> … led to boredom, despair, often substance abuse, sometimes criminal activity, incarceration, domestic violence and a crisis level incident rate of youth suicide. [Yet we knew] All research points to the

Jacqueline Amagula and Helen CD McCarthy

one finding: retention of students at this stage of their education is critical in breaking the cycle of a future adult life of deprivation.
(Steering Committee for the Review of Government Service Provision, 2005, p. 7).

Fortunately, at this time in the Northern Territory there was a growing movement both from Aboriginal and non-Aboriginal educators towards the Two-Way Learning Model, where the "students' learning experiences count as much as the teachers' knowledge. This 'Two Way' learning is also reflected in sharing authority in which learners assist in formulating and evolving a relevant and engaging emergent curriculum" (Burns, 1995, p. 233). By incorporating negotiated course content, and in both Standard Australian English and the local language, students were supported to operate as effectively as they possibly could in both worlds. At the time Yirrkala Principal, Dhupuma College alumni Dr M. Yunupingu, kept saying,

What we want is BOTH WAYS education – Balanda (non-Indigenous) and Yolŋu (Indigenous) ways – but we want the Yolŋu to have control over both sides of the curriculum. We want our children to learn Yolŋu culture and history from the Yolŋu point of view. We do not want to keep the Balanda content out of the school, but we want control over the Balanda content. We want to decide for ourselves what our children learn about the Balanda world. We all, Balanda and Yolŋu are trapped by our past experiences of school the Balanda way.
(as cited in Marginson, 2002, p. 197)

The first case study, which we describe below, resulted from an extended period of negotiation with key Balanda and Yolŋu stakeholders who sought educational reform. This resulted in the creation of Dhupuma College in Arnhem Land. It was badged as the school to make the difference in the lives of young Aboriginal people. When it began the mood was buoyant: for the first time there was a sense of something right being created, a culturally sensitive and appropriate place of learning for their children.

Dhupuma College

The Gumatj speaking Yolngu School, Dhupuma College, which means 'looking up and ahead', was established at Nhulunbuy in Arnhem Land in the Northern Territory in 1972. Utilising portions from the abandoned missile tracking station, the college facilities were reconstructed to support the education of an entire cohort of both Yolngu (Aboriginal) and Balanda (non-Aboriginal) educators and students in a Two-Way education approach. This involved highly innovative bicultural/bilingual programs which were carefully implemented. Its success was unprecedented in the Northern Territory both in terms of academic and leadership accomplishments. In fact, a significant number of graduates went on to become influential in both the mainstream and Aboriginal communities. Jacqueline, who attended from 1978, is testimony to that. Despite this, it was largely unknown by the wider Australian community. After the facilities had become quite dilapidated, promises were made to rebuild the campus in two phases, but instead the Government closed the college abruptly on the 21st August 1980 without any prior notice. When asked why the college was closed, Dhupuma College staff member, Dr M Yunupingu, replied, "Well I think the Northern Territory Government didn't want black people to be smart" (Corn, 2009, p. 26).

Tiwi College – Northern Territory

As you acquire more experience as a teacher working in a variety of schools, you will find that many things in education are indeed cyclic and history does tend to repeat itself. As with those who worked to establish and deliver programs at Dhupuma College, the Tiwi people of Bathurst and Meville Islands in the Northern Territory hoped that their children and grandchildren would receive a better education than they had received. However, "This did not happen, so as a result the Tiwi took control of their own future by taking control of Tiwi education, starting with building their own secondary school" (https://www.tiwilandcouncil.com/, para, 1). Unlike the story of Dhupuma College, however, Tiwi College, located on Melville Island, continues to exist and to provide successful Two-Ways education.

The college is a secondary boarding school governed by the Tiwi people. Their aspiration is for their children to graduate and have opportunities to make good life choices so that they may live full, rewarding, and healthy lives. Initially operated by the Northern Territory Christian Schools Association, the college was taken over in 2010 and is now completely owned and managed by the Tiwi people through the Tiwi Education Board, which is made up of ten senior men and women from the eight landowning groups.

The college is unique, as it provides a weekly boarding facility where the 133 students (My School 2020, https://www.myschool.edu.au/) are accommodated in Family Group Homes and bussed home for the weekend. The whole school bicultural program has been designed and guided around the vision of parity and equality. The school program promotes strong Tiwi and non-Tiwi collaboration, with due respect, mutual trust and understanding given so that everyone can learn from one another, and, where 'both worlds' are recognised and respected.

The Northern Territory bilingual program

Naturally the bilingual learning program that was adopted in many Aboriginal schools in the Northern Territory during the 1980s was also intricately linked to culture. Learning activities encompassed the Indigenous seasons, the ceremonial cycles and community events. Importantly it also provided a role for community members to be closely involved in their children's learning, with many working as educators and some taking up leadership roles within the program and in schools more generally. Even when their involvement was less formal, their contributions were still important. For example, community members would sit under the bough shelters in the soft-river or beach sand close to where the classes were taking place, and observe what was happening. If students weren't behaving in a way deemed by them appropriate, a custodian would casually walk over, sit down and work with them until they settled into the task.

Once again, despite positive outcomes from the program, the Northern Territory Minister for Education directed the Department to close down all bilingual programs and centres and Bilingual Education was abolished in the Northern Territory on 1st December 1998. According to Nicholls (2005) the axing of the bilingual programs, "ran counter to the oft-articulated wishes of the overwhelming majority of Aboriginal community members" (Nicholls, 2005, p. 161). She argued that no hard evidence was ever provided to prove that bilingual education was failing students; "the government's lack of endorsement of Indigenous languages programmes ultimately discredits the status of Indigenous languages by undermining their legitimacy in Australian classrooms, and by extension, in other social settings as well" (Nicholls, 2005, p. 165). As a result of this action a profound void was left and the opportunity for strong connections between culture, language, and cognition were lost.

Jacqueline Amagula and Helen CD McCarthy

The ramifications of the government decision caused a furore across the Northern Territory with schools, unions, and communities demanding the closure to be rescinded. A petition was presented to the Northern Territory Parliament with over 3,000 signatures. Following determined lobbying, such as by Friends of Bilingual Education, the NT government commissioned the "Learning Lessons" Review. "The review documented intense community support for bilingual education and gave qualified support to continuing it – albeit with the name changed to 'Two-Way' learning" (nintione.com.au/resources/rao/learning-lessons-an-independent-review-of-indigenous-education-in-the-northern-territory/, para 21). And so, the decision was then made to re-establish a bicultural Two-Way program.

Once more, however, the repeated history of closing Indigenous programs occurred. This time, as a consequence of the 2009 National Assessment Program Literacy and Numeracy (NAPLAN) results, the NT government mandated that English was to be the language of instruction for the first four hours of each school day. In 2010 a complaint was lodged with the Human Rights and Equal Opportunity Commission invoking the Commonwealth Racial Discrimination Act, stating this action was discriminatory and, therefore, unlawful. As a result, in December of that year the compulsory first four hours of English policy was replaced with a new policy, 'Literacy for Both Worlds'.

Viewed by many as a lamentable decision, on January 13, 2011, the replacement policy was withdrawn and the compulsory teaching of English for the first four hours of the day was reinstated. But again, the fluctuations continued and in 2012 a report was released by the House of Representatives Standing Committee on Aboriginal and Torres Strait Islander Affairs with 30 recommendations. One key one was that, "Indigenous language education should be introduced to all schools with Aboriginal students, and Indigenous languages included as an official Closing the Gap measure" (Karvelas, 2012). This has been translated into action and currently there is a bilingual program that uses the students' first language to teach appropriate aspects of the Australian Curriculum, as well as local cultural knowledge through the Northern Territory Indigenous Languages and Cultures (NTILC) curriculum. It achieves this by having "Students … immersed in their first language for most of the school day in the Early Years of Schooling, and for at least 5 hours a week from Years 4–9" (https://education.nt.gov.au/, para. 5).

To date this program has not been shut down. There is now inclusive and localised collaboration between communities, schools, and the Education Department in more than 50 schools. They are delivering programs in 27 different languages and employing local Indigenous teachers to do so. Such a program enhances respectful and purposeful interactions generating greater local community input and leadership. It also reduces the language barriers for those learners who have English as an additional language. As a consequence, learners have been reported as exhibiting increased engagement and interest and staying on longer at school.

The following case study provides an example of one such bilingual program and shows that 'magic happens' when people believe in what the right thing to do is.

The Anindilyakwa and English bilingual program

Since the 1970s English was the single language of instruction in all Eylandt schools and students were expected to learn and write using it. When I first arrived on the Eylandt it was immediately clear that I would need to go to Anindilyakwa classes since English was only spoken in the school and not the wider community. Every Tuesday night I would go off to the library for my classes. The kids would wait for me to come out and ask me what I had learned. When I replied in Anindilyakwa they would roar with laughter. After the apparent appropriate time of teasing they would walk me home telling me how to say the words correctly. I realised very quickly that these kids were far more patient and much better at explaining linguistic concepts than me. The following vignette is included as a means to show why bicultural, bilingual education is essential for learners as it influences their identity, their self-esteem, and their sense of self.

I was walking past the early childhood classrooms today on my way to the staffroom when I happened to look in to see one of the new, non-Indigenous teachers, seated on a high chair holding up a huge poster while the children sat around at her feet.

It was a picture of a jungle, luscious and green and thoroughly alluring. The kids were really excited by it and were up on their knees leaning forward, straining to get a better view. As they were studying the photograph, I could hear them talking in Anindilyakwa about the animals that lived in the jungle and all the delicious foods that could be sourced there, as well as sideline chatting about their recent foray for jungle vine to make dilly-bag string.

Then I heard the teacher ask the children, "What do you call this?" The kids yelled out their rich and well-informed responses enthusiastically in the vernacular "eka-manja!" (trees) "erriber-riba-manja!" (open forest/jungle). "No," she said very slowly. "It is called a jungle."

(McCarthy, 2016, p. 40)

In November 2012, as a result of the coming together of key leaders from the Anindilyakwa Land Council (ALC) and from the Groote Eylandt communities, a 15 Year Strategic Plan 2012–2027 was created. It mapped out a specific bilingual approach using 'Partnerships with the Families as First Teachers program' to teach foundational pre-literacy and language learning platforms in Anindilyakwa and English.

> The centres will provide a first language education program delivered by linguists and in partnership with schools as an embedded part of the curriculum. Every child will have the opportunity to develop a strong foundation in Anindilyakwa. Students will also be engaged in learning about Anindilyakwa history, kinship system and other subjects pertinent to a child's development and understanding of their heritage and identity as part of their clan and community.
>
> (Anindilyakwa Land Council, 2012, p. 9)

This Education Implementation Plan for Groote Eylandt became law in April 2020. This meant that the Anindilyakwa people were able to take control and take responsibility for their own schools, and to have a bicultural curriculum to enable Anindilyakwa people to live in both worlds. It was overseen by an independent education authority. Similar to the Tiwi model, it provides training

Jacqueline Amagula and Helen CD McCarthy

to local staff and also a residential boarding college for students on Bickerton Island.

The Anindilyakwa Land Council have dedicated the Education Implementation Plan Local Decision-Making Agreement to Ms Jacqueline Amagula, reflecting her long-standing commitment to education on Groote Eylandt:

> This Implementation Plan is signed in the memory of Ms J. Amagula, who worked tirelessly to progress the Education of her people. As she was growing up, every day she went to school. When she finished school, her mind was focused on helping children at school. From there, she kept on working at the school, then she went to Batchelor College for training. Her pathway to teaching started as a young student teacher who wanted to achieve literacy and numeracy in her community. When she finished at Batchelor, she got the certificate 4 for teaching and became the principal at Angurugu school. Then, she became sick and she went to Darwin, but still she never forgot her community. Through the work she was doing in Darwin, she helped Wurrumangkadirra and she never gave up, kept on working both ways. It was her vision to educate our kids by having community control, and she fought to make an improvement in the lives of our people because education leads to a better lifestyle, and is the key to a pathway towards a career. She set an example for adults, younger generations and her children to follow in her footsteps. Whenever a person got sick anywhere, she was there to help them. She never gave up caring about education until she left her people and her children.
>
> The signatories also acknowledge the contributions of all past, present and future Warnumamalya and Wurrumangkadirra educators whose contributions assisting Anindilyakwa children across the Groote Archipelago to be successful in both worlds is both valued and recognised.
>
> (Groote Archipelago Local Decision-Making Agreement, 2020, para 1).

In this way Jacqueline's enduring struggle for educational reform has finally become a reality. Success has been hard won, with many challenges faced and only made possible through collegial and community collaboration. Her story, and that that of the various programs and schools (or colleges), serves as a role model and demonstrates what is possible.

As pre-service teachers about to launch yourselves into your careers we conclude our chapter hoping that you will have opportunities to contribute to, but also learn from Indigenous students and their families. Fortunately, I was able to do this – collaborating and emulating Aboriginal ways of teaching into my own pedagogy. In fact, with my growing experience I could differentiate between the classroom behaviour of students whose non-Indigenous teachers used these ways of learning and those who did not. Likewise, I could differentiate the relationships between non-Indigenous teachers who spent time in the community they worked in with the local people and those who took off to the neighbouring non-Indigenous communities each weekend.

This is all possible to learn by going out On Country at every opportunity, caring and sharing your life with the community. The following yarn describes how privileged I was to live and learn with my Mob.

Erriberriba-wa (On Country)

It was never planned – just in the moment. Families would fling everything including kids and dogs in the back of vehicles and off we would go. One Friday night, like many others, we drove south firstly along the jungle track then along the sand beach. The full moon rose in total brilliance while we set up camps and drank steaming billy tea. When the tides were right, we went crabbing while the clan screamed and laughed and ordered others, especially the younger ones, to do jobs – playing on the pecking order like only large families can.

I fell asleep to the sound of the incoming tide as it lapped upon the shore line. Sunrise was spectacular, as was the smoked damper and billy tea. After breakfast we went back over to Salt Creek to go shell fishing amongst the densely populated mangrove swamp, famous for crocodiles. The family with all their self-adopted white kids – me, Greeny and Brett-Boy, bent over like the number seven for hours, plucking and cursing, ripping and tearing our bodies and clothes to reap a pillow case of cockles.

Later we sat around the fire with Aunty and Uncle listening as they yarned and Uncle carved his totem designs into the soft wood he was working. They talked about what it meant to them to be survivors of the Stolen Generations, taken from their families on the island to the missions on the mainland and how the island had changed with the coming of the mining company.

I was conscious that this world of theirs was so fragile and how outsiders from the southern cities … made precarious decisions that impacted on locals' lives. In that moment I felt ashamed to be white.

I came to understand that what we did and when we did it was intricately connected to the tides, the moon and seasons, and reading this world was lusciously visceral and continual.

(McCarthy, 2012, p. 27)

Conclusion

The cautionary, but also positive tales presented in this chapter provide an opportunity for you to reflect on and learn from the experiences of others. No doubt, challenges will continue for all teachers, particularly with regard to the struggle for educational reform and so there is a need for ongoing resilience. Educators, both Indigenous and non-Indigenous, will need to continue to challenge the rhetoric about equitable educational opportunities and outcomes. Finally, there is a strong need to continue to work together collaboratively so that culturally appropriate ways of learning can be used in ways that give Indigenous learners a chance to have both choice and voice.

Reflective questions

1. Why do you think there has been a constant cycle of opening and closings of Aboriginal programs and schools?
2. What strategies might you use to help establish and build a strong collaborative connection with the school and community you are living and working in?

3. Why is creating strengths-based pedagogy a good starting point for relation-ship building in schools?

Dedication

This chapter is dedicated to the late Ms Jacqueline Amagula, who refused to stay silent and spent her lifetime agitating and struggling to create culturally sensitive and relevant educational pathways for her people.

She came and whispered the idea while I slept. Whispered in my ear, "Let's ask to put our story in this book, yo eningarba (good), help new pre-service teachers who will soon come to our schools, who will be overwhelmed and challenged and need our help". Always one to help.

We met when we were just young girls (dadiyaras). It was in 1981. From the outset Jacqueline talked long and passionately about education and how she felt learning needed to be reformed in the school, recognising Aboriginal kids had to be taught 'both ways' in the Aboriginal and non-Aboriginal ways. "Coming from a family of innovative artists and community leaders, she had grown up surrounded by motivated revolutionary thinkers. This was the ilk that Jacqueline emulated from. Her persistence to transform education in her community led her to continue with formal studies and take on complex senior leadership responsi-bilities" (McCarthy 2012, p. 23).

Note

1. Parts reprinted with permission from Batchelor Press.

References

Amagula J., & McCarthy H. (2015). Red ochre women: Sisters in the struggle for educa-tional reform. In H. Huijser, R. Ober, S. O'Sullivan, E. McRae-Williams, & R. Elvin (Eds.) *Finding common ground: Narratives, provocations and reflections from the 40 Year celebration of Batchelor Institute*. Batchelor, NT: Batchelor Press. https://www.batch-elor.edu.au/biite/wp-content/uploads/Common-Ground-ebook.pdf.

Anindilyakwa Land Council. (2012). 15 Year Strategic Plan (2012–2027). https://www.anindilyakwa.com.au/uploads/images/ALC-15-YEAR-STRATEGIC-PLAN-FINAL.pdf

Burns, R., (1995). *The adult learner at work*. Sydney: Business and Professional.

Connell, R. (2013). The neoliberal cascade and education: An essay on the market agenda and its consequences. *Critical Studies in Education*, 54(2), 99–112.

Corn, A. (2009) *Reflections and voices*. Sydney: Sydney University Press.

Chang, H. 2008. *Autoethnography as method*. Walnut Creek, CA: Left Coast Inc.

Gandini, L. (2012). Connecting through caring and learning spaces. In C. Edwards, L. Gandini, & G. Forman (Eds.) *The hundred languages of children: The Reggio Emilia experience in transformation* (3rd ed.). Greenwich, CT: Praeger, pp. 317–341.

Gobby, B. (2017). What is curriculum? In B. Gobby, & R. Walker (Eds.) *Powers of curriculum: Sociological perspectives on education*. Victoria, Australia: Oxford University Press, pp. 5–34.

Gray, J., & Partington, G. (2003). Attendance and non-attendance at school. In Q. Beresford & G. Partington (Eds.) *Reform and resistance in Aboriginal education: The Australian experience*. Perth, WA: University of Western Australia, pp. 133–163.

Groote Archipelago Local Decision-Making Agreement (2020). Schedule 3.4 Education Implementation Plan. Department of the Chief Minister Northern Territory Government. https://dcm.nt.gov.au/.

Karvelas, P. (2012). *The house of representatives standing committee on Aboriginal and Torres Strait Islander affairs*. Evaluating the Northern Territory Bilingual Program. https://www.nt.gov.au/

Marginson, S. (Ed.) (2002). *Investing in social capital: Postgraduate training in the social science Australia*. St. Lucia, Queensland: University of Queensland Press.

McCarthy, H. (2012). Beginnings… Living and learning in remote Aboriginal schools. In Q. Beresford, G. Partington, & G. Gower (Eds.) *Reform and resistance in Aboriginal education: The Australian experience* (2nd edn). Perth: University of Western Australia, pp. 1–34.

McCarthy, H. (2016). Auto/ethnography: a pathway to share the story. *International Journal of Humanities Education*, 14(1), 35–46.

Northern Territory Department of Education (1999). Learning Lessons Review. https://www.nintione.com.au/resources/rao/learning-lessons-an-independent-review-of-indigenous-education-in-the-northern-territory/

Northern Territory Education Department (2020). Northern Territory Indigenous languages and cultures curriculum. https://education.nt.gov.au/support-for-teachers/indigenous-languages-and-culture-curriculum-resources

Nicholls, C. (2005). Death by a thousand cuts: Indigenous language bilingual education programs in the Northern Territory of Australia, 1972–1998. *International Journal of Bilingual Education and Bilingualism*, 8(2 & 3), 160–177.

Sharifian, F., Rochecouste, J., Malcolm, I. G., Konigsberg, P., & Collard, G. (2004). *Improving understanding of Aboriginal literacy: Factors in text comprehension*. Perth: Department of Education and Training.

Yunkaporta, T. (2019). *Sand talk: How Indigenous thinking can save the world*. Victoria: The Text Publishing Company Melbourne.

Index

Note: Page numbers in *italics* refer to figures and page numbers in **bold** refer to tables.